Proclaiming the Gospel:

Spencer W. Kimball Speaks on Missionary Work

Proclaiming the Gospel:

Spencer W. Kimball Speaks on Missionary Work

Edited and Arranged by Yoshihiko Kikuchi

Bookcraft
Salt Lake City, Utah

Library of Congress Catalog Card Number: 87–71825

ISBN 0–88494–638–X

Second Printing, 1988

Printed in the United States of America

I wonder if we are doing all we can. Are we complacent in our approach to teaching all the world? We have been proselyting now 144 years. Are we prepared to lengthen our stride? To enlarge our vision?

Contents

Part Three: Finding

Part Four: A Great Increase in the Conversions

Preface

Having received the call in October 1977 to be a member of the First Quorum of the Seventy, I attended numerous training sessions to prepare me to serve in that General Authority capacity. I was also searching independently to know how I could more effectively serve in the Lord's kingdom. As I did so the Spirit whispered to me that I should follow the counsel and direction of the living oracle, the prophet of God.

I therefore began to compile all of President Kimball's messages to the new mission presidents and to the Regional Representatives delivered since he became Church President in December 1973. As I read those messages many times, I felt strongly what the Lord was asking us to do in this last dispensation. I now started collecting the prophet's messages presented in Church magazines and in area conferences, firesides, and various other gatherings. As my understanding developed and deepened, President Kimball's own understanding of his dynamic vision profoundly touched my soul. In particular I recognized that his great faith had secured for us a tremendous insight and depth of understanding about missionary work, and I felt a burning desire to share with others the mind and will of the Lord on this subject as revealed to his prophet.

In presenting the missionary message, President Kimball coined or otherwise made his own a number of compelling expressions that embrace the challenge and the blessing, expressions such as "Lengthening our stride," "Increase the missionaries," "Explore every possibility," "Open the doors of the nations," "Thousands of conversions," "A nation born in a day," "Make no little plans," "Move forward in a major way," "Is anything too hard for the Lord?" I am convinced of the need for all of us to *feel* the power behind such expressions, to catch the spirit of missionary work, to believe, and—as President Kimball would say—"Do it."

The scope and magnitude of the Lord's will on this subject as given to us through his prophet were manifest partly in the size of the compilation that resulted from my research—almost 2,500 pages. Publishing and other practical considerations nevertheless necessitated reductions in manuscript size. This book is not an official Church publication, however, and I alone am responsible for the selections made and for the final content and structure.

I express my thanks to those who encouraged me in this project or who helped or cooperated with me in the preparation of the manuscript. I mention particularly the family of President Kimball, especially his son Dr. Edward Kimball, and D. Arthur Haycock, President Kimball's personal secretary. I am indebted to Cory Maxwell of Bookcraft and his staff for their patience and support. I wish to thank my dear friends Dillon and Jeannie Inouye, and many other wonderful people too numerous to name here. Most of all, I am grateful to my dear wife, Toshiko, for her tireless support and the sacrifices she made in helping me prepare the manuscript.

I pray that this book will touch the hearts of many missionaries and other Church members. I testify that if you will read the will and mind of the Lord expressed here through his prophet, Spencer W. Kimball, you can gain and develop the spirit of missionary work. Any royalties the book generates will go to that cause via the Missionary Fund of the Church.

Yoshihiko Kikuchi

PART ONE

The Prophet's Vision

Go ye therefore, and teach all nations, baptizing them in the name of the Father, and of the Son, and of the Holy Ghost (Matthew 28:19).

CHAPTER ONE

Go Ye into All the World

[We have] accepted the solemn obligation of build-
ing God's kingdom here on earth and, through
exemplary living and missionary work, spreading
the gospel message throughout the world.

The Mission of the Church

To Proclaim, to Perfect, to Redeem. My brothers and sisters,
as the Brethren of the First Presidency and of the Twelve have
meditated upon and prayed about the great latter-day work the
Lord has given us to do, we are impressed that the mission of
the Church is threefold:

To proclaim the gospel of the Lord Jesus Christ to every
nation, kindred, tongue, and people;

To perfect the Saints by preparing them to receive the ordinances of the gospel and by instruction and discipline to gain
exaltation;

To redeem the dead by performing vicarious ordinances of
the gospel for those who have lived on the earth. All three are
part of one work—to assist our Father in Heaven and his Son,
Jesus Christ, in their grand and glorious mission "to bring to
pass the immortality and eternal life of man." (Moses 1:39.) ("A
Report of My Stewardship," General Conference Address, April
4, 1981.)

Go Ye Therefore and Teach All Nations. From the Church's
humble beginning of six members at Fayette, Seneca County,
New York, April 6, 1830, we have grown to approximately four
and one-half million members. When I was a missionary in the
Central States Mission in 1914, the Church had approximately

1,500 missionaries in 21 missions. We now have more than 30,000 missionaries in 189 missions around the world. This is wonderful, my brothers and sisters, and for this we are grateful. But it is not good enough! We must do more! We must lengthen our stride so that we may fulfill the commandment of our Savior to "Go ye into all the world, and preach the gospel to every creature." (Mark 16:15.)

If you haven't seen the beautiful mural on the first floor of [the Church Office] building, you should make it a point to do so before you leave today. You will see on the east wall of the foyer a painting there, sixteen and one-half feet high and sixty-five feet wide. It portrays the Savior standing on the Mount of Olives just before his ascension, as he gives his final instructions to his Apostles: "Go ye therefore, and teach all nations, baptizing them in the name of the Father, and of the Son, and of the Holy Ghost: Teaching them to observe all things whatsoever I have commanded you: and, lo, I am with you alway, even unto the end of the world." (Matthew 28:19-20.)

We are here to fulfill that commandment of the Lord that all the world may hear the message. It is for all the world, the inhabitants of all nations. The Lord has also told us that they are to hear the gospel in their own tongue. Speaking to the Prophet Joseph Smith, the Lord said: "For it shall come to pass in that day, that every man shall hear the fulness of the gospel . . . in his own language, through those who are ordained unto this power, by the administration of the Comforter, shed forth upon them for the revelation of Jesus Christ." (D&C 90:11.)

It is for every nation, kindred, tongue, and people, and that includes the minorities in English-speaking areas. Don't over-look them, brothers and sisters, or the Lord will hold us respon-sible.

We know that under the direction of the Lord this work will go forward to the blessing of all his children. Where there are now thousands of the faithful, there will be millions, and whereas The Church of Jesus Christ of Latter-day Saints is now established in eighty-one nations, it must and will cover the whole earth until men everywhere shall bow the knee and con-fess that Jesus is the Christ!

Let us all press on confidently in this work as we look for-ward to the glorious promises ahead. Through our faithfulness all that God has promised will be fulfilled! (New Mission Presi-dents Seminar, June 20, 1980.)

We Are Really Serious About This. We are really serious about this, brothers and sisters. We are not just fooling. This is important. It is the Lord who gave the responsibility to us. It isn't I; it is the Lord who said, "Go ye into all the world."

We haven't touched the world yet.

We have missionaries working in quite a number of countries. There are seventy countries probably receiving the gospel; but we have hardly touched the world. Just think of the millions of people in *East Pakistan*, for instance. When the great flood came there due to the disturbances of nature, they died by the thousands. Of course, we are going to have to take care of them after they die, too, but we ought to get some of those missionaries to people who are hungering for the truth now.

Now the Lord is able. He is powerful. It is possible for him to prepare the way. (Area Conference Address, Glasgow, Scotland, June 21, 1976.)

The Savior's Command

He Seemed to See. When the Savior stood on the Mount of Olives in Palestine just outside Jerusalem with eleven of his Apostles and cast his eyes into the heavens, he seemed to see the great work that would need to be done to gather scattered Israel in, and I cannot feel that he was overlooking the children of Lehi as he gave this command to his Apostles, to "Go . . . into all the world, preach the gospel to every creature" (D&C 68:8).

I think he was seeing *Russia*, and *China*, *India*, and *all Asia*. I believe he was seeing with his super-human sight the isles of the sea, and *North* and *South America*. And I believe he was seeing the *Arab* world which has come into prominence these last years, and I believe that he saw the problems that would be theirs in connection with their sufferings and the wars and the contentions, the misunderstandings, the discoveries, the total war for supremacy between the Lamanites and the Nephites, the intertribal battles and the subjugation by European conquerors of the great people of the Americas. ("The Lamanite," Regional Representatives Seminar, April 1, 1977.)

Whosoever Ye Shall Send in My Name, It Must Be Official. The answer to our prayers as we reread this is ". . . whosoever ye shall send"—all of these missionaries, the 21,000, plus their leaders and plus all the others—". . . whosoever ye shall send in

my name"—it must be official—". . . whosoever . . . in my name
. . ."—and called in his name, the name of Christ—". . . by the
voice of your brethren, the Twelve . . ."—that brings the responsibility back to the very spot where the Lord placed it and left it
nearly 2,000 years ago from the Mount of Olives—". . . duly
recommended and authorized . . ."—there again, these are the
ones who shall do it. And the promise is, they "shall have power
to open the door of my kingdom." Remember that. The earth is
the Lord's; he has control over it; he can handle it. He can touch
the hearts of leaders. He can change their attitudes. He can
impress people to move into these communities where they can
help us. (Regional Representatives Seminar, October 2, 1975.)

Without Converts, the Church Would Shrivel and Die.
Surely there is significance in the words of the Lord: "all
nations," "every nation," "every land," "uttermost part of the
earth," "every tongue," "every people," "the ends of the earth."
There was and is a universal need; there must be universal cov-
erage. Mankind is the universal family of our Heavenly Father,
and we have received a universal command to take the gospel to
the members of his family.

*If there were no converts, the Church would shrivel and die.
But perhaps the greatest reason for missionary work is to give
the world its chance to hear and accept the gospel.* The scriptures are replete with commands and promises and calls and
rewards for teaching the gospel. I use the word *command* advis-
edly, for it seems to be an insistent directive from which we,
singly and collectively, cannot escape. Furthermore, the command is clear that not only must all members of his Church give
missionary service, but we must take the gospel to all the
children of our Heavenly Father on this earth.

The Lord has indicated that we can expect his power to be
with us when we proclaim his word. He has said, "All power is
given unto me in heaven and in earth." ("It Becometh Every
Man," *Ensign*, October 1977.)

The Lord Has Promised Us. The Lord has promised us that
*he would give us all the help and the strength and the inspira-
tion that we need,* and so all he says is, "*Feed my sheep; feed
my lambs.*" And there are thousands, tens of thousands, hundreds of thousands of little sheep, little lambs that need feeding
in all these countries in the world. ("Let Us Move Forward and
Upward," General Conference Address, April 1, 1979.)

President Kimball's Direction

They Accepted the Solemn Obligation. They accepted the solemn obligation of building God's kingdom here on earth and, through exemplary living and missionary work, spreading the gospel message throughout the world. It was a noble ambition—one that we, their descendants, still share. ("Images of the Past: The Mormon Pioneer Heritage," Rededication of Mormon Pioneer Memorial Bridge, April 21, 1979.)

Go Forward with a New Dedication. Now, brethren, you have been set apart, you have received your errand from the Lord. Go to, and may God bless you and be with you. I have no fear whatever that the candle lighted in Palestine years ago will ever be put out. It will shine more brightly always. *This is the work of the Lord. We are doing his service. He has commanded us specifically and over and over to go into all the world and preach the gospel to every creature, every corner of the earth, every nation, every tongue, and that includes many that we have never touched yet.* We are unknown among many, many of the people of the world, and it is time now that we began to gird up our loins and go forward with a new dedication to this great work. (New Mission Presidents Seminar, June 20, 1975.)

We Must Move. I plead, therefore, with all of you to understand, while we must always move wisely to move the Lord's work forward—that *we must move!* ("The Uttermost Parts of the Earth," Regional Representatives Seminar, September 29, 1978.)

Go with a Faith like That of Moses. In the next room is a beautiful mural—I had to stop and absorb it a little as I came in this morning. It shows the Lord and his Apostles on the Mount of Olives. I imagine his feet were weary and his body strained, but his spirit was alive and alert. He is giving the last instructions to his leaders who will carry on. Perhaps he is thinking: "Go with a faith like that of Moses, that the impossible can happen—the sea can open, the enemy pursuers can be stopped, the east wind can be controlled and the children of Israel can be given a new world, a new vision, a new opportunity."

Perhaps he is thinking: "There are bushes aflame with God in every desert; if one can see and hear and understand, revelation is there."

Perhaps he is saying: "There is a smooth stone in every shepherd's pouch and a sling in every hand and a faith in every heart, a true marksman David for every Goliath."

Maybe he is thinking: "There is a Brigham Young with perception and faith and understanding for every wandering company of pioneers—a leader who will see them through to their eternal destination."

Perhaps he was seeing many Wilford Woodruffs hallowing our little ponds and baptizing thousands of followers. He is saying, *Go ye into all the world and preach the gospel to every creature.*

Perhaps he is thinking of *Yugoslavia* and *Iran* and *India* and *Greece* and *Czechoslovakia* and *Russia*, that will come into being after his crucifixion and ascension, with closed doors which will need to be opened. Maybe he is thinking also of *Romania* and *Poland* and *China* and *Burma* which may need a burning bush and revelation, and maybe of places where a Moses might strike his rod and cause water to flow. He is saying without all of the explanations of the how's and why's, "Go ye into all the world and preach the gospel to every creature."

Brethren, we do not worry about how and when and why. *We say why not.* (Regional Representatives Seminar, October 3, 1974.)

Who Is Going to Do It? The gospel must be preached to the world, *but who is going to do it?* Not the Baptists and the Methodists; not the Catholics or any other Protestants. You and I are going to do it. You and I must do it because we have the gospel; they do not have it. This is really serious, and we expect that you will take it seriously and that the regional representatives and the mission presidents and the stake presidents will call this to your attention frequently so that no boy will think he has the option. There really isn't any option, only that he has free agency, of course. However, there is not an option as to whether he will fill a mission or not.

If we are going to serve the Lord, we are going to teach the gospel in all of these countries. These countries are rather significant and it frightens us a little bit when we think of the number of countries that need the gospel. Let me read just two or three of them. Here's *Afghanistan* with eighteen or nineteen million people, none of whom have been touched by the gospel. Here is *Burma* with over thirty million people, and I don't suppose that there is a member of the Church there in that whole country; *Cambodia* with eight or nine million people; *Ceylon* or *Sri Lanka* with fifteen million people and untouched. Who is going to do it? You are and I am. We are because it is that important. Then there is *China* with its eight hundred million people untouched. (Area Conference Address, Manchester, England, June 19-20, 1976.)

This Is Something We Are Bound to Do. Now brethren, this is not just a matter of suggestion. This is something we are bound to do. The Lord looks straight at us through the Apostles and says, "Wherever you can't go, you send the other brethren." (See D&C 84:62.) It is not a matter of, "Well, if it happens to be convenient and if it happens that you are financially well fixed and if you have a few extra hundred dollars you do not know what to do with, you could send a boy on a mission." That is not it at all. No matter what situation we are in, the Lord says, "Sacrifice brings forth the blessings of heaven." (Hymns, no. 27.) And so we expect that. We expect that of *New Zealand* over here. *Tonga* and *Samoa*, we have found, are already heavy with missionaries. They send more missionaries than we can use there. (Area Conference Address, Sydney, Australia, February 28, 1976.)

Our Message Is to Bring Light into the World. Our great need, desire, and obsession is to bring to the people of this world the candle of understanding to light the way out of obscurity and darkness. Our message is to bring light into the world and our charge to convert the people of the world to accept the truth. (Regional Representatives Seminar, September 30, 1976.)

CHAPTER TWO

Convert the World

At the top of the Mount of Olives with Apostles, eleven of them, our Lord stands looking off into the limitless world of ours and says with serious intent, "Go."

A Divine Promise

He Will Be in Their Midst. Jesus will accompany the missionaries, *he will be in their midst,* he shall be the advocate with the Father, and nothing shall prevail [against them], nothing. This is a divine promise we have waited for a long time. Brethren, it's a promise I would like to apply to every one of us. I believe that as we circle the globe and preach the word to the people of the world, that nothing shall prevail against us if we are persistent. (New Mission Presidents Seminar, June 27, 1974.)

Lesser Work Crowds Out the Important. Sometimes lesser routines and lesser work crowds out the important. The brethren going to Missouri in the early days received this revelation: "But verily I say unto you, that it is not needful for this whole company of mine elders to be moving swiftly upon the waters, whilst the inhabitants on either side are perishing in unbelief." (D&C 61:3.) (New Mission Presidents Seminar, June 25, 1976.)

The Kingdom Shall Fill the Earth

All Corners of the Earth Will Be Proselyted. If any of you should question having been sent officially to do the work, please read Doctrine and Covenants 88:81-82, which says, "Behold, I sent you out to testify and warn the people, and it becometh every man who hath been warned to warn his neighbor. Therefore, they are left without excuse, and their sins are upon their own heads."

He takes away all limitations and obstructions and has given this responsibility to *all* of the people to the ends of the earth that *all* who might hear will hear. (Regional Representatives Seminar, September 30, 1977.)

It is inconceivable that the Lord actually expected those eleven wonderful early Apostles to cover the earth, even when it was much more limited in numbers. They did their best and planted the seed in many places and many cities. The responsibility still is with the Twelve, and they have been given authority to call others to assist them. . . . All of us are engaged in this important work. (Regional Representatives Seminar, April 3, 1975.)

The Kingdom of God Will Fill the Earth. The question that the press and others ask us is, "Whither goest thou?" And the answer is: We are going to our destiny—through to the kingdom of God. As the prophet Daniel said hundreds of years ago, "In the days of these kings shall the God of heaven set up *a kingdom,* which . . . shall not be left to other people, but *it shall break in pieces and consume all these kingdoms,* and *it shall stand for ever.*" (Daniel 2:44.)

That's the kingdom that you and I are building today in Australia and elsewhere in the world, a kingdom that is permanent. It is the kingdom of God, not established by men but established by the Lord himself. (Area Conference Address, Melbourne, Australia, February 28, 1976.)

A Mountain of Considerable Size. Now again we come to the world aspect. The kingdom of God has been established, and it has moved forward and *become a stone.* Then it's *become a mountain* of considerable size. There's still much of the whole earth that is untouched by the gospel of Christ. I looked through the atlas and found hundreds of states and countries, most of which are still untouched. I was surprised at the number of islands in the Pacific and elsewhere which still seem to be sectarian. I was surprised at the great number of countries and provinces in numerous countries and cities with populations almost without number. And yet we go on and on with limited strides toward covering the land and touching the people. (New Mission Presidents Seminar, June 27, 1974.)

The Gospel Has Been Restored. In 1820 the Savior of the world came back to this earth. He came back in person as the angel said he would; he with his Father, Elohim. They came back, visited the young man whom they had selected to be the prophet of this dispensation, and they brought with them the authority and the power and blessings for the people. A great volume of sacred scripture emanated from this prophet as revelations from God, revealing truth to the people, and knowledge about the straight and narrow way leading back into his presence. This is the testimony of Latter-day Saints; that the gospel has been restored in all of its beauty, in all of its power, in all of its strength. (Area Conference Address, London, England, June 20, 1976.)

Enoch Was a Great Missionary. Enoch was a great missionary. With his associates he had proclaimed the gospel of repentance to many people. But he came to realize that they would not repent and that Noah built an ark to save himself and his immediate family from the destruction of the flood. "And it came to pass that Enoch looked; and from Noah, he beheld all the families of the earth; and he cried unto the Lord, saying: When shall the day of the Lord come? When shall the blood of the righteous be shed, that all they that mourn may be sanctified and have eternal life? And the Lord said: It shall be in the meridian of time, in the days of wickedness and vengeance." (Moses 7:45-46.)

For the Harvest Is Ripe

We Must Gather the Wheat. We've been told by the Lord as he sent us into the world, that the field is ripe already to harvest, that we must gather the wheat from among the tares and we're to search out the elect of God. Put ye in the sickle, for the harvest is ripe. Come get ye down for the press is full, the fats overflow, for their wickedness is great. Multitudes, multitudes in the valley of decision, for the day of the Lord is near in the valley of decision. (New Mission Presidents Seminar, June 27, 1974.)

This Day of God's Power. "I am looking to the day," said Wilford Woodruff, "[of] the fulfillment of all the prophecies the Lord has ever made." I quote him in this particular. "When this day comes, returning to the Lamanites, we will feel a day of God's power among us, and a nation will be born in a day. Their chiefs will be filled with the power of God and receive the gospel and then will go forth and build the New Jerusalem and we shall help them." They are branches of the house of Israel. This day of God's power—we are waiting for it, this day when we baptize a nation in a day. *Hail that day! Oh, our beloved Father in Heaven, bring about the day when we may be able to bring in large numbers as Ammon and his brethren did, thousands of conversions, not dozens, not tens or fives or ones, thousands of conversions.* The Lord promised it: He fulfills his promises. (Regional Representatives Seminar, April 3, 1975.)

The Spirit of the Lord Is Brooding over the Nations. Now, I repeat what I have said many times before: we have an obligation, a duty, a divine commission to preach the gospel in every nation and to every creature.

But I ask you, are we advancing as fast as we should? *We feel that the spirit of the Lord is brooding over the nations to prepare the way for the preaching of the Gospel.* ("The Uttermost Parts of the Earth," Regional Representatives Seminar, September 29, 1978.)

The Gospel Will Cover the Earth. President Romney called to the attention of the General Authorities the other day a verse in Moses 7:62, which noted how righteousness and truth *"would sweep the earth as with a flood."* This spreading of the gospel will occur, therefore, in a time of great iniquity; righteousness and evil will exist side by side. We must not, therefore, fail to do our part to help the gospel cover the earth, even though the circumstances around us may be very difficult and trying. (Regional Representatives Seminar, October 3, 1974.)

For Thousands of Conversions. Remember the "unto such" promise given in the missionary work, that "he that *repenteth* and exerciseth *faith,* and bringeth forth good *works,* and *prayeth* continually without ceasing—unto such it is given to know the mysteries of God; yea, unto such it shall be given to reveal things which never have been revealed; yea, and it shall be given unto such to bring thousands of souls to repentance, even as it has been given unto us to bring these our brethren to repentance." (Alma 26:22.)

And we are thinking and hoping for thousands of conversions by individual missionaries and missions. (New Mission Presidents Seminar, June 20, 1975.)

A Chapel on Nearly Every Corner. In the small city of Salt Lake, we have a chapel on nearly every corner and a great number of stakes. That must carry forward throughout the world for limitless time—and we see it coming, we are sure! (Area Conference Address, Tokyo, Japan, October 31, 1980.)

The Greatest and Most Important Duty. My brethren, our effort must be *well planned, well governed, well directed.* The reservoir of power and authority is full to overflowing. We must learn to tap it. Remember, the Prophet Joseph said, *"After all that's been said, the greatest and most important duty is to preach the Gospel."* And remember also that the Lord emphasized to the Whitmers that *"the greatest and most important duty is to preach the Gospel."* And remember also that the Lord emphasized to the Whitmers that *the greatest blessing that could possibly come to a preacher of righteousness is that he convert souls and change lives and inspire people* so they could enjoy eternity with him, the missionary. Remember, President John Taylor said on one occasion, "If you do not magnify your callings, God will hold you responsible for those you might have saved had you done your duty." (New Mission Presidents Seminar, June 27, 1974.)

There Is No Reason . . . Why You Cannot Go Forward. We are going forward with this program and shall soon have some special missionaries working in this field. There is no reason in the world why you cannot go forward immediately. . . . It could bring joy and peace to many people, if they will live the commandments of the Lord. That is basic and important. We will move forward with slowness. We want to be sure that we know what we are doing, moving with care, and we will go forward with the great program. (Area Conference Address, Johannesburg, South Africa, October 23, 1978.)

Why Aren't They in the Mission Field? I am looking for the day when we will have five thousand missionaries from South America. There are more than five thousand boys in South America. Why aren't they in the mission field? I think they did not understand. They thought it was something you could just choose to do or choose not to do. But a mission is like paying tithing. Of course, you don't have to pay tithing, but every boy who loves the Lord is going to get the tithing habit. And every boy and girl should get that habit of paying tithing. There are many things we are not compelled to do, but we want to do them because it is right to do them. We want to keep our lives clean because it is right to keep them clean. We want to hold home evenings because it is right to do it. And so we want to go on missions because it is the Lord's way. (Area Conference Address, Luna Park, Buenos Aires, Argentina, March 8, 1975.)

The Greater Opportunities Ahead. You have seen an emphasis on simplification of Church programs so that these programs can move wherever the gospel goes in the world without too much difficulty and without too much complexity. We have seen further emphasis on enriching family life. Recently, we established the new consolidated schedule which is aimed at enriching family life even further, together with the greater opportunities for *individual and family gospel scholarship and for more Christian service.* (Regional Representatives Seminar, April 4, 1980.)

We Have Paused on Some Plateaus Long Enough. We have paused on some plateaus long enough. Let us resume our journey forward and upward. Let us quietly put an end to our reluctance to reach out to others—whether in our own families, wards, or neighbors. We have been diverted, at times, from fundamentals on which we must now focus in order to move forward as a person or as a people. ("Let Us Move Forward and Upward," General Conference Address, April 1, 1979.)

To Have Christ for a Missionary Companion! Again, think of the promise made to the Prophet Joseph Smith [and] to Parley P. Pratt and his associates being sent into the Indian mission. "I myself will go with them and be in their midst. I am their advocate with the Father, and nothing shall prevail against them." (D&C 68:12.)

What a promise to have Christ for a missionary companion and a promise that they cannot fail! (Regional Representatives Seminar, October 3, 1974.)

There Is So Much Yet to Do. The work of the Lord is going forward as never before—but, as always, there is infinitely more to be done as we contemplate the whole world and its four billion inhabitants as our field of missionary labor. Do not misunderstand me—we are grateful and know the Lord is pleased with your efforts. He is mindful of your devoted service and does and will bless you for so serving. But there is so much yet to do and the adversary is so unrelenting. So we pray and encourage you not to weary in well doing. (Regional Representatives Seminar, March 30, 1979.)

All Races and All Creeds

We Are a Proselyting Church. By divine commandment we are a proselyting church. More than 23,000 missionaries are abroad in the world today, unselfishly giving of their time, means, and talents to spread this message of the Restoration. They are in most nations of the free world. Their message is to all mankind everywhere—to the world of the Catholic, the Protestant, all the so-called Christian world; to the world of the Hindu, the Buddhist, the Muslim, the Jew, the Shintoist, the follower of Confucius—to all people of all races and all creeds. ("The Stone Cut Without Hands," General Conference Address, April 3, 1976.)

Missionary Work Is Continuing Beyond the Veil. Our great and growing missionary program among mortals is the most extensive it has ever been in this dispensation as we preach, teach, and baptize tens of thousands of our fellowmen. However, missionary work is not limited to proclaiming the gospel to every nation, kindred, tongue, and people now living on the earth. Missionary work is also continuing beyond the veil among the millions and even billions of the children of our Heavenly Father who have died either without hearing the gospel or without accepting it while they lived on the earth. Our great part in this aspect of missionary work is to perform on this earth the ordinances required for those who accept the gospel over there.

The spirit world is full of spirits who are anxiously awaiting the performance of these earthly ordinances for them. I hope to see us dissolve the artificial boundary line we so often place between missionary work and temple and genealogical work, because it is the same great redemptive work! ("The Things of Eternity— Stand We in Jeopardy?" *Ensign*, January 1977.)

The Lord May Inspire Us. We should constantly strive to develop a deep and broad knowledge from which the Lord may inspire us to speak for he makes clear to us through the Prophet Joseph Smith just what our responsibility is with reference to preaching the gospel. (Regional Representatives Seminar, March 31, 1978.)

Go Forth Boldly, Nobly, and Independent. I have lived for more than half the 150 years the restored Church has been upon the earth in this last dispensation. I have witnessed its marvelous growth until it now is established in the four corners of the earth. As the Prophet Joseph said:

> Our missionaries are going forth to different nations, and in Germany, Palestine, New Holland, Australia, the East Indies, and other places, the Standard of Truth has been erected; no unhallowed hand can stop the work from progressing; persecutions may rage, mobs may combine, armies may assemble, calumny may defame, but the truth of God will go forth boldly, nobly, and independent, till it has penetrated every continent, visited every clime, swept every country, and sounded in every ear, till the purposes of God shall be accomplished, and the Great Jehovah shall say the work is done. (*History of the Church* 4:540.)

("No Unhallowed Hand Can Stop the Work," General Conference Address, April 5, 1980.)

Move Forward in a Major Way. Now, my brothers and sisters, it seems clear to me, indeed, this impression weighs upon me—that *the Church is at a point in its growth and maturity when we are at last ready to move forward in a major way.* Some decisions have been made and others pending, which will clear the way, organizationally. But the basic decisions needed for us to move forward, as a people, must be made by the individual members of the Church. The major strides which must be made by the Church will follow upon the major strides to be made by us as individuals. ("Let Us Move Forward and Upward," General Conference Address, April 1, 1979.)

Our Ally Is Our God

He Is Our Commander. Remember, our ally is our God. He is our commander. He made the plans. He gave the commandment. Remember what we have quoted thousands of times as told by Nephi:

> And it came to pass that I, Nephi, said unto my father: I will go and do the things which the Lord hath commanded, for I know that the Lord giveth no commandments unto the children of men, save he shall prepare a way for them that they may accomplish the thing which he commandeth them. (1 Nephi 3:7.)

And as I read that scripture I think of the numerous nations that are still untouched. I know they have curtains, like iron curtains and bamboo curtains. I know how difficult it is because we have made some efforts. Surely the Lord knew what he was doing when he commanded. And like Nephi we can say:

> For the fulness of mine intent is that I may persuade men to come unto the God of Abraham, and the God of Isaac, and the God of Jacob, and be saved. (1 Nephi 6:4.)

And certainly the command to the original Apostles of this dispensation followed the command of the others of earlier years, and you Twelve have that same command.

The 112th section of the Doctrine and Covenants was addressed to Thomas B. Marsh, the President of the Twelve in 1837, and concerns the Twelve Apostles. The keys of the kingdom were given to the Presidency and the Twelve. Apparently President Marsh had been praying for his brethren and the Lord listened:

> . . . thine alms have come up as a memorial before me, in behalf of those, thy brethren, who were chosen to bear testimony of my name and to send it abroad among all nations, kindreds, tongues, and people. . . . (D&C 112:1.)

Further:

> . . . thou shalt bear record of my name, not only unto the Gentiles, but also unto the Jews; and thou shalt send forth my word unto the ends of the earth. (D&C 112:4.)

He [Marsh] was commanded:

... let not the inhabitants of the earth slumber, because of thy speech.

... thy path lieth among the mountains, and among many nations. (D&C 112:5, 7.) (Regional Representatives Seminar, April 4, 1974.)

This Work Is Vital. It Is Vital! Brethren and sisters, this work is *vital*. It is *vital!* If we don't do it, we could just fade out and be eliminated from this old world, if we get too careless. We had better be doing what the Lord said when He went on the mountain, and said, "Go ye into all the world." He said, "Go! GO! GO! into *all* the world." And that means *China*, and *India*, and *Burma*, and *Russia*, and *Pakistan* and *Germany*, and *Brazil* and *Japan*, and *Korea*—"Go ye into all the world and preach the gospel to every creature." (Dedication Address, Fair Oaks, California, October 9, 1983.)

CHAPTER THREE

The Impossible Dream

Are we advancing as far as we should? How can we be satisfied with 200,000 converts in a year out of 4 billion people in the world who need the gospel?

The Impossible Dream

The song that is often sung, "The Impossible Dream," is a real inspiration to me every time I read it, because it sets aside the impossible mission and puts before us the idea that if we are determined, we can easily have the blessings the Lord wants us to have. (Regional Representatives Seminar, October 2, 1975.)

To Reach the Unreachable Star. As I read, "Is anything too hard for the Lord?" I think of the verses of Mitch Leigh:

The Impossible Dream

To dream the impossible dream,
To fight the unbeatable foe,
To bear with unbearable sorrow,
To run where the brave dare not go.

To right the unrightable wrong,
To love, pure and chaste from afar,
To try when your arms are too weary,
To reach the unreachable star.

This is my quest,
To follow that star,
No matter how hopeless,
No matter how far;
To fight for the right,

Without question or pause,
To be willing to march into hell
For a heavenly cause.

And I know if I'll only be true
To that glorious quest,
That my heart will lie peaceful and calm
When I'm laid to my rest.

And the world will be better for this,
That one man, scorned and covered with scars,
Still strove with his last ounce of courage
To reach the unreachable star.

(Regional Representatives Seminar, April 5, 1976.)

The More Enlarged Our Perspective Becomes. The righteous life is achieved as we magnify our view of life, and expand our view of others and of our own possibilities. Thus, the more we follow the teachings of the Master, the more enlarged our perspective becomes. ("President Kimball Speaks Out on Service to Others," *New Era*, March 1981.)

A Great Movement. A year ago now I was in Japan and Korea, and as I saw the many handsome young men joining the Church and giving leadership to its organizations, I seemed to envision a great movement when there would be thousands of local men prepared and anxious and strong to go abroad. As I have been in Mexico since that time, I seemed to envision again Mexican youth and Latins from Central and South America in great numbers qualifying themselves for missionary service within their own country and then finally in other lands until the army of the Lord's missionaries would cover the earth as the waters cover the mighty deep.

I have stated the problem. I believe there is a solution. I think that if we are all of one mind and one heart and one purpose that we can move forward and change the image which seems to be that "We are doing pretty well. Let's not 'rock the boat.' "

In all the countries I have ever visited I have found many intelligent and qualified people who give leadership in their countries, and I also remember numerous people from deprived countries enjoying benefits from the gospel.

Every Member a Missionary. In our stake missionary work at home we have hardly scratched the surface.

Brother T. Bowring Woodbury told us of ninety-three cooperating families in one Utah stake who were working with ninety-three non- or part-member families. Clifton Johnson told us of bringing five of twenty-six non-members into the Church in a few months.

It can be done.

We can change the image and approach the ideals set out by President McKay, "Every member a missionary." That was inspired!

I know this message is not new, and we have talked about it before, but *I believe the time has come when we must shoulder arms. I think we must change our sights and raise our goals.*

The Gospel to Every Creature. When we have increased the missionaries from the organized areas of the Church to a number close to their potential, that is, every able and worthy boy in the Church on a mission; when every stake and mission abroad is furnishing enough missionaries for that country; when we have used our qualified men to help the Apostles to open these new fields of labor; when we have used the satellite and related discoveries to their greatest potential and all of the media—the papers, magazines, television, radio—all in their greatest power; when we have organized numerous other stakes which will be springboards; when we have recovered from inactivity the numerous young men who are now unordained and unmissioned and unmarried; then, and not until then, shall we approach the insistence of our Lord and Master to go into all the world and preach the gospel to every creature.

To Walk with God. Brethren, I am positive that the blessings of the Lord will attend every country which opens its gates to the gospel of Christ. Their blessings will flow in education, and culture, and faith, and love, like Enoch's city of Zion, which was translated, and also will become like the 200 years of peaceful habitation in the country in Nephite days. There will come prosperity to the nations, comfort and luxuries to the people, joy and peace to all recipients, and eternal life to those who accept and magnify it.

Someone gave us this:

To walk with God, no strength is lost.
Walk on.
To talk with God, no breath is lost.
Talk on.
To wait on God, no time is lost.
Wait on.

("When the World Will Be Converted," *Ensign*, October 1974.)

Did You Catch the Words, "Every Man"?

Every Young Man Should Fill a Mission. It is interesting to me that some statistician told us that in A.D. 33 when the Savior himself was stressing so strongly "every nation, kindred, tongue, and people" that there were on the earth possibly a quarter billion.

Eighteen hundred years later, when the command came through Joseph Smith to proselyte the world, our experts estimated there were one billion people (1,000,000,000) or about four times as many as in the meridian of time. And now as we renew the injunction to cover the earth with the gospel, it is estimated that there are probably three-and-a-half billion.

The question is frequently asked, "Should every young man fill a mission?" And the answer has been given by the Lord. It is "yes." Every young man should fill a mission. He said, "Send forth the elders of my church unto the nations which are afar off; unto the islands of the sea; send forth unto foreign lands; call upon all nations, first upon the Gentiles, and then upon the Jews." (D&C 133:8.)

We now ordain young men at nineteen years of age to be elders. . . . Every man should also pay his tithing. Every man should observe the Sabbath. Every man should attend his meetings. Every man should consummate his marriage in the temple and properly train his children, and do many other mighty works. Of course he should. He does not always do it.

We realize that while all men definitely should, all men are not prepared to teach the gospel abroad. Far too many young men arrive at the missionary age quite unprepared to go on a mission, and, of course, they should not be sent. But they should all be prepared. There are a few physically unfit to do missionary service, but Paul also had a thorn in his side. There are far too many unfit emotionally with the spirit of missionary work. They should have been prepared. Should! But since they have broken the laws, they may have to be deprived, and thereon hangs one of our greatest challenges, to keep these young boys worthy. Yes, we would say, every able worthy man should shoulder the cross. What an army we should have teaching Christ and him crucified! Yes, they should be prepared, usually with saved funds for their missions, and always with a happy heart to serve.

The Lord says: "*And that every man [did you catch the words, "every man"?] should take righteousness in his hands and faithfulness upon his loins, and lift a warning voice unto the inhabitants of the earth; and declare both by word and by flight that desolation shall come upon the wicked.*" (D&C 63:37.) Note that he said "every man," but we must find a way to have "every man" prepared. (Regional Representatives Seminar, April 4, 1974.)

We Are Still Just Scratching the Surface. We now have more than 30,000 full-time missionaries and 189 missions, but we are still just scratching the surface of the needs of our Father's other children who dwell upon the earth. Many still hunger and thirst after truth and are kept from it only "because they know not where to find it." (D&C 123:12.)

There are still more places to go than there are full-time missionaries and organized missions to serve them. There are still millions more being born, living and dying, than are hearing testimonies borne to them by the servants of the Lord. (Regional Representatives Seminar, October 3, 1980.)

The World Is Full of Men Who Aimed. I am told that a good golfer never plays against his opponent — he plays against par! A good runner runs against time — a good bowler works for 300 — when they play against time, par, or a perfect 300, top performance is obtained through it. A mediocre game may be good enough to beat a poor opponent. The world is full of men who aimed only to be a little better than the other man of mediocrity. The history of the world is made by men who shoot for par and make it or better it. (Regional Representatives Seminar, April 3, 1975.)

Determined to Meet It and to Conquer It. This is a picture of a teenage boy. He's nineteen. That's still teenage. He's standing on the seashore at San Francisco. His left hand holds his shoes. His rolled up pants uncover his ankles. His hair, newly trimmed by a real barber, is reddish. He stands on the wet sand, a moment ago made damp and hard when a larger than average wave swelled out before him. Jack was amazed. Never had he seen water like this before. He grew up in Thatcher and the largest body of water he had ever seen was the Gila River. These waves never seemed to stop. They roll and break and spread and roll out again. Only hours ago he had boarded an airplane. This big moment he had anticipated every time a big plane had flown over Thatcher, which was rare. First he tested the seat, soft as a sofa. Then he devoured a six-course lunch. Then he chatted with the stewardess, prettiest girl he had ever seen, even when she wasn't smiling, and that was twice. Then he listened to six channels of music, stereo even. Suddenly they were in San Francisco and now the Pacific and Jack is discovering what an ocean looks like, swells like, smells like, sounds like. Jack is discovering America and a big new world.

An hour ago he was on Market Street and was amazed at the great crowds of people. He wrote a card home to his family and described this experience, saying, "There's so many people. It's just like when conference lets out in Thatcher." Jack is on the threshold. He's going to see even more people in Hong Kong, to learn that there are even more millions in the new world he's coming to know. He will cross part of the 69 million square miles of ocean and will see many of the 3½ billion people and will become bewildered when he knows that he and his 18,000 fellow missionaries are supposed to proselyte all these people. He's discovering a fabulous world. When he'd climbed Mt. Graham, he'd tried to count the giant trees and was bewildered. When he and his friends had slept out in an Arizona clear night, he had tried to count the stars and got lost and now he'd tried to conceive of 3½ billion people all in his world. Jack remembered one of the scriptures he had read. "And if it so be that you should labor all your days in crying repentance unto this people, and bring, save it be one soul unto me, how great shall be your joy with him in the kingdom of my Father!" (D&C 18:15.)

And then he wondered what was the worth of a soul such as he'd been sent out to recover. He remembered how he had read of one little boy kidnapped in Los Angeles who was recovered by his father upon payment of a quarter million dollars to the vicious ones. At that rate that would be 87½ thousand billion dollars or 875 trillion dollars, and he became bewildered at the responsibility that he had assumed. Who was it that said, "If you want to launch big ships, go to deep water, the ocean." Jack was beginning now to feel a part of this big new world and was determined to meet it and to conquer it, regardless of how big it was. (New Mission Presidents Seminar, June 27, 1971.)

Major Causes for the Holding Back

First, Sin; Second, Reluctance. It seems to me that basically there are two major causes for the holding back which we see in the Church: *First*, sin which results in disinterest or immobilization and guilt; and *second*, the reluctance of good members of the Church to stretch just a little bit more in the service, instead of being too slow to see the power of their example or too shy about letting their light shine. It is time for us all to take those seemingly small steps forward which will, when compounded, mean major progress for the Church! ("Let Us Move Forward and Upward," General Conference Address, April 1, 1979.)

We Must Not Tarry Too Long. He will not ask us to bear more than we can bear nor thrust upon us that for which we are not yet ready. But likewise, we must not tarry too long when we are ready to move on. Let us trust the Lord and take the next steps in our individual lives. He has promised us that he will be our tender tutor, measuring what we are ready for: "And ye cannot bear all things now; nevertheless, be of good cheer, for I will lead you along." (D&C 78:18.) *Let us not shrink from the next steps in our spiritual growth,* brothers and sisters, *by holding back, or side-stepping our fresh opportunities for service to our families and our fellowmen.* ("Let Us Move Forward and Upward," General Conference Address, April 1, 1979.)

If We Do Our Part. Even though my strength will not permit me to do all that I would like at the moment, I am blessed and I will continue to do my part to the best of my ability. I wish I had more strength, but as long as I have any strength, I will continue to bear my testimony to the truth of this great latter-day work and to pray for the Lord's blessings and His guidance to be upon us all! ("Remember the Mission of the Church," General Conference Address, April 3, 1982.)

If One-Half the Membership Became Totally Involved. Now if only ONE-HALF THE MEMBERSHIP OF THE CHURCH BECAME WHOLLY INVOLVED and assum[ing] they brought into the Church one convert for each of the two million, in one year they would bring in some millions of new members. And that, of course, is what we want—the total membership of all the world as indicated by the Lord. That would grow to three million, to five million, to seven million, and on until we would, before we awakened almost, we would have 20 million people. THAT MAY SOUND FRIGHTENING, AND YET IT IS THE GOAL. (Regional Representatives Seminar, September 30, 1976; emphasis added.)

An Upsurge in Spirituality—Are We Ready? Are we ready, brothers and sisters, to do these seemingly small things out of which great blessings will proceed? I think we are. *I believe the Lord's Church is on the verge of an upsurge in spirituality. Our individual spiritual growth is the key to major numerical growth in the kingdom.* The Church is ready to accomplish these things now which it could not have done just a few years ago. So also we are ready as members. If you will accept my counsel, you will come to feel that there is a readiness in our people which must be put to work. ("Let Us Move Forward and Upward," General Conference Address, April 1, 1979.)

He Has a World That Needs Converting. Dr. Allen Stockdale wrote: "God left the world unfinished. If he had completed it you wouldn't have liked it. He left the electricity in the clouds. He left the paper in the pulp; he left the rivers unbridged and the cities unbuilt and the forests unfelled; he left the music unsung and the poetry undreamed and the dramas unplayed . . ." and, I might add, he has a world that needs converting. (Regional Representatives Seminar, October 3, 1974.)

We Expect Him to Do His Utmost. We do not expect every missionary to get 200 or 32 or 82, but we expect him to do his utmost and to have his sights raised. (New Mission Presidents Seminar, June 25, 1976.)

One More Quiet Act of Christian Service. Think of the blessings here and on the other side of the veil if each holder of a temple recommend were to do just one more endowment this next year! And how would our nonmember neighbors and friends feel if we were each to do just one more quiet act of Christian service for them before October conference—regardless of whether or not they are interested in the Church! ("Let Us Move Forward and Upward," General Conference Address, April 1, 1979.)

This Is Only a Prelude. Do not fail to let your missionaries know that they are not filling a two-year assignment, but this is only a prelude to the lifetime of proselyting that they must so completely gear their lives to, that there will never be any slowing of the process. (New Mission Presidents Seminar, June 1977.)

Our Almighty Father Will Increase Our Faith

Lead Our Missionaries to All Nations. Our Almighty Father, *increase our faith* as we remember the glorious deliverances of the past. We remember that thy powerful hand did reveal thyself in the unconsumed "burning bush," in the desert. Thou didst reveal thy power in delivering the Children of Israel from captivity in Egypt; thou didst deliver Noah and his posterity from the raging sea; thou didst lead the Lehite family across impossible deserts and uncrossable seas; thou didst protect Daniel in the lions' den; thou didst open prison doors and thou didst lead the modern Saints across the plains to the mountain valleys.

With these and numerous other events, *we know that thou canst unlock gates and open doors,* that we may present to the people of this world thy exalting program as thy Beloved Son has decreed. So we pray, lead our missionaries to all nations with their testimonies of the truth and successfully bridge all barriers. (Washington Temple Dedicatory Prayer, Washington, D.C., November 19, 1974.)

I Know It Won't Be Easy. This is the work of the Lord, my brothers and sisters. It's glorious to contemplate it, to dream about it, to think about it, to see the great possibilities. I know it won't be easy. I know it will not go fast. I know it will be difficult, but I'm sure that the Lord is with us and he will be with us until, as he says, "It has penetrated every continent, visited every clime, swept every country, and sounded in every ear till the purposes of God shall be accomplished." (New Mission Presidents Seminar, June 27, 1974.)

The Man of Faith. To ordinary reasoning and ordinary human calculations, there was no chance for the youth. His death in moments was certain. What a horror in seconds would meet their gaze, but what could they do about it? Impossible, must have been in their minds. Futile and senseless, must have been in their thoughts. A sheep boy and a calloused, trained, muscular man of war experience. What chance could there be? But nothing is impossible with God. The Lord uses normal situations to bring his purposes to fruition.

The boy of years, the man of *faith*, the servant of God, running across the no man's land, drew from his bag a stone, fitted it into the pocket of his sling, swung the weighted, simple projectile. It must have been a breathless moment for the armies on both sides. The lad had undoubtedly used this sling and similar stones numerous times to drive off wild predator animals from his sheep or to kill a vulture which planned to carry away a lamb. He was prepared, trained, able, and armed with the equipment of *faith*, a *faith* such as Nephi's, like Abraham's, like Enoch's. (Salt Lake Valley Young Adults Fireside, Salt Lake Tabernacle, April 28, 1974.)

I Have Great Faith. If we do all we can, and I accept my own part of that responsibility, I am sure the Lord will bring more discoveries to our use. He will bring a change of heart into kings and magistrates and emperors, or he will divert rivers or open seas or find ways or touch hearts. *He will open the gates and make possible the proselyting.* In that, I have *great faith.* (Regional Representatives Seminar, April 4, 1974.)

He Gave You Your Voice to Teach the Gospel

Tell the World. The cancer was so bad I could not talk. As we went up the elevator that day in the hospital, some man was there with a hole in his throat. And his voice was terrible, and I said to my wife, "I could not stand that."

Then Brother Lee said to the doctor, "This is an important man. He goes all over the world and preaches the gospel to the world. He could not get along without his voice."

And this great doctor said, "Oh, people can get along without voices." And then we said, "But I could not because that would be the end of my life because my work is to preach the gospel to all the world."

At any rate, he took me into surgery. He cut my throat, and he took out certain things. But after a few months I had regained my voice. That is, I had regained part of it. I have not been able to sing since that date. But you don't have to be able to sing to continue to live. You do not have to sing to preach the gospel. So my voice gradually came back until I now have the ugly one that I do have.

When I was eleven years old, a little boy in the country, my father took me to a patriarch. Among other things, he said to this little boy, "You will preach the gospel to many people, but more especially to the Indians, the Lamanites, and you will see them grow to be a great people in the Church." And so I knew I had to preach the gospel, and I could not quit and do without a voice.

Let me ask you how many of you would be willing to give up your voice? Did you buy it or trade it? Did somebody give it to you? Did the Lord give you a voice so that you could express yourself? Then why don't you go out into the world and express the greatest story in the world, and tell the people that the truth has been restored; that the Lord has a continuation of prophets from Adam to now; and that you yourself have the holy priesthood, and you are going to magnify it all the days of your life? Tell the world that! They need it!

And so I ask you again, who gave you your voice? Why?—just so that you could sing or talk or have fun with people? Or did he give that voice to you so you could teach the gospel? Why did he give you eyes and ears and the other parts of your bodies? He gave them to you to use for his purposes.

Now I think we had better go in the mission field, don't you?—every boy that is worthy. (Area Conference Address, Luna Park, Buenos Aires, Argentina, March 8, 1975.)

We Can Join in Serious Continuous Petitions. There is one thing we all may do. We can join in serious, continuous petitions to our Father in Heaven to open the doors of nations and to soften the hearts of people to the extent that missionaries and each of us may be blessed to teach the gospel to all who need and want it. ("Are We Doing All We Can?" *Ensign*, February 1983.)

Every Night and Every Morning. We have already asked you, and we now repeat that request, that every family, every night and every morning as the family has its family prayer, and in secret prayers, too, pray to the Lord to open the doors of the other nations so that their people, too, may have the gospel of Jesus Christ. Until we get the permission of political authorities, we are unable to go into a country and proselyte there. And so we are praying that the Lord will touch the hearts of the prime ministers, the queens, the emperors, the presidents, and the rulers of all the nations in the world, so that they will make it possible for our young missionaries to go into those fields. (Area Conference Address, Ann Arbor, Michigan, September 21, 1980.)

As With Your Faith, So Shall It Be. Do you believe the doors of *Russia* can be pushed wide open? Do you think the gates of *China, Egypt, India, Burma,* and *Arab* countries can be swung wide so that we may enter and teach the gospel to them? Is it possible? As with your faith, so shall it be.

If We Do Not Do Our Duty . . . Therefore, as missionaries we are not to question whether or not to serve, but we are to prepare and then do. There are not impenetrable "iron curtains" or "bamboo curtains" or national curtains or neighborhood curtains so far as teaching the gospel is concerned. I see no good reason why the Lord should open doors we are not prepared to enter, but *I believe he will open every missionary door we are prepared to enter.* And if we do not enter, then the responsibility will be upon us. If we do not do our duty in regard to missionary service, then I am convinced that God will hold us responsible for the people we might have saved had we done our duty. ("It Becometh Every Man," *Ensign*, October 1977.)

That Is the Kind of Faith the Lord Wants. You remember when the Apostles had followed the Lord across the sea and a storm arose in the vicinity of the Sea of Galilee. There is a deep depression, with hills all around, and . . . when the wind comes down those mountains and touches the water, it sets about a great torrent. That had happened in this case, and as the Lord came to the ship, the brethren spoke to him and said, "It is the Lord." Then Peter said, (and he was the chief Apostle), "Ask me to come and join you." And the Lord put out his hand and told him to come. Peter walked on the water, probably as no other man in all the world had ever done, outside of the Lord himself. He walked on the water, and the water was placid under his feet, and he walked, but that doubting nothing began to work on him and he must have begun to think, "Water doesn't hold up a body like that, water just doesn't. It gives way and you start to sink." Just then he did sink, and his *faith* was not strong enough, was not long enough, so he began to sink into the water, which is a natural consequence, and the Savior grabbed him and gave him support so that he could get back into the ship.

That is an indication of the kind of *faith* that we must have, but it is much greater than most of ours would be because he did walk on the water; but when he began to doubt and wonder if this could happen, if he could do the thing that the Lord had done, then his support began to melt and he slipped into the water. In spite of this, he has exhibited a *faith* that very few people in the whole world have ever exhibited, though it did last a little while. But that is the kind of *faith* that we have when we receive the blessings. That is the kind of faith the Lord wants us to have, *faith* that is unwavering; doesn't change, doesn't rationalize. It is very difficult for us not to do a lot of rationalizing these days when we have such skilled men among us who know so many details of our lives, it is rather difficult, and it seems that nearly all of us, the moment there is difficulty in the family, we get on the telephone to get to the doctor. That, of course is all right, but very frequently we wait until the doctor has pretty well exhausted his efforts, and when the person is going to pass away, then they think all at once, "We must pray, We must pray," but as a *last* resort, not as a *first* resort. (General Priesthood Meeting Address, Monument Park Stake, Salt Lake City, September 12, 1976.)

Let Us Bless the Land

We Can Bless the Land. And I ask myself this question, "Could we better prepare all our Mission Presidents to stir and stimulate?"

Nearly twenty years ago I was in a place in England in which I felt very curious. But I did not know at that time what it meant. I went through a town called Chatburn, Clithero. Before I went there, some persons told me that there was no use in my going and asked me what I wanted to go to Chatburn for, saying it was the worst place in the country; for the sectarian priests had preached there faithfully thirty years without making any impression. Notwithstanding that, I went and preached once, and baptized twenty-five persons where the priests had not been able to do a thing. I went through the streets of that town feeling as I never before had felt in my life. I pulled off my hat and felt that I wanted to pull off my shoes. I did not know what to think of it.

When I returned, I mentioned the circumstances to Brother Joseph, who said, "Did you not understand it? That is a place where some of the old prophets traveled and dedicated that land and their blessing fell upon you." I know that we can bless the land and through the blessing it will be filled with the spirit and power of God, and that in great profusion. (*Life of Heber C. Kimball.*)

And now I am wondering if the lands you traverse, the missions and the stakes, have been dedicated and blessed and sanctified. Do you Brethren of the General Authorities see to it that the countries and the stake areas are made holy by your presence and by your walking on the soil?

My grandfather said again:

Let us bless the land we cultivate and the fountains of water, and they will be blessed, and then men will drink of those waters and they will be filled with the spirit and power of God.

Then go to work and build up this kingdom, establish righteousness and prepare yourselves. . . .

[They will come by] hundreds and by thousands—yea, fifty thousand in a year and very many will come trudging along with their bundles under their arms. (Ibid.)

And while we talk about this, do you folks live in dedicated homes? If you have paid for your home, why don't you set a date for your family to gather and have a dedication service. I tell you, brethren, much value can come to us when living in a dedicated home.

When my house was finished and ready to be lived in, we had a family home evening, and had our youngest son who had just returned from a mission do the honors. He dedicated the building as a safe and comfortable home in which to live. I commend this practice to you. (Regional Representatives Seminar, April 5, 1976.)

Rededicate Our Homes. We move forward, with clear vision and sound judgment, and rededicate our homes and our families to high moral and spiritual values. ("Seeking Eternal Riches," General Conference Address, April 6, 1976.)

To Use All Inventions and Opportunities

Surely This Is a Great Day. Surely this is a great day, when there are so many inventions, so many glorious things we can enjoy. Long centuries ago the Lord made this statement to Samuel, the prophet: "Behold, I will do a thing in Israel, at which both the ears of every one that heareth it shall tingle." (1 Samuel 3:11.)

The nineteenth century theologians thought they saw the fulfillment of these predictions in the coming of the steam engine, the sewing machine, and the motor car.

What they saw was merely the dim beginnings of the most spectacular increase of knowledge man has had since the beginning. If they could emerge from their graves today and behold a giant rocket in flight, a man-made satellite that bounced off their songs back to the earth, these people would recognize that numerous space marvels of fulfillment were with us. (Area Conference Address, Guatemala City, Guatemala, February 21, 1977.)

To Use the Technology Provided in Our Time for This Work. I have spoken often of the need to use the technology provided in our time for this work.

Even though there are millions of people throughout the world who cannot read or write, here is a chance to reach them through radio and television. The modern transistor radio can be mass-produced by the thousands in a size that is small and inexpensive. We can preach the gospel to eager ears and hearts. These could be carried by people in the market places of South America, on the steppes of Russia, the vast mountains and plains of China, the subcontinent of India, and the desert sands of Arabia and Egypt. Some authorities claim that this tiny miracle will be recorded by future historians as an event even greater than the invention of the printing press. The transistor is an eloquent answer to illiteracy and ignorance. The spoken voice will reach millions of hearers who can listen through an inexpensive transistor but could not read even an elementary little book or tract.

There are over seven thousand AM and FM radio stations in the United States, with thousands more in other parts of the world. There are innumerable opportunities for us to use these stations overseas, if we only prepare the message in the native languages.

Also, missionaries could be supplied with small portable cassette tape players and go into the homes with prepared messages to humble family groups all around the globe. Millions of people are anxious and willing to learn, if only they can hear the 'sound' in their own tongue and in a manner that they can grasp and understand.

Just think what can be accomplished when we broadcast our message in many languages over numerous radio stations, large and small around the world, and millions of good people listening on their transistors, and being indoctrinated with the truth.

With the Lord providing these miracles of communication, and with the increased efforts and devotion of our missionaries and all of us, and all others who are "sent," surely the divine injunction will come to pass: "For, verily, the sound must go forth from this place unto all the world, and unto the uttermost parts of the earth—the gospel must be preached unto every creature." (D&C 58:64.) And we must find a way. ("The Uttermost Parts of the Earth," Regional Representatives Seminar, September 29, 1978.)

The Television and Radio. I believe that the telephone and telegraph and other such conveniences were permitted by the Lord to be developed for the express purpose of building the kingdom. Others may use them for business, professional or other purposes, but basically they are to build the kingdom. I believe that the television and radio have been released to general knowledge by the Lord for the special purpose of building his kingdom, to produce programs which will build the testimonies of the Church members and take messages to numerous people. I urge our missionary committee to explore every possibility, to use all inventions and opportunities afforded them to bring the gospel to the world and to build the kingdom. (Regional Representatives Seminar, April 3, 1975.)

Small Efforts of Each Member Could Do So Much. Seemingly small efforts in the life of each member could do so much to move the Church forward as never before. *Think, brothers and sisters, what would happen if each active family were to bring another family or individual into the Church* before next April conference. We would be joined by several hundred thousand new members of the Church. Imagine, if only one additional mature couple were to be called on a full-time mission from each ward—our missionary force would go from 27,500 to over 40,000! Contemplate the results if each family were to assist—between now and next April conference—an inactive family or individual into full activity. How we would revel in the association of those tens of thousands! ("Let Us Move Forward and Upward," General Conference Address, April 1, 1979.)

I Can See This Miracle. Now, my brothers and sisters, I am converted to this great miracle that we have talked about. I can see this miracle becoming a big one instead of a little one. I can see it grow and prosper. I can see great numbers of these good people on the streets of Manila and elsewhere joining the Church and being baptized in the waters of the rivers here.

I pray that the Lord will bless you, every one of you, every one of your children, every one who makes this promise, "Lord, I want to help you do the thing that is necessary to be done." (Area Conference Address, Manila, Philippines Area Conference, October 19, 1980.)

CHAPTER FOUR

Urgency

Evangelistic harvest is always urgent. The destiny of man and of nations is always being decided. Every generation is strategic. We may not be responsible for past generations, but we cannot escape full responsibility for this one.

There's Urgency in Our Program

My brothers and sisters, I must warn you that this is not a new sermon, it's not a new subject, but our theme song, and maybe a few changed trinkets to add to the costumed picture. For years we've been speaking of the life-giving blood of which we continue to grow and our ever present responsibility which we've barely touched as yet. *There's urgency in our program. We're directed and commanded to convert the world.* And this brings us to the statement of young Jesus, "Wist ye not that I must be about my Father's business?" He has given us a time in which to accomplish his purposes. (New Mission Presidents Seminar, June 27, 1974.)

Baptize Tens of Thousands. Our great missionary program among mortals is the most extensive it has ever been in all dispensations as we preach, teach, and baptize tens of thousands of our fellowmen. However, missionary work is not limited to the proclaiming of the gospel to every nation, kindred, tongue, and people now living upon the earth.

Missionary work is also continuing beyond the veil among the millions and even billions of the children of our Heavenly Father who have died either without hearing the gospel or without accepting it while he lived on the earth. Numerous of our dead to mortality since Adam are teaching and being taught the saving principles of the gospel.

Our great part in this aspect of missionary work is to perform on this earth the ordinances required for those who accept the gospel over there. The spirit world is full of spirits who are anxiously awaiting performance of these earthly ordinances.

I hope to see us dissolve the artificial boundary line we so often place between missionary work and temple and genealogical work, because it is the same great redemptive work! ("The Things of Eternity—Stand We in Jeopardy?" *Ensign*, January 1977.)

In Jeopardy Every Hour. After all, is it not security instead of jeopardy for which we seek? The president of this great country caught a glimpse of this security recently when the Church presented him a book containing a record of his ancestors. As he stood in the Oval Office of the White House holding the book closely to him, he said with some feeling of emotions, "Now I feel secure."

This man who commands the manpower of the world's greatest nation must have sensed at that moment the only real security which comes through the family. His ancestry meant much to him, and he no doubt sensed the truth of what we know full well, that "they without us cannot be made perfect—neither can we without our dead be made perfect." (D&C 128:15.)

There is no real and lasting security apart from this spiritual security, from the peace of conscience gained in perfecting ourselves and our ancestors. It comes in part from knowing who our ancestors are and in doing for them what they cannot, or did not, do for themselves. In so doing, we become, in a very real sense, saviors of our people. While genealogical research and temple work can help build security, ignoring these responsibilities leaves us in "jeopardy every hour." ("Temple Work for the Dead as Urgent as Missionary Work," Priesthood Genealogy Seminar, August 4, 1977.)

The Urgency of the Task Noah Undertook. In our day, those who keep the commandments will be set apart from the world, just as surely as Noah was by his seemingly strange act of building an ark before the floods came. As we strive to serve by doing simple, mundane things, and as we strive to keep the commandments of God in our day, we will no doubt meet some of the same kind of ridicule that came to Noah and that party of eight—before it began to rain and kept on raining.

Noah's neighbors simply could not understand the urgency of the task Noah had undertaken. Neither should we expect many others to understand *our sense of urgency* about simple things like family, chastity, and doing missionary work! (Opening Address, June Conference, June 21, 1974.)

The Social Symptoms in the Time of Noah. We are told that society in the last days would display some of the social symptoms that existed in the time of Noah. We have very few adjectives that describe Noah's contemporaries, but his neighbors were apparently very "disobedient" to the commandments of God, and the earth was "corrupt," and, significantly, society then was "filled with violence" (Genesis 6:11). Violence and corruption usually occur because of selfishness. In a time of violence and corruption, how fitting it is that our theme should focus on service to our fellowmen! (Opening Address, June Conference, June 21, 1974.)

The Trends of the Times. If you are acquainted with the trends of the times, you will be greatly disturbed, as I am; you will notice the dissolution of the morals of our communities. Sin has had a holiday, it now celebrates throughout the entire world and has in all ages. It had a great hold on the people in Noah's day; in the days of Sodom and Gomorrah it had the whip hand, and in the days in which we now live, Lucifer has the whip hand. Every sin that is imaginable is upon the earth today, and I would like to enlist your help this day to pledge your unqualified support toward calling the hand of Satan and of bringing repentance to a confused and sickly world. ("The Trends of the Times," Utah State University Address, April 30, 1978.)

Appreciate Values by Contrast. Sometimes we can appreciate values by contrast, and so may I quote to you a few paragraphs from my journal of 1961:

January 1, 1961. We are now in Calcutta—Calcutta the great—Calcutta the populous—Calcutta the filthy— Calcutta the seething mass of humanity—Calcutta with its breathing, groaning, yelling, begging, hungry populace.

It is the Sabbath day. The sun is still sleeping, so also are the millions all over the great metropolis; so also are the poor devils across the way. We are on the fifth story of the Oberei Grand Hotel. Our quarters are comfortable, but I have had little sleep this night. The window is a high one, three feet square. It is barred with heavy wire half-inch mesh, and the panes of the window are too small to admit a thief. . . .

Through our window I see down and across the street, possibly two hundred feet from me, the huddled creatures on the cold, wet sidewalk, curled up or stretched out, and covered by dirty shawls. There is a little straw—perhaps it makes their concrete bed a little easier. They were there when we went to bed last night, part of them huddled around a little fire on the sidewalk. They are still there this morning. Something under a dark gray cloth—a dirty one. It moves—I think it is a woman. It is, and there is something else now moving under the filthy cover. It wiggles until it is a little uncovered. It is a little baby, perhaps eight or nine months old, sleeping on the mother's breast on the cold, concrete sidewalk. Men and women there are—they stir—they sit up—they rub their eyes—they stretch out again for what is there to do? Where may they go? This is a back street. To the left across the intersecting street is another sidewalk under the porch of a big red brick building. It looks like a long row of sleeping beggars there also. They were just dark little mounds, but now as they stir, I see that they are people. People? I wonder. What can be their thoughts, their ambitions, their hopes?

The sidewalks are full—Sunday seems to mean nothing to these people. We can hardly jostle our way through the crowds. Beggars appeal to us from every side. Poor, emaciated little bodies of old and young, holding out their hands. *What can I do?* A poor little woman follows—a little babe in her arms. Can she be starving? Only in the hotel can one get away from the constant barrage. Can I help them? Yes! Yes! I can give away my few dollars, bring smiles to a few, but there is the ever-increasing number, all eager, all hungry.

A poor woman is kneeling at a little pool of water on the sidewalk—it has been raining. She is washing her face, drinking the same water from her hands, the dog by her side getting his drink also. The naked little boy up the sidewalk—he must be about six. There is another one a little older. Each of them is as nude as when he was born, and it must be a little chilly out there, too. It is January.

There are the rickshaws, hundreds of them. The street is full of them. The pullers are barefoot and wear short diaper pants. The little carriage they pull has shelter for the rider but none for the puller—the human animal who pulls and runs. Does he run as demanded by the "fare" or by the necessity to get this penny "fare" delivered so he can pick up another? . . .

These poor human wretches pulling rickshaws! Is it inhuman to have them pull you or human to patronize them? Pulling and running in the rain! Wet and bedraggled, but they must run on. Perhaps there is another customer around the corner. . . .

Then I pray, and my prayer is one of gratitude for my blessings—for a warm bed at home, for warmth, for pure water, for food, for comforts—yes, even for hope.

January 3, 1961 . . . We are now at Benares—Varanasi—the holy city. It is a city of a half a million people located on the high bank of the famous Ganges River.

We are excited about our tour of the morning. . . . It is colder here—but we are higher and closer to the mountains. . . . Cows, some of them, have burlap covering—better than many humans. . . . We reach the sacred Ganges River in the holy city —The holiest, they claim. . . . The streets are so full of seething humanity that we shudder a thousand times as our car weaves in and out among them. . . . We thought Calcutta was sore and dirty and ugly. This holy city surpasses them all. What could the gospel do for these people? Oh, how they need the truth to set them free! There goes an old man with hair near six feet long, matted, apparently never combed.

There are hordes of pilgrims here coming from far away places to worship and be cleansed and washed in their holy river, the Ganges. . . . They take them to the river, "Mother River" they call it. . . . The Hindu, our guide said, will come to this holy river at least once in his lifetime and his sins are forgiven when he bathes in this sacred river. "If I die in Benares," the guide said, "I am forgiven of all my sins and go to Nirvana.". . .

Now we are out in the middle of the wide river with our guide who tells us many weird stories. A dead body is carried on the shoulders of four men on the bank. The corpse is probably wrapped in a sheet and lies on a loose framework. It may be taken down to the water's edge and placed on a small skiff, a rock tied to its neck, and it is rowed out into the center of this wide river and the body is pushed off into the river. It sinks immediately to the bottom to join its fellows which have not yet been devoured by the fish.

Or the body is placed on a burning ghat. They have brought willows and wood to burn the body and the mourners circle the burning ghat as the body is consumed. There are many people bathing in the river with little or no covering. Some are dipping up bottles of the sacred water to take home. The guide tells us that there is no pollution or contamination here. This is the purest water, he said, perfectly pure and holy. . . .

Now we are back to the landing, and we can hardly get up the steps for the numerous beggars, many starving. . . . My pockets are already empty. I have only my tickets left. Market Street is probably eight feet from wall to wall with many tiny shops . . . and up and down this narrow alley . . . we jostle with the cattle, the holy cows, the dogs, the lepers, and others of the sick. Manure is everywhere. They spit their betelnut saliva and worse, and it looks like bloody ground. The holy cows push us out of the way. So many beggars assail us that my wife begins to weep—I fear she will go into hysterics. I feel like retching. We thought we had seen everything. We had seen nothing. Pilgrims, barefoot in rags, carrying holy water from the Ganges. . . . We are not supposed to be worthy to enter the temple but a holy cow walks boldly into the temple in its inner precincts. . . .

And so we leave the holy river—the pure water river which is paved with dead bodies in its center, contaminated with the sewer from the banks, diseased with the germs from the lepers, smallpox victims, the T.B. coughers and the spitters, the dung of the animals, and the ashes of countless cremated ones.

As we come from them, we pass a body lying in the street. It is covered with a dirty rag. When we went down two hours ago, it lay there. Our guide says it is probably a dead person. . . . What must the Lord think? How must he feel? So many of his sons and daughters so wretched! (Thanksgiving Address to Holladay Stakes, November 26, 1975.)

We Will Wait Too Long to Move. I fear sometimes lest some people, near and far, who are already partially converted will grow tired of waiting for us. I fear that sometimes we will wait too long to move and miss certain golden opportunities to build the Church or to feed our Father in Heaven's children. We can be careful and yet move forward. It is better for something to be underway than under advisement. It is better for a facility to be under construction than under consideration. ("The Uttermost Parts of the Earth," Regional Representatives Seminar, September 29, 1978.)

We're Very Short of Missionaries for This Big World. We're very short of missionaries for this big world. We need your sons. Every boy should be considered. We hope that when he is eight and twelve and fourteen and sixteen and nineteen, he will be properly interviewed by his bishop and prepared for his baptism covenant, his growing priesthood responsibilities and his approaching mission. All worthy, normal boys should fill missions. The mission is part of this priesthood responsibility. (Regional Representatives Seminar, April 3, 1975.)

Can We Raise Our Sights?

We Are Not Increasing Our Missionary Force Fast Enough. Our responsibility at the present time is three-and-a-half to four billion people with whom we must share the gospel. We have at the present time, as I have said, nearly 19,000 or 20,000 missionaries. Without accounting for the deaths and the births in the world and the losses through apostasy, it would take us three or four regimes of mission presidents to baptize a million people. It would take more than our lifetimes combined to baptize ten million. It would take us a thousand years or three or four hundred regimes of mission presidents to reach a hundred million and ten thousand years for us to reach one billion, and we still have two and a half billion to go—plus the numerous births that we are not accounting for, and of course, some deaths and some few apostasies. You can see, brethren, that 80,000 or 90,000 or 100,000 converts a year is not good enough. We are not increasing our missionary force fast enough nor are we baptizing real converts rapidly enough. We seem to remember that Wilford Woodruff baptized 2,000 people on his mission in England in a short few months and that Heber C. Kimball baptized 1,800 in a few months and that there are hundreds of other brethren who have baptized tens and fifties and hundreds during their missions. *Is it possible that each of you could develop some Wilford Woodruffs and Brigham Youngs who could baptize hundreds and thousands?* Can we raise our sights? (New Mission Presidents Seminar, June 20, 1975.)

As I Have Urged Before. As I have urged before, we must increase our devotion so that we can do the work that is here for us to do. There are numerous people in the world who are hungering for the Lord and his word. They are thirsting for associations with the Lord's truths and work, and yet they neither know exactly what they are hungry for nor what will quench their thirst. It is your and my responsibility to quench their thirst. ("Are We Doing All We Can?" *Ensign*, February 1983.)

Let Us Not Shrink from the Next Steps. Are we ready, brothers and sisters, to do these seemingly small things out of which great blessings will proceed? I think we are. I believe the Lord's church is on the verge of an upsurge in spirituality. Our individual spiritual growth is the key to major numerical growth in the kingdom. The Church is ready to accomplish these things now which it could not have done just a few years ago. So also we are ready as members. If you will accept my counsel, you will come to feel that there is a readiness in our people which must be put to work.

Let us not shrink from the next steps in our spiritual growth, brothers and sisters, by holding back, or side-stepping our fresh opportunities for service to our families and our fellowmen. ("Let Us Move Forward and Upward," General Conference Address, April 1, 1979.)

CHAPTER FIVE

Is Anything Too Hard for the Lord?

*I believe the Lord can do anything He desires, and
certainly He desires that the gospel be taught to
every person on the earth.*

Is Anything Too Hard for the Lord?

Pray for Opening of Doors. Brethren, do you always pray for
the work, for the nations, for the leaders of nations, that we may
have them open the gates for our missionaries and theirs to
penetrate these great populations?

Do your children pray for this thing? Are they trained to
pray thusly?

Let every man, woman and child and youth take this
seriously. *Pray for opening of doors.*

Now, brethren, shall we not go forward in so great a cause?

"Verily I say, men should be anxiously engaged in a good
cause, and do many things of their own free will, and bring to
pass much righteousness." (D&C 58:27.)

Brethren, let us see that the fast developing stakes shall be
fully organized and trained to do this vital duty and cause that
all the world may hear his voice.

"Is anything too hard for the Lord?" (Genesis 18:14.) (Regional Representatives Seminar, September 30, 1977.)

Is Anything Too Hard for Me? "Is anything too hard for the
Lord?" He asked, when Sarah laughed when she was told that
she would have a son. She heard this in the tent door and knew
that both Abraham at a hundred years and she at ninety years

were past the age of reproduction. She could not bear children. She knew that, as well as it has been known that we could not open doors to many nations.

Brethren, Sarah did have a son, from Abraham, the father of nations.

Also to Jeremiah he said: "Behold, I am the Lord, the God of all flesh; is there anything too hard for me? (Jeremiah 32:27.)

If he commands, certainly he can fulfill.

We remember the exodus of the children of Israel crossing the uncrossable Red Sea.

We remember Cyrus diverting a river and taking the impregnable city of Babylon.

We remember Father Lehi getting to the promised land.

We remember the revolutionary war and the power of God that gave America triumph.

I believe the Lord can do anything he sets his mind to do. ("The Uttermost Parts of the Earth," Regional Representatives Seminar, September 29, 1978.)

I Believe the Lord Can Do Anything He Desires. If missionary work is indeed the Lord's work, which it is, and if it is to go forth by His power, which it will, then why should we, as Latter-day Saints, fear or hesitate in taking the gospel to others?

The Lord Is God; He Is Our Maker. Brothers and sisters, the work goes on. The Lord is God; He is our Maker. He has filled us with purpose. He did this for a purpose. We didn't just happen into the world. He organized our body. He gave us each a body. He arranged where they could be perpetuated and multiplied, and He gave us roles to play. The woman has a role to play and the man has a role to play and everybody in the world has a role to play; that's a part of our lives, but our lives are much more comprehensive than that. We are born for a purpose. We are born to teach the gospel and to bring people to a knowledge of the truth, to change lives. That's the important part, and to that end our Lord and Savior, Jesus Christ, came to the earth, to change lives. The Evil One was given liberty to be a taskmaster, to tempt, because the Lord in the first place gave us our free agency. If we didn't have free agency, we couldn't progress and grow. It is a matter of evaluating things that are given to us in order that we can select the right things, the developing things, the precious things. (Fireside Address, Orlando, Florida, December 19, 1976.)

God Does Nothing by Chance. We need to help those we seek to serve to know for themselves that God not only loves them, but he is ever mindful of them and of their needs. Surely God our Father and his Son, Jesus Christ, who appeared to an Aaronic Priesthood-age youth, Joseph Smith, to give that lad instructions for all mankind, did not simply make a random appearance to a person on this planet. Rather, the Lord says that this appearance which was precisely planned occurred because "I the Lord, knowing the calamity which should come upon the inhabitants of the earth, called upon my servant Joseph Smith, Jun., and spake unto him from heaven, and gave him commandments." (D&C 1:17.)

God does nothing by chance but always by design as a loving father. You know his purpose. We have purpose also in our lives. (Opening Address, June Conference, June 21, 1974.)

Nothing Is Impossible with God. Yet there are men among us who wade in the puddle instead of accepting the immensity of the ocean, and some who think of our earth as the great creation when it is but a small portion of the works of God.

And Enoch, the Prophet, had revelations and visions and heard the voice of the Lord say, "I am God: I made the world, and men before they were in the flesh." (Moses 6:51.)

Sometimes we became provincial. When I was a child, I thought the Gila Valley in Arizona was the world. When I grew up and learned that many people lived in Salt Lake City, thousands in Los Angeles, and millions in other parts of the world, I came to increase my admiration for the Lord who made it all. When I learned later that there were places in the world across oceans so wide that it took a month to get from one shore to the other, I began to stretch my imagination and realize in an ever expanding way what God had done for his children. And as I pondered and expanded, I came to realize that where I could dig a posthole, or open a canal or build a mound, that my Creator could fill a world with land and water and living things for the use of his posterity and his offspring.

As my knowledge increased, my faith seemed to multiply. As I saw things happen which to my small, finite mind seemed impossible, I realized that my knowledge was but a thimbleful as compared to all outdoors for my Creator. So my faith began to grow greater and greater toward the faith that nothing is impossible with God. (Salt Lake Valley Young Adults Fireside, Salt Lake Tabernacle, April 28, 1974.)

If We Do Our Duty, We Cannot Fail. We must keep in mind always, also, that in the Wentworth Letter the Prophet Joseph assured us that if we do our duty, we cannot fail. (New Mission Presidents Seminar, June 27, 1974.)

The Lord Is Waiting for Us to Move. Well, I believe that the Lord is waiting for us to move. I think the Lord is sitting there on his throne and is saying, "Whenever those good people down there catch the vision, I am going to bless them as they have never seen blessings or heard of them. But as long as they are content and they are satisfied to send a few of their boys and a few of them go on missions themselves, a few of them give a few hundred dollars, a thousand dollars to the missionary program, as long as they are content to just go right on as they have been doing for a long while, well, there is not much use of me, their Lord, to open the doors if nobody wants to go through them. Why open a gate? Everybody's standing out here not daring to move in." (Spokane, Washington, July 24, 1974.)

When We Are Ready. So I have expressed to the brethren time and time again . . . , "Brethren, *I have the faith that when we are ready, and the Lord knows when, he is going to open gates and doors that you could not believe.*" He says, "I'll do things that you cannot believe." Perhaps that day is just around the corner, I don't know just where . . . I don't know just how soon you and I are going to meet all these requirements. (Spokane, Washington, July 24, 1974.)

Instructions to Mission Presidents

Give All Our Time and Energy. Brothers and sisters, this is the work of the Lord that we are doing. We're called to go out and be his servants, special servants, and to give all our time and energy. What a glorious thing it is to give all of your time to the Lord, to have no other responsibilities and that, it seems to me, is one reason why mission presidents are so devoted. They have had this experience to not have a worry about their finances or other things and they have grown and developed. The Lord has given us the command. The Lord has said this is our duty. So we go forward with this in our minds. May the Lord bless you brethren and sisters. We call down upon you the blessings of heaven as you move from this place to your missions. It is true. There is no question about it. The Lord lives and his Father lives and he watches all our doings and he will appreciate it and show his appreciation for it. (New Mission Presidents Seminar, June 1977.)

It is easy to sit back in the shadows and say, "Well, the people are not ready for it," or that "the people have been drained. They have already taken from this country all of the souls that belong to the Church or will come into the Church." I know one young man who, with his family, baptized a whole family every year here in Zion. He just made a special effort and did it. (New Mission Presidents Seminar, June 25, 1976.)

To Be Trusted Now with These Many Precious Souls. Millions of people have spoken of Paul and Peter and James and John. You new mission presidents are to be trusted now with these many precious souls, local and foreign and it will be your privilege to lead these numerous missionaries to the fountain of truth unsullied, unfolded in the majesty of light and splendor from the opening heavens in all the simplicity of its nature. (New Mission Presidents Seminar, June 1977.)

You Become a Kind of Creator. As a mission president, you will be set apart by a member of the First Presidency of the Church or of the Council of the Twelve to stand foursquare on your own feet with your advisor and supervisor to do the important work in this great day.

You become a kind of creator, taking new people who have been differently trained and making them great leaders and inspired family people, to love the Lord, the Master.

It will be your privilege to take hundreds of boys, barely out of their swaddling clothes, sometimes spoiled and pampered boys, and to change their lives. Yes, to change their lives, to make their lives richer and more meaningful.

You become a creator in the sense that you take the unimproved, untrained, uninspired, sometimes selfish young men, and in two years make of them adults, sons of God.

You will take of these young men, unpolished shafts, and make them smooth and attractive. You will, in fact, make of these young men hunters and fishers as spoken of by Jeremiah, for you will act with the Missionary Committee and for the Lord wherein he said: "Behold, I will send for many fishers, saith the

Lord, and they shall fish them; and after will I send for many hunters, and they shall hunt them from every mountain, and from every hill, and out of the holes of the rocks." (Jeremiah 16:16.)

You will inspire them that they may do for the Lord what he did when he was on the earth. (New Mission Presidents Seminar, June 25, 1976.)

Go to the Emery Stone and Sharpen Your Ax. You mission presidencies, in your preparation, need to take time between each of your assignments to go to the emery stone and sharpen your ax. When I was a little boy, the pain of my life was the haying time when the numerous knives of the mowing machine had to be sharpened, when my older brother sat and held the blades to the emery stone while I stood on my feet and turned the great emery stone until my back ached and my legs were tired and my hands were blistered. I was glad when I was older and could sit on the seat and hold the knives against the stone while someone else turned it.

The beloved preacher said, "If the iron be blunt and he do not whet the edge, then must he put two more strings." (New Mission Presidents Seminar, June 27, 1974.)

Five Observations on Missionary Effectiveness. As I look back on several decades of close personal involvement with the missionary program of the Church, certain things seem to stand out from all the others.

FIRST, the Church seems to grow most rapidly where we are best known and where we have a high concentration of Church members. This is why we stress the member-missionary effort as a must in order to obtain the major growth which now is possible.

SECOND, we have had sudden spurts of success in missionary work based upon high pressure and gimmicks, but the real sustained growth such as we have achieved in several places in the world is almost always a result of solid proselyting in which the full-time mission president and his missionaries work very closely together.

THIRD, missionaries are happiest when they are succeeding, just as is the case with all of the rest of us. When missionaries are not succeeding in baptizing, they will tend to search for substitutes for success. Please don't force them into measuring their success by hours of tracting, gospel conversations, Books of Mormon distributed, etc.

FOURTH, we generally do better where the general population is larger and offers a greater field for labor and when we build outward from the centers of strength, which in our day, is where our stakes are. In this connection, please build the relationship between yourselves as a mission president and the regional representatives and the stake presidents in your area. They and the members must not only do more of the finding of the prospective members of the Church whom your missionaries will teach, but they must later receive, love, and train these new members so that appropriate levels of retention are realized.

FIFTH, missionaries watch the mission president to see whether or not he is a true missionary. When missionaries see a president who knows how to be bold, they will take the exhortation seriously. If missionaries feel they are simply tending or that you are merely serving time instead of serving the Lord, they will adjust their attitudes downward, also.

Now, I pray the Lord to bless you as you embark upon this glorious and demanding assignment. I express once again the thanks and gratitude for all your willingness and for your service. (New Mission Presidents Seminar, June 22, 1979.)

Get Busy and "Do It!" Speaking of the motivating of people, and getting them to work, that's our responsibility — to give. Eloquent sermons may brighten the life; to use expressive words may stimulate; but the evidence of our greatness, the proof of our effectiveness is in the area of motivation, to get them to do something.

I think Brother Simpson brought me a little card which is on my desk yet: "Do it!" And I like the thought that is behind it, and I think you need to have one of them on your desk, and when an idea comes to you, get busy and "Do it!" And find a way, if there isn't already one.

If we can stir our leaders in the stakes and the missions to set higher goals and encourage them in their accomplishments, we have proved our mettle. *If we can stir missionary leaders to get their missionaries to awaken their souls and then, in turn, to motivate the people to believe and repent; then we have achieved.* (New Mission Presidents Seminar, June 23, 1978.)

A Spark from Within Yourself. Mission presidents and regional representatives must realize that you can never light a candle unless there is A SPARK FROM WITHIN YOURSELF. You can never give the priesthood unless you have it. You can never convey enthusiasm without a liberal supply. (New Mission Presidents Seminar, June 27, 1974; emphasis added.)

Setting Part of the World on Fire. When he had been baptized, he himself began to choose his helpers. He saw Simon Bar-jonah and Andrew. He said to them: "Follow me, and I will make you fishers of men" (Matthew 4:19). As we follow through the scriptures, we can see to what extent he made them great fishers of men.

Did that mean that he would change their bodies or that he would change their minds and attitudes?

He could have gone to Nicodemus and other educators, perhaps, and presented the program to them. Perhaps they might even have accepted it. Some of them would, but he made them fishers of men, as we follow through the lives of Peter, James and John, and the other brethren and Paul.

We realize to a great extent that he made them over. He made them fishers of men.

It was this same Peter who stood defiantly before magistrates and officials who had the persecuting mania. Peter said, "We ought to obey God rather than men." (Acts 5:29.) Here were Peter and the other Apostles before the officials of the law and with such conviction and such courage and such power, they said: "The God of our fathers raised up Jesus, whom ye slew and hanged on a tree. Him hath God exalted with his right hand to be a Prince and a Saviour, for to give repentance to Israel, and forgiveness of sins. And we are his witnesses of these things." (Acts 5:30-32.)

This is your duty—to take these young, fresh, sweet young men and make them fishers of men; remembering, too, that it is your responsibility in large measure within your own area to take of these fresh recruits, strengthen their testimonies and build up their abilities.

Can you see the Lord standing on the Mount of Olives above the city of Jerusalem looking out into the wide world and speaking to all nations, all tongues and people? Perhaps He was the only one of the group that could see the future.

Can you see yourself as the number one man in your mission setting that part of the world on fire? Can you find a way to stir an appetite on the part of all men and women that they may have a hunger and a thirst for righteousness which can only be assuaged by the Holy Ghost following their proper baptism into the kingdom?

Can you see yourself as the father of a nation—a father by adoption and conversion? Can you appease their hunger and their thirst? (New Mission Presidents Seminar, June 25, 1976.)

See That They Have Real Warning. You personally will not be held responsible for the other millions of people in the world, but you will be held responsible for those within the boundaries of your own mission, to see that they have a real warning, and for the lives and souls of your hundreds of missionaries.

President John Taylor said that you will be held responsible for all those souls who would have received the gospel had they been warned. Oliver Cowdery, by appointment, gave this commitment to the brethren. It is somewhat comparable to the commitment we give to you, the charge.

> You will have the same difficulties to encounter in fulfilling this ministry, that the ancient Apostle had. You have enlisted in a cause that requires your whole attention; you ought, therefore, to count the cost; and to become a polished shaft, you must be sensible; [it] requires the labor of years. . . . It is required of you not merely to travel a few miles in a country, but in distant countries: you must endure much labor, much toil, and many privations, to become perfectly polished.
>
> Your calling is not like that of the husbandman, to cultivate a stinted portion of the planet on which we dwell, and when heaven has given the former and the latter rain, and mellow autumn ripened his fruit, gathers it in, and congratulates himself for a season in the intermission of his toils, while he anticipates his winter evenings of relaxation and fireside enjoyments. But, dear Brother, it is far otherwise with you. Your labor must be incessant, and your toil great; you must go forth and labor till the great work is done. . . . You will be dragged before the authorities for the religion you profess; and it were better not to set out, than to start and look back, or shrink when dangers thicken around you, or appalling death stares you in the face. I have spoken these things, dear brother, because I have seen them in visions. These should not appal you. . . . The ancients passed through the same experience. . . . You must bear the same testimony; or your mission,

your labor, your toil, will be in vain. . . . you shall see a nation born in a day. (*History of the Church* 2:192-93.)

We congratulate you on the call that has come to you. Of the million men, probably, in this Church, perhaps there are great numbers, many thousands, who would be glad to have the calls that have come to you this day. It is a great opportunity when a few of you are chosen out of the great number. This is a choice experience and such an opportunity that frequently some step over the boundaries of modesty and request such experiences.

This is an unusual experience in the sense that you will be with your beloved companion almost night and day all the time, and you will consider numerous matters of importance with her. This is a time when your position places you in an elevated place where you have decisions to make and where you will be looked upon by many people as their chief leader and where you will begin the training of hundreds of missionaries. (New Mission Presidents Seminar, June 25, 1976.)

These Young Missionaries Are Precious. These young missionaries are precious, fresh, new, unsullied, impressionable. It is our hope that you may be able to return every one of them without exception to his home at the termination of his mission with a strong testimony and a clean upright life. He will grow up and love you as his parents, mission president, and his wife, as I have loved my mission president all of my life. These budding flowers will become completed buildings, completed workers. (New Mission Presidents Seminar, June 1977.)

Teach Your Missionaries to Study the Scriptures. I hope you will teach your missionaries to study the scriptures as well as the lessons. Encourage them to learn the scriptures, to memorize some. I hope you will teach your missionaries tithing and that you will keep them reminded of it. They are exempt from tithing when they have no income, and most of them have no income except that which is given to them for their missions, but there are sometimes missionaries who have income that is separate and which continues on through their missions. They have a few head of cattle or they have some interest-bearing programs and they should not forget their tithing. They shouldn't get out of the habit of paying tithing. They pay it to their bishops, of course. (New Mission Presidents Seminar, June 20, 1975.)

Let the Missionaries Set Goals. I am not convinced that mission presidents should ever set goals for missionaries. They may set *goals* for their mission if they like and for themselves, but let the missionaries set *goals* for themselves and then the president will praise and give them adulation for succeeding in the *goals* which they set. (New Mission Presidents Seminar, June 20, 1975.)

Organize Carefully and Well. We hope you presidents will organize carefully and well. Do not over-fill your office force. Do not use your missionaries for messengers commonly, more than is absolutely necessary. You are responsible for their time and for their efforts. You must see that their time is so carefully monitored that they will not have time nor opportunity to become casual. Too many visitors sometimes visit your missions. I think there are times when you would be in the right way to excuse yourself from them. People from the Church who come sightseeing and want somebody to take them around—you have not time. You have a big job to do, to bring the gospel to all the people in your area. You cannot be nurse-maids or guest leaders to take people around and show the sights. There has been a tendency to do that in many places, and the president seems to feel many times that he had the obligation to take them around or have his missionaries do it. (New Mission Presidents Seminar, June 25, 1976.)

Have Your Missionaries Love You. Now, your responsibility is more than merely to train and assign. Have your missionaries love you, not merely respect you. Make them want to visit with you and to confess to you, if that be necessary, and to eagerly accept your directions. Remember your interviews with them, when they come, when they go, and all between as necessity seems to dictate. They are your first responsibility. They should be complete and total and sympathetic, these interviews with them. They should be individual and comprehensive, coupled with great understanding and affection. They should be private and confidential, and you will find many bits of information that should never be relayed to or through your assistants. I have seen that done in missions in the past where one missionary was degraded before other missionaries, and that is not proper. (New Mission Presidents Seminar, June 20, 1975.)

Love Turns the Wheels of This World. We hope that you will love your missionaries and cause them to love you, for love turns the wheels of this world. Make them your sons and daughters as did Paul make his fellow workers. He said of them, Timothy and others, ". . . my own son in the faith . . . my own beloved son . . ."

I hope that all are your beloved sons, for love will develop far more than critical leadership. I wish that every missionary would love his mission president as I did Samuel O. Bennion, who presided over me, for though I somewhat feared him, I respected his judgment, accepted his recommendations and did my utmost to sustain him fully. I loved my mission president. (New Mission Presidents Seminar, June 20, 1975.)

Effective Proselyting Methods. President Rhee Ho Nam in the Korea Pusan Mission, with the help of the regional represent-atives and the executive administrator . . . has given a strong emphasis to member-missionary work. He has only five districts and no stakes in his mission, but has instituted a program between missionaries and district and branch presidents and members. They've had special workshops to train members on how to be member missionaries. Baptisms in that mission when President Rhee got there were about 16 a month. Now they are around 120 a month. The Korean members are bringing friends to their homes and providing referrals and the priesthood leaders are not asking members to do any missionary work which the district and branch presidents are not doing them-selves. Further, President Rhee stresses that those who come into the Church through tracting often must leave their old friends behind and hope to make new ones in the Church, but when members bring their friends into the Church, these new members automatically have ready-made friends within the Church. President Rhee says that the priesthood leaders and members not only help bring their friends into the Church, but they watch over them once they are in the Church with specific affection and concern. (New Mission Presidents Seminar, June 22, 1979.)

Work with Circles of Friends. President Robert Stout in the Japan Kobe Mission has stressed member-missionary work in a fresh way under the direction of his executive administrator . . . and with the help of his regional representatives, he has involved members and particularly the local priesthood leaders who are asked to be the first to refer their friends to the missionaries to teach further. In this mission, 90 percent of their referrals come from the just-baptized new members. This is a mission which was baptizing around 25 a month a year or so ago. There were 144 baptisms in May and there should be 200 this, the month of June. This is with the involvement of leaders and members in the stakes. Furthermore, President Stout is using group teaching so that those prospective members who are being taught are asked to bring in their friends to be taught simultaneously. This permits the Japanese to work with their natural circles of friends in a very effective way. Local priesthood leaders and members are excited by this solid growth. (New Mission Presidents Seminar, June 22, 1979.)

Teach Those Whom Members Convert. In the Costa Rica San Jose Mission which involves three countries, President Joseph Muren has been emphasizing member missionary work. Just a short year ago, baptisms in that mission were running at about 135 a month. They seemed to have hit one of those plateaus. Over a two- or three-month period, the priesthood leaders in the four stakes were involved and the emphasis was given that there would be no more tracting, but that missionaries would teach those whom members converted. We're building the converts, we're building up the kingdom, and we're building the missionary. (New Mission Presidents Seminar, June 22, 1979.)

Do Proselyting Yourselves. It will be your responsibility to not only tell your missionaries how but to show them how. You who are highly motivated, you should proceed with proselyting yourselves: each of you should be a great proselyter and accept every opportunity, this in addition to your direction of your missionaries. (New Mission Presidents Seminar, June 20, 1975.)

CHAPTER SIX

More Conversion Productivity

From now on, brethren, we expect that every year there will be a great increase in conversions and baptisms.

Are We Getting As Many Conversions As We Should?

Are You Satisfied? Think then of the hundreds of millions who live out among the Saints in the big world we have now.

Miracles have always happened; they still happen and will continue to happen. The Lord used Cyrus, the Persian, to do his bidding, to send the Jews back to their land, to build the temple again. Cyrus was a king of the world. The Lord used him. He will use him and all the others as it is proper and necessary.

Are you satisfied with either the stake mission or the full-time mission? Are we getting as many conversions as we should? I don't know if there is any blame, I don't know where it is. We wouldn't want to blame anybody, but is it the missionaries? Is it our program? Is it our leaders? Is it the way we handle the matter? What is the reason that we are receiving less than 100,000 people a year with a third that many missionaries, ever growing? That's something for us to be thinking about. (Regional Representatives Seminar, October 2, 1975.)

We Must Convert More People. Now I want to say a word about missionary productivity—particularly *goals.*

Some years ago there grew up an error in the method of proselyting and many people were baptized who were not converted. This caused concern among the Brethren. We want people to have a testimony, but, when we expressed some concern about many of these baptisms, the pendulum swung the other way, all the way across, and there were many mission presidents who came to feel, mistakenly, that they should never discuss baptism with investigators at all. That is the trouble with pendulums—they nearly always swing all the way in one direction or the other. That problem has been corrected. We have had some difficulty, however, in getting the pendulum to stay in the center. From now on, brethren, we expect that every year there will be a great increase in conversions and baptisms. We hope that stake and full-time mission presidents will understand this. We do believe in setting goals. We live by goals. In athletics, we always have a goal. When we go to school, we have the *goal* of graduation and degrees. Our total existence is *goal-oriented*. Our most important *goal* is to bring the gospel to all people. We must convert more people. We must find ways and means.

Our *goal* is to achieve eternal life. That is the greatest *goal* in the world. We are not opposed to *goals*. We do not want stake and full-time mission presidents to establish quotas for the missionaries. Rather, we expect them to inspire missionaries to set their efforts, and work to achieve them. We expect them to inspire missionaries to set their own *goals*, and make them high enough to challenge their very best efforts, and work to achieve them. We expect you brethren to convey this message to them. We look to you to teach these principles and follow up. (Regional Representatives Seminar, April 3, 1975.)

We Can Increase Our Production

We Want to Be Productive. I have mentioned before that in rice production in the Orient, they have found that *they can produce 24 times* as much as they used to by improving the growing conditions and then buying better seed. There are many areas in life where, by improving the conditions and methods of production, the output can be greatly increased. I think I have mentioned to you that in Tempe, Arizona, in their university dairy they have found four cows that produced just an unbelievable amount of milk and butter fat. *Their four cows produced 88,000 pounds. That's 44 tons of milk, with 2,672 pounds, or over a ton, of butter fat.* They don't eat much more hay than any other cows—[But they receive] simple grain, *careful feed management, careful milking and proper feeding and breeding. If cows can do it, people can do it.* We can increase our production and that's what we're talking about, and we want it to be real production, of course. We're not talking about baptisms—we're talking about conversions. (Regional Representatives Seminar, October 2, 1975.)

Could We Bring Concerted Action? If you brethren agree with my thinking in this matter, *could we bring concerted action to a "lengthening stride" movement that would bring into the missionary activity the good members of the Church the world around?* The approach and the attack will need to be planned very carefully. We will need to impress upon stake, ward, and branch leaders around the globe their opportunity and responsibility. There will be need for strong, well-organized stake, ward, and district missions. It cannot be left to a mere suggestion, and a comprehensive score must be kept as a stimulant to the workers. Such a special, organized, developed program could bring many other of the blessings of the Church to more people as we have said. (Regional Representatives Seminar, April 3, 1975.)

Lengthen Your Stride

Now we have another revealed program which has in it the power of heaven. Several decades ago when President David O. McKay presided over the Church, he gave impetus to the missionary work in the stakes of Zion. He coined the [phrase], "Every member a missionary," and it is obvious that would be a giant step toward the accomplishment of our directives, with 3.5 million member missionaries. However, if only two million of the Latter-day Saints energetically and fully accepted the challenge of President McKay to work with the full-time missionaries, or separate from them as seemed wise, certainly we could extend our efforts and "lengthen our stride" and greatly increase the conversions and build the kingdom and eventually knock at every door. That would be only about 2,000 to each missionary but the ratio would rapidly change if we really did this. (Regional Representatives Seminar, April 3, 1975.)

Members Must Be Finders. In summary then, *there are two keys to productive missionary work.*
1. Family to family friendshipping (when a member family shares the gospel with a nonmember family).

2. Cooperation between members and the missionaries to reach people.

Missionaries are called and ordained to preach the everlasting gospel.

It is impractical for us to expect that 19,000 missionaries alone can warn the millions in the world. Members must be finders. The valuable time of our teaching missionaries is too often spent in "finding." (Regional Representatives Seminar, April 3, 1975.)

Overworry and Too Little Work

If You Get One or Two Converts. There seems to have grown up in many quarters a feeling that "we will just plod along and take the two or three or four converts that happen to come along." One sharp young man was saying goodbye to his home folks when a friend of the family said to him, "Where you are going, it is going to be a tough mission. You will do well if you get one or two converts in all your mission." The boy stiffened up and said, "No, sir, I am going out to convert the world." He had that spirit, and of course, he would be rewarded to the extent that he put that into practice. (New Mission Presidents Seminar, June 25, 1976.)

They Can Do a Greater Work Than Our Own Boys. We are not interested merely in numbers, but we have a great task to take the gospel to all the world. Generally the men most capable of teaching the gospel are those native sons. When you give the responsibility to a young native boy, who has the language, who has the customs and who has the acquaintances, oft times they can do a greater work than our own boys. (New Mission Presidents Seminar, June 25, 1976.)

And Then We Wonder. Frequently we ask the missionary, "How did you get along?" and his answer is, "Oh, I did the best I could." And then we wonder. "Only a mediocre person is always at his best," says Somerset Maugham. (Regional Representatives Seminar, October 3, 1974.)

Destroyed by Overworry and Too Little Work. You are not going to overwork your missionaries. There are few missionaries, if ever any, that have been destroyed by overwork.

They have been destroyed by overworry and too little work and by immoralities and other things, but generally not by over-work. (New Mission Presidents Seminar, June 20, 1975.)

They Are Doing Everything but Preaching the Gospel. I asked one of the brethren once how he was getting along in a certain mission, and he said, "It's a wonderful mission, wonderful missionaries. They are doing everything but preaching the gospel." There are so many leaks of time and effort that the new product is greatly reduced. Each mission president should study prayerfully his own program and be sure that there are no leaks of energy or time, for in the end you are responsible for the two years that these wonderful missionaries give to the Lord. (New Mission Presidents Seminar, June 20, 1975.)

We Must Find Ways to Inspire

We Can Hardly Be Content with the Record. As to converts, the number [has risen], and of course we do hope these are *well-converted* new members. As indicated, it rose from 75,000 a year ago to the happy figure of 95,000 this year [1975].

Now, the increased number of missionaries accounts for much of this increase in baptisms, for the "per-missionary baptisms" increased only from 4.3 to 4.9 per missionary. So we would say that the increase in actual missionary work was not so great as it might appear by the increased baptisms.

Now we can hardly be content with this record. *We must find ways to inspire and teach better ways of doing missionary work.* We see no objection to every missionary setting himself a goal. We do not want others setting his goals for him—it becomes too mechanical. But there is no reason why each missionary should not set his own goal.

Let us figure a little. Four billion people, not accounting for the increase in population, is many, many people. If we baptized only 100,000 converts per year, which we approached this past year, I figure that it would take us 40,000 years to accomplish the feat. That may be all right for you, but it's a little long for me.

Suppose we increased to 100,000 missionaries and each baptized 4.9 per missionary; that would be only a half million in a year, and in even your lifetime, it would leave many good people unproselyted.

We had a wonderful visit in Mexico two weeks ago, when we were in Mexico City and discussed the various phases of the program with the leadership there. We found such a quality of devotion that we seldom see.

We learned that, in 1975, 4.7% of the missionaries of the Church were in the Mexican area, but that the 4.7% of the missionaries had baptized 22.1% of the converts of the whole world.

They have been giving eager attention to the families, and of the 16,000 plus baptized families in the world last year, the Mexico area had baptized 4,849 families or 28 plus percent.

We note that in this south area they had baptized 21.47 converts per missionary as against 4.9. Why can't we come a little nearer to that figure in all the world?

This reminds us that 23,000 missionaries at 21.47 converts per missionary would mean just a little less than a half million conversions. This we never have yet attained or approached.

In another period, from Mexico only, it seems that the annual converts were 32.07 per missionary, and this would mean 670,700 baptisms if all the missionaries in the world were having that kind of success.

Now there is one more surprise. The Hermosillo Mission with their missionaries for February 1976 baptized 159.6 per missionary. If all the 23,000 missionaries in the world were baptizing similar numbers, that would be 3.5 million people in the Church in a year and would double our Church population in one year, and even that would take a long time to reach the world and to cover it. I realize the numerous problems that come with a greatly increased number of members, but we would have to meet that as it came and would have to arrange and develop for it.

We recollect that in January 1975 these missionaries baptized 1,323 in the one month, whereas in January 1976 they baptized 3,007 converts. Three thousand converts for one mission would be 36,000 in a year from one mission, but for 23,000 missionaries, it would be eight hundred million people. We'd begin to get the world at that time. I realize we are talking, not in impossibilities but improbabilities, perhaps.

I don't know how we would train them, but let us get them baptized first and then move as we need to.

I certainly would not like to appear critical of our missionaries generally, but *I wonder if our stride is long enough.*

And I realize, too, that these converts in Mexico are Lamanites and from a fertile field, but I am sure we can greatly exceed the 4.9 converts per missionary in the world. (Regional Representatives Seminar, April 5, 1976.)

They Are So Thrilled and Happy. Almost every mission in the Church is now saying that last year they *more than doubled or tripled the conversions* that they've made in the same world [where] just a half dozen years ago, they could hardly touch the family, they could hardly get a man and his family to come into the Church and yet, today, we are getting families, fathers and mothers. They like this home evening. They like this family business that we think so extremely important.

We just had one of our grandsons return from Central America where he went all over the hills down there doing the work of the Lord, and that they are so thrilled and happy as they bring whole families, father and mother, into the Church so that they can rear their children. (Missionary Farewell, Scottsdale, Arizona, May 14, 1978.)

We Must Use Our Talents. In the account of the barren fig tree (See Matthew 21:19) the unproductive tree was cursed for its barrenness. What a loss to the individual and to humanity if the vine does not grow, the tree does not bear fruit, the soul does not expand through service! One must live, not only exist; he must do, not merely be; he must grow, not just vegetate. We must use our talents in behalf of our fellowmen, rather than burying them in the tomb of a self-centered life. Personal purity and veracity and stability in leadership are essential if we are to give sanctified service to others. We must expend our energies and use our skills for purposes larger than our own self-interest if we desire true happiness. ("President Kimball Speaks Out On Service to Others," *New Era*, March 1981.)

CHAPTER SEVEN

Make No Little Plans

The Lord was saying to his despondent prophet, "If I told you what I'm going to do in the world, you wouldn't believe it."

We Can Raise Our Sights

You Wouldn't Believe It. How do you feel about 144 years of proselyting and the relatively small number of converts that we have made, compared to what we could have made? We feel to cry with Habakkuk: "O Lord, how long shall I cry and thou wilt not hear!" (Habakkuk 1:2.)

Habakkuk had almost reached the point of despair as he saw the overwhelming odds against the word of the Lord. God gave him a glorious answer: "I will work a work in your days, which ye will not believe, though it be told you." (Habakkuk 1:5.)

The Lord was saying to his despondent prophet, "If I told you what I'm going to do in the world, you wouldn't believe it."

We repeat that to ourselves. (Regional Representatives Seminar, October 3, 1974.)

As Though They Had All Time and Eternity. We are greatly concerned about the timing of this campaign. Some few missionaries move toward their work as though they had all time and eternity to convert a few people in their part of the world. *The word is urgency*—it is now.

We have something to say about this also: We do hope that while the boy is being groomed for a mission, that he will be impressed also with the thought that he must make himself heard; he must make himself believed and use his time profitably. (Regional Representatives Seminar, April 5, 1976.)

Missionary Goals

Make No Little Plans. Now may I use one of my favorite verses from Daniel H. Burnham, an architect, who says,

MAKE NO LITTLE PLANS
They have no magic in them
To stir men's blood, and
probably themselves will not be realized.

MAKE BIG PLANS, aim high and hope and work.
Remembering that a noble, logical diagram
Once recorded will never die, but long after
we're gone will be a living thing asserting
itself with ever-growing insistency.

(New Mission Presidents Seminar, June 20, 1975.)

Our Efforts Must Be Unbending. Remember that our sons and grandsons are going to do things which would stagger us. Remember that a lighthouse without a light is not as good as the absence of the lighthouse. And so our lights must shine, our lives must penetrate, our efforts must be unbending. (New Mission Presidents Seminar, June 20, 1975.)

It Will Be Unbelievable If We Do Our Part. Indicative of the great, new, increased enthusiasm for the work is the fact that not only are the people coming into the Church in large numbers, but *the missionaries have the spirit and have nearly doubled their baptisms per missionary. Also there is the great increase in the missionaries* for those same countries, increasing more than 400 percent among the Lamanite missionaries, young men and young women from these countries who have devoted themselves to two years of spreading the program of the Church. For instance, 167 young men and women are now proselyting in the Chile Santiago Mission, with another 42 in another mission in the same country. A greatly increased activity is predicted for the coming five years, and it will be unbelievable if we do our part. "The Lamanite," Regional Representatives Seminar, April 1, 1977.)

We Must Think in Large Numbers. Brethren and sisters, *we must think in larger numbers. We must prepare our missionaries better not only with language but with scripture and*

above all with a testimony and a burning fire that puts power to their words. (Regional Representatives Seminar, April 5, 1976.)

Set Substantial Goals. I tried out the goal process in a number of stakes when I was visiting regularly. We presented to the bishoprics of the wards of the stake the setting of their own goals, then putting forth the effort to make the goals a reality. We went into great detail in the suggesting of the goals and explaining how and by what means they could be reached.

After a few months I received a letter from one of the stake presidents who said that in several categories covered, the twelve wards in those months had raised their standards from 32% to 39%. This increase, which was the beginning in a few short months, represented a substantial increase in activity. Each bishop had made his own goals and had been influenced by the things that were said to encourage him. A letter just received from the Osaka Stake indicates, "We have some good news. After the last stake conference in February, we have sent in ten recommendations for full-time missionaries. For the month of March we plan to send five full-time missionaries more." This kind of message is coming from all over the world now, and we are grateful for that and we are grateful to you brethren who are stimulating this encouragement. (Regional Representatives Seminar, April 3, 1975.)

This Is More Than a Hundredfold Increase. For many centuries oysters were cultivated in the Orient even before the Christian era, but now a new science is developing in which waste solids, waste fluids, waste gases are converted to new organic ecosystems supporting aquatic life. It is suggested that if it were possible to turn just 1,000 square miles of New York's Long Island Sound into the cultivation of mussels, this relatively small area could produce a quantity of protein equal to three times the total world fish catch. Put it another way. Japan has raised the productivity of oysters from *600 pounds per acre under natural conditions up to 32 tons or 64,000 pounds per acre under a special culture. This is more than a hundredfold increase.* Now, if we could take our delightful, fresh, spiritual young men and ladies and cultivate them to the point where an *increase of 100% were possible* for them, that would certainly be the day. (New Mission Presidents Seminar, June 20, 1975.)

There Is Always a Better Way to Do It. I remember when I started in my family life, we were raising alfalfa almost totally in the valley where I lived. Alfalfa was our main crop. We also had grain and such, but cotton came into the program, so we all ploughed up our alfalfa fields and put them into cotton. We could get a great deal more per acre by raising cotton than we could alfalfa. We had to return to alfalfa once in a while because it enriched the soil and we needed the alfalfa once in a while to do that; but consistent with every good reason, we grew cotton because it brought us more money to take care of our family. That is the way it is in missionary work. There is always a better way to do it. Always something that will be *more efficient to use, some plan, organization or otherwise, and that we continue to pray for.* (Area Conference Address, Johannesburg, South Africa, October 23, 1978.)

We Must Become Sanctified Before Him. We continue to desire the growth of the Church, and we are pleased, but not overwhelmed, with the progress being made. We look to the day when Zion can be fully built, but the Lord reminds us: "But first let my army become very great." (D&C 105:31.)

And that, of course, refers to the missionaries, which army is growing, but also to the people of the Church which army isn't growing quite so fast.

The Lord wants us to grow numerically and eventually to cover the world, but also "we must become sanctified before him." We are not overly impressed with our size or our growth, but we know that it is a circumstance of our development. (Regional Representatives Seminar, September 30, 1976.)

CHAPTER EIGHT

The Example of Former Missionaries

I think we remember that early-day Apostles in their sincerity and inspiration reached goals which we are now coveting.

They Went Out into the World

Emulate the Great and Good Things. What a marvelous thing it would be if we could all emulate the great and good things accomplished by our pioneer forebears. Think of it! Imagine this valley and dozens of others like it as they appeared a century and a half ago. Imagine the great challenge that faced your ancestors and mine as they moved into a strange, uninviting territory—a desolate territory. Would we—we who so take for granted our automobiles and comfortable homes with their cool air in summer and warmth in winter—would we who do not have to break the dry and parched ground to plant crops for our survival, have the courage and fortitude of those great nineteenth century people who simply rolled up their sleeves, gritted their teeth, and carved out of the desert the forerunners of the great Rocky Mountain communities of today? (Territorial Ball, July 22, 1978.)

The Boldness of the Early Brethren. When I read Church history, I'm amazed at the *boldness of the early brethren* as they went out into the world. They seemed to find a way. Even in persecution and hardship, they pressed forward and opened doors which evidently have been allowed to sag on their hinges and many of them to close. I remember that these fearless men were teaching the gospel in Indian lands near headquarters before the Church was even fully organized. As early as 1837 the Twelve were in England. We were in Tahiti in 1844 and Australia in 1851, Iceland 1853, Italy, Switzerland, Germany, Tonga, Turkey, Mexico, Japan, Czechoslovakia, China, Samoa, New Zealand, South America, France, Hawaii in the 1850s. When you look at the progress we have made in some of these countries and no progress in many of their nearby neighbors, it makes us wonder. Much of this early proselyting was done while the leaders were crossing the plains and planting the sod and starting their homes. *It was faith and super faith.* To the Twelve the Lord said, "You have a work to do that no other men could do . . .; there will be times when nothing but the angels of God can deliver you out of their hands." (*History of the Church* 2:178.) (Regional Representatives Seminar, September 29, 1978.)

They Had to Make New Ditches and Canals. I mentioned to the other group also that many people who had crossed thousands of miles of water and then the many, many hundreds of miles up the Mississippi and then 1200 miles across a trackless plain, they hardly got settled when Brigham Young felt that it was necessary to use them again. There were many beautiful little valleys in the mountains here in Idaho, Utah, Arizona, Colorado, Nevada. He had sent out exploring parties and they had found these valleys. There was a little trickle of water coming down from the mountain and there was level, good land. So they would just up in conference and say, "Brother so- and-so will go to Carson City. Brother so-and-so will go to Idaho. Brother so-and-so will go down to another place, Arizona maybe." And without thinking, they would say, "Why, of course, when the brethren of the Church, the leadership, tell us to do this, that we are going to do." They abandoned their newly made homes, though they were not so much to speak of perhaps. But they went to new places where they had to start from scratch; where they had to cut the trees; where they had to build their homes from the elements that were common there. They had to make new reservoirs. They had to make new ditches and canals to get water on their places. Then they brought in a few seeds and started with a very meager crop. (Special Flood Conference, Rexburg, Idaho, June 13, 1976.)

One-Half Million Missionary Years. We are deeply grateful to the numerous missionaries who have proselyted since the beginning of time. For some six thousand years, they have been proselyting. The missionaries today, with their contemporaries, have proselyted nearly one-half million missionary years collectively. In one-half million years of teaching, much has happened. Adam and Eve were in the Garden of Eden. Cain took the life of his brother, Abel. Noah carried his family through the flood. Civilization moved from the Mississippi River to Mount Ararat. Abraham taught the Egyptians astronomy. Moses led the children of Israel across the Red Sea. Lehi led his people to the promised land. Columbus discovered America. The American revolutionary war brought freedom to this land. Joseph Smith, the Prophet, was instrumental in restoring the gospel. (Regional Representatives Seminar, March 31, 1978.)

Sacrifice Must Become an Even More Important Element

This Was the Beginning of the Missionary Work. This work, begun in A.D. 33 at the time of the resurrection, was not set on a never-ending sequence.

I read with pleasure of leaders long since gone to eternal fields. There were certainly numerous others there — Enoch and his ancestors, and Adam, and possibly thousands of those generations of righteous leaders and prophets who dwelt among the Nephites. They had all felt to be in bondage.

Joseph Smith, Hyrum Smith, Brigham Young, John Taylor, Wilford Woodruff, and numerous other choice spirits — Heber C. Kimball, Lorenzo Snow, and possibly others who had helped in the restoration, exodus, and the reconstruction were there.

Beginning with the organization of the Church, specific men were sent into neighboring communities to teach the gospel to their relatives and friends.

This was the beginning of the missionary work in this dispensation, and the numbers of missionaries were rapidly increased as many of the nations were approached, and a relatively few converts were made. Now the CALL is for all of the people, members of the Church old and young, aged people, middle-aged people, younger people, youth and children, to carry forward this work to the nations. (Regional Representatives Seminar, September 30, 1977.)

Get Brother Brigham Up. The day for carrying the gospel to ever more places, to ever more people, is here. Are we ready for the CALL?

We must come to think of our obligation rather than our convenience. The time, I think, is here when sacrifice must become an even more important element in the Church. Remember the story of how Brigham Young and Heber C. Kimball went on their missions to England? They were both ill and poverty stricken, but they accepted the call to serve. The day they were to leave, Brigham Young was so ill that he fell down and could not get up. Heber C. Kimball went over and tried to lift him up but could not because he was so weak. So he called across the street to another brother and said, "Come on over here and help me get Brother Brigham up!" The next day both of them were on the way to their missions. ("Are We Doing All We Can?" *Ensign*, February 1983.)

He Baptized Thousands of Converts

Baptized a Whole Community. Wilford Woodruff, later to become President of the Church, went down from the Potteries and baptized a whole community numbering six hundred and more and about 60 ministers. He did not know it could be done. He did not know that there was any limit. He did not know that two or three or four or five people, converts, was satisfactory. (New Mission Presidents Seminar, June 25, 1976.)

He Baptized Thousands of Converts—Wilford Woodruff. President Woodruff was one of the great spiritual giants of this dispensation. The Lord gave him many dreams and visions; he baptized thousands of converts, as was explained to us today, and he performed many, many miracles. Few men have enjoyed more of the guidance of the Holy Spirit than did President Woodruff. He was an Apostle of the Lord Jesus Christ, was valiant and true all his days, and, in the provinces of the Lord, he was the fourth president of The Church of Jesus Christ of Latter-day Saints. He is the one who dedicated the Salt Lake Temple in 1893, and it was to him that the founders of the American nation appeared in the St. George Temple, seeking to have the temple ordinances performed for them. That was very unusual, brethren, and those kinds of miracles and visions and revelations were rather unusual, as you would know. These men of the American Constitution had lived in a day when the gospel was not upon the earth, but they were upright, good men who were entitled to all of the blessings which come to us. ("Preparing for Service in the Church," General Conference Address, March 31, 1979.)

The Lord Blessed Him and Preserved Him. President Woodruff sought the privilege to go on a mission when he was a teacher, and he went forth as a missionary when he was a priest. The Lord blessed him and preserved him and gave him many revelations. ("Preparing for Service in the Church," General Conference Address, March 31, 1979.)

The Gospel Established in Great Britain. We are grateful that the gospel is being spread. We are grateful that many people are hearing the word. We hope the work will be greatly expanded. The work began here in the British Isles, as you will remember, in 1837. My own grandfather, Heber C. Kimball, led a group of the brethren to the shores of these islands and brought the gospel here. This was ten years before Salt Lake City was settled, before there was a house built by the Saints in that area. Ten years before the Church was established in the western United States, the gospel was established here.

The last two days we have been in Manchester, which was the site of the first great conference of the Church held abroad. There were as many as twenty-seven branches in the Manchester area at the time of this conference in the early 1840s. It pleases us very much to come back to the British Isles and to express our love and appreciation for you. (Area General Conference, Glasgow, Scotland, June 21, 1976.)

CHAPTER 9

The Missionary Messages of the Church

This has happened again in our own dispensation when both separate beings, the Father and the Son, came again to the earth in person and appeared unto man.

The Fatherhood of God

We Proclaim the Fatherhood of God. The gospel of Jesus Christ is a gospel for all the world and for all people. We proclaim the fatherhood of God and the brotherhood of all mankind. We proclaim the divine sonship of Jesus Christ and him crucified, that his divine sacrifice was a ransom for all mankind. We bear witness of his resurrection and that he lives today, standing at the right hand of God, to guide the affairs of his earthly kingdom. ("The Stone Cut Without Hands," General Conference Address, April 13, 1976.)

An Absolute Truth. God, our Heavenly Father—Elohim —lives. *That is an absolute truth.* All four billion of the children of men on the earth might be ignorant of him and his attributes and his powers, but he still lives. All the people on the earth might deny him and disbelieve, but he lives in spite of them. They may have their own opinions, but he still lives, and his form, powers, and attributes do not change according to men's opinions. In short, opinion alone has no power in the matter of an absolute truth. He still lives. And Jesus Christ is the Son of God, the Almighty, the Creator, the Master of the only true way of life—the gospel of Jesus Christ. The intellectual may rationalize him out of existence and the unbeliever may scoff, but Christ still lives and guides the destinies of his people. That is an absolute truth; there is no gainsaying. ("Absolute Truth," *Ensign*, September 1978.)

God, Elohim, Came to the Earth. It is noteworthy that the Father, God, Elohim came to the earth upon each necessary occasion to introduce the Son to a new dispensation, to a new people; then Jesus Christ, the Son, carried forward his work.

This has happened again in our own dispensation when both separate beings, the Father and the Son, came again to the earth in person and appeared unto man. This holy occurrence was described by the devout and prepared young man who was the principal recipient of the vision.

There are many different approaches toward our Creator. There are many who profess belief in a God but have little idea what he is. Or perhaps they do not ever expect to see their Creator. Perhaps they would not recognize him when he comes, not knowing what to expect. ("Jesus the Christ," General Conference Address, October 2, 1977.)

God Lives, Jesus Christ Lives. My beloved brothers and sisters, God lives, and I bear testimony of it. Jesus Christ lives, and he is the author of the true way of life and salvation.

This is the message of The Church of Jesus Christ of Latter-day Saints. It is the most important message in the world today. Jesus Christ is the son of God. He was chosen by the Father as the Savior of this world. His coming was foretold centuries before his birth upon this earth. It was seen in vision by Adam, Moses, Isaiah, Jeremiah, Ezekiel, Lehi, Nephi, King Benjamin, Alma, Samuel, and many others, including Mary, his eternal mother.

A modern prophet, the late Elder James E. Talmage of the Council of the Twelve Apostles, declared who Jesus was and is: "Jesus Christ was and is Jehovah, the god of Adam and of Noah, the God of Abraham, Isaac, and Jacob, the God of Israel, the God at whose instance the prophets of the ages have spoken, the God of all nations, and He who shall yet reign on earth as King of kings and Lord of lords." (*Jesus the Christ*, 12 ed., Salt Lake City: The Church of Jesus Christ of Latter-day Saints, 1924, pp. 1-2, 4.) ("The True Way of Life and Salvation," General Conference Address, April 1, 1978.)

The Sonship of Christ

"This Is My Beloved Son, in Whom I Am Well Pleased."
What was the purpose of Christ's mission in life? "God created
man in his own image, in the image of God created he him: male
and female created he them." (Genesis 1:27.)

Man, created in the image of God, was placed on the earth to
experience mortal life, an intermediate state between premortal
life and immortality.

Our first parents, Adam and Eve, disobeyed God. By eating
the forbidden fruit, they became mortal. Consequently, they
and all of their descendants became subject to both mortal and
spiritual death (mortal death, the separation of body and spirit;
and spiritual death, the separation of the spirit from the presence of God and death as pertaining to the things of the spirit).

In order for Adam to regain his original state (to be in the
presence of God), an atonement for this disobedience was necessary. In God's divine plan, provision was made for a redeemer to
break the bonds of death and, through the resurrection, make
possible the reunion of the spirits and bodies of all persons who
had dwelt on earth.

Jesus of Nazareth was the one who, before the world was
created, was chosen to come to earth to perform this service, to
conquer mortal death. This voluntary action would atone for the
fall of Adam and Eve and permit the spirit of man to recover his
body, thereby reuniting body and spirit.

Jesus Christ has influenced humanity more than anyone
else who ever lived. Born in a manger of an earthly mother and a
Heavenly Father, he lived on earth for thirty-three years. He
spent thirty of those years preparing for his life's mission and his
ministry. Then he traveled to the River Jordan to be baptized by
immersion by his cousin John, called the Baptist. By participating in this symbolic ordinance, he demonstrated to all that baptism is the door into this church. From heaven, his Father
acknowledged the important occasion, saying, "This is my
beloved Son, in whom I am well pleased." (Matthew 3:17.)("The
True Way of Life and Salvation," General Conference Address,
April 1, 1978.)

Jesus of Nazareth Came into the World. Jesus of Nazareth
came into the world to bring to pass the Atonement, which gives
to all men everywhere immortality through the gift of the resur-

rection. Thus Jesus' teachings can clearly help us to live a righteous life and to be happier here, but his great sacrifice guarantees to us immortality and the extension of our individual identity and life beyond the grave. Of course, there are those who do not accept the reality of the resurrection—and that is their privilege and their loss—but it is impossible to speak of the abundant life without speaking of life as a continuum. This life, this narrow sphere called mortality, does not, within the short space of time we are allowed here, give to all of us perfect justice, perfect health, or perfect opportunities. Perfect justice, however, will come eventually through a divine plan, as will the perfection of all other conditions and blessings—to those who have lived to merit them. ("The Abundant Life," *Ensign*, July 1978.)

Jesus Christ Is the Center of Our Faith. Above all, I declare that Jesus Christ is the center of our faith; I testify to you that he lives. He leads his Church today; he hears our prayers when we humbly, earnestly, unceasingly seek to know his will, making this, too, a day of miracles and of revelation. I witness that this is the truth as my father and I, and your fathers and you, have been teaching it to the world—this gospel is true and divine. ("Give The Lord Your Loyalty," BYU Devotional Address, September 4, 1979.)

The Great White Spirit. I should like to say it was he, *Jesus Christ, who came forth from the tomb a resurrected being.* It was he, Jesus Christ, in his glorified state who came to the ancestors of the Indians, who is variously known by them as the Great White Spirit, the Fair God, and numerous other names.

It was he, Jesus Christ, our Savior, who was introduced to surprised listeners at Jordan (see Matthew 3:13-17), at the holy Mount of Transfiguration (see Matthew 17:1-9), at the temple of the Nephites (see 3 Nephi 11-26), and in the grove at Palmyra, New York (see Joseph Smith 2:17-25); and the introducing person was none other than his actual Father, the holy Elohim, in whose image he was and whose will he carried out.

Many people have grown up with the idea that it was the Father who was in charge through the Old Testament history days whenever the title God or Lord was used. ("Jesus the Christ," General Conference Address, October 2, 1977.)

We Have a Hope in Christ Here and Now and for Eternity.
We have a hope in Christ here and now. He died for our sins.
Because of him and his gospel, our sins are washed away in the
waters of baptism; sin and iniquity are burned out of our souls
as though by fire; and we become clean, have clear consciences,
and gain that peace which passeth understanding. (See Philip-
pians 4:7.) But today is just a grain of sand in the Sahara of eternity. We have also a hope in Christ for the eternity that lies
ahead; otherwise, as Paul said, we would be "of all men most
miserable." (1 Corinthians 15:19.)

How great would be our sorrow—and justly so—if there were
no resurrection! How miserable we would be if there were no
hope of life eternal! If our hope and salvation and eternal reward
should fade away, we would certainly be more miserable than
those who never had such an expectancy. ("An Eternal Hope in
Christ," General Conference Address, October 1, 1978.)

The Calling of the Prophet Joseph Smith

Joseph, This Is My Beloved Son. But the day had come when
the major elements were ready for this stupendous revelation.

It was a simple prayer of inquiry and request, but the faith
that accompanied it seemed to open the heavens. He had vanquished Satan; the Father, God, and his Son Jesus Christ were
again speaking to men. In proper protocol the Father introduced
the Son, saying, "Joseph, this is my Beloved Son. Hear him."
With two eternal deities standing above the kneeling boy, he
came to the beginning of instructions which would eliminate
spiritual darkness from the earth and open the heavens for continued revelation to make the path of men to return to their
Heavenly Father.

The heavens which had been closed in large measure for
many centuries were now opened. The voices that had been still
and subdued and unheard through many centuries now began
to speak. The revelation that had been well-nigh obliterated and
reasoned out of existence was again available. Prophets who
had been eliminated for many generations were now there.
They now began to spring up as a bulb in a new, rich soil in
warm spring weather. And now a young man, named Joseph
centuries ago, selected and foreordained before mortality, had
an unsatisfied urge for the answer to questions, and truth

sprang from the earth. For this young boy, clean, free from all antagonistic and distorted ideas and with a sincere desire to find the truth, knelt in a secluded spot in a New York forest and poured out his soul to God, and with a faith the size of mountains he asked serious questions that none of the sects upon the earth had been able to fully answer.

A new truth, a concept not understood by the myriads of people on the earth, burst forth, and in that moment there was only one man on the face of the whole earth who knew with absolute assurance that God was a personal being, that the Father and Son were separate individuals with bodies of flesh and bones as the boy who had been created in their image. As the Son was in the image of His Father, the Father God was the same kind of image as the Son. (Special Missionary Program, A.S.U., Tempe, Arizona, June 7, 1974.)

Commissions Were Given and Authority Was Bestowed. This formal introduction by the Father of the Son was most important, for this would be the word of Jesus Christ and the Church of Jesus Christ and the kingdom of Jesus Christ.

Questions were asked and answered, and eternal truths were given. It was made clear to the young, unspoiled Joseph that if he retained his worthiness and kept clean before the Lord, he would be responsible for the restoration of the Church and the gospel and the power and authority of God.

As maturity came to the young, unsullied man, there came also a flood, a deluge of ministrations from heaven. Commissions were given; authority was bestowed; information was given; and the revelations from on high continued almost without interruption, for the time had come. Conditions were ripe; many people were ready to receive the truth in its fullness.

In quick succession there came other visitors. *Peter, James, and John*—men who last held the keys of the kingdom, the power of the priesthood, and the blessings of eternity—appeared to the young man and restored the power and authority which they had held on earth.

John the Baptist, beheaded by Herod but now a resurrected being, returned to the earth and laid hands on the Prophet Joseph to give him the Aaronic Priesthood.

The great *Moses* of antiquity returned to the earth, a celestial being, and restored the keys of the gathering of Israel.

Elijah, the prophet of the eternal work for the dead, returned to make way and prepare for the great temple work and for the restoration of the gospel to those who had died without an opportunity to hear it. ("The Stone Cut Without Hands," General Conference Address, April 3, 1976.)

The Book of Mormon Establishes the Divinity of the Lord

A Further Testimony of the Coming of Christ. The organizers of the Church were told by the Lord: "No one shall be appointed to receive commandments and revelations in this church excepting my servant Joseph Smith, Jun., for he receiveth them even as Moses." (D&C 28:2.) And the prophet *Moroni* appeared unto Joseph and spent long hours explaining the peopling of the American continents by the Lehites and also the Book of Mormon, which would be unearthed and translated. *This book would be a further testimony of the coming of Christ to America and would give testimony that Jesus was the Christ, the Eternal God, for both Jew and Gentile. This record, the Book of Mormon, would help to establish the divinity of the Lord Jesus Christ.*

These were the beginnings of accomplishment; and the gospel was revealed, line upon line, and precept upon precept, and truths were restored, and power was given and authority was revealed, and gradually enough light and enough people were there for the organization of this kingdom of God which Daniel saw two-and-a-half millennia ago. ("The Stone Cut Without Hands," General Conference Address, April 3, 1976.)

A Second Scriptural Witness—the Book of Mormon. We should be given a second scriptural witness in the form of the Book of Mormon. The Book of Mormon supplements, but does not supplant, the Bible. The two books together declare the divinity of Jesus Christ and the importance of mankind's keeping the commandments of God, lest his judgment come upon them. The Church of Jesus Christ of Latter-day Saints both bears the name and the form of Jesus Christ and is built upon the fullness of the gospel. It is a true and living church. ("The Family is Forever," Los Angeles, California, May 15, 1977.)

This Book Bears Testimony of the Living Reality. I testify that the Book of Mormon is a translation of an ancient record of nations who once lived in that western hemisphere, where they prospered and became mighty when they kept the commandments of God, but who were largely destroyed through terrible civil wars when they forgot God. This book bears testimony of the living reality of the Lord Jesus Christ as the Savior and Redeemer of mankind. (General Conference Address, *Ensign*, May, 1980.)

Because of a Fourteen-Year-Old Boy. I want to tell you a little about another miracle . . . a miracle that occurred when a boy, just fourteen years old, went into the woods to pray. Before he was through with that experience, he had seen the Lord God of heaven, his Son, and others; and he had had a marvelous experience. The earth and all the powers of earth met him on that occasion. The Father and the Son came to earth and spoke to him. They met with this fourteen-year-old boy and delivered to him the precious message of the restored gospel.

Because a boy of fourteen years of age went into the woods to pray, great multitudes of people from all over the world have heard the gospel message and have joined the true Church of Jesus Christ.

Because a fourteen-year-old boy went into the wood of New York to pray, more than 30,000 young men are now in the mission field, plus many young women and older couples. And this is to share the marvelous gospel with the rest of the world—the gospel which we have talked about considerably today. That miracle will not happen again tomorrow, and it may not happen again in your lifetime, but it did happen in the lifetime of some of your forebears. The Lord God of heaven, the Eternal Father, came to this earth and bore witness to this boy of only fourteen years of age, that the gospel was true and that what he had to give back to the world was precious and very, very valuable.

Now, by assembling the two miracles together, we see where the effort of all of us put together will take the gospel—this precious gospel that was restored by the Lord in His own time. And we will see it work another miracle: When a great populace of wonderful people like you will join the Church, will change your lives, will teach your families in righteousness, then you will receive all of the blessings which are in store for you. (Area Conference Address, Manila, Philippines, October 19, 1980.)

The Divinity of the Church

The Kingdom of God. As you investigate the Church of Jesus Christ, you will find it is not a religion claiming succession from those who shared Christ's earthly ministry; nor is it a Protestant religion. It is a divine restoration of Christ's earthly kingdom, organized, as was his primitive church, with "apostles, prophets, pastors, teachers, evangelists, etc." (Sixth Article of Faith.) ("The Stone Cut Without Hands," General Conference Address, April 3, 1976.)

The Divinely Restored Powers and Authorities. In your study of this restored church, you will find herein the divinely restored powers and authorities of the holy priesthood. By this divine authority, and in no other way, the saving ordinances of the gospel are performed and are made binding for all time and eternity. I testify of this to all of you who hear my voice. ("The Stone Cut Without Hands," General Conference Address, April 3, 1976.)

The Church Was Organized. The Church was organized. Small it was, with only six members, compared to the stone cut out of the mountain without hands which would break in pieces other nations and which would roll forth and fill the whole earth.

Rough days were ahead for the little kingdom. Prophets were assassinated. Persecutions and drivings have taken place and have vexed the fast-growing little church. A great exodus to the mountains of the West was directed by revelation. The colonization of the West occurred. Great tribulations were suffered. Blood was spilled. Hunger has taken its lives, but today the stone rolls forth to fill the earth.

Twenty-three thousand young missionaries proclaim these truths to thousands of people in their home areas. The gospel spreads to the nations of the earth in its approach toward the promise made by God through Daniel to fill the whole earth, and numerous people of all nationalities and tongues are accepting the gospel in many nations, and the Church and kingdom grow and develop, and we say to you and testify to you that it shall, in Daniel's words, "never be destroyed: and the kingdom shall not be left to other people, but . . . it shall stand forever." (Daniel 2:44.) ("The Stone Cut Without Hands," General Conference Address, April 3, 1976.)

Another Banner Held Up. The Church of Jesus Christ also holds another banner up, our commitment to the gospel of work, and this in an age of increasing idleness. Ours is an age in which more and more and more of the idle seek to eat the bread of the workers. We do not believe in the dole, but rather we teach and strive to help those in need to help themselves. There is great satisfaction in working for one's own needs and desires. ("The Family Is Forever," Investigators Meeting, May 15, 1977.)

The Plan of Salvation

The Salvation of All Who Will Believe and Obey. But it is much more than this. The gospel of Jesus Christ is the eternal plan of salvation. It is the plan devised and announced by God, the Eternal Father, for the salvation of all who will believe and obey. ("An Eternal Hope in Christ," General Conference Address, October 1, 1978.)

He Marked for Us the Plan. My heart was filled with joy to know that he marked for us the plan, the way of life, whereby if we are faithful we may someday see him and express our gratitude personally for his perfect life and his sacrifice for us. ("Christmas Remembrances of the First Presidency," *Friend*, December 1976.)

We Should Become Perfect. I would emphasize that the teachings of Christ that we should become perfect were not mere rhetoric. He meant literally that it is the right of mankind to become like the Father and like the Son, having overcome human weaknesses and developed attributes of divinity.

Because many individuals do not fully use the capacity that is in them does nothing to negate the truth that they have the power to become Christlike. It is the man and woman who use the power who prove its existence; neglect cannot prove its absence.

Working toward perfection is not a one-time decision but a process to be pursued throughout one's lifetime.

Through Moses the word of the Lord came down from the mountain. The commandments which the Lord gave to the children of Israel set minimum standards of conduct. These commandments, said Paul, are "our schoolmaster to bring us unto Christ, that we might be justified by faith." (Galatians 3:24.) ("Hold Fast to the Iron Rod," General Conference Address, September 30, 1978.)

We Are the Children of God

A Unique Sense of Man's Dignity. First, let us pause to remind ourselves that we are the spiritual children of God, and that we are his supreme creation. In each of us there is the potentiality to become a God—pure, holy, true, influential, powerful, independent of earthly forces. We learn from the scriptures that we each have eternal existence, that we were in the beginning with God. (See Abraham 3:22.) That understanding gives to us a unique sense of man's dignity. ("President Kimball Speaks Out on Morality," *New Era*, November 1980.)

The Human Body Is God-Created. The human body is God-created. It was created for a *solemn purpose.* It was not to abuse or weaken or destroy. God gave grass, herbs, and fruit trees and seeds of all kinds to give man's body growth and strength and power.

Among the direct commandments he gave to man was, "Thou shalt not kill," and in this directive or commandment, he meant one should not kill himself, either by violent means or gradual means, and the use of these forbidden things are the cause of death and they shorten life. ("Revelation and the 89th Section," Public Meeting, Cleveland, Ohio, January 30, 1976.)

We Are Eternal Beings. We are eternal beings. We have no way of comprehending how long we dwelt in the presence of God as his spirit children. We are here in mortality for a moment of testing and trial. Then we will come forth in the resurrection, receive an inheritance in whatever kingdom we deserve, and go on living the commandments to all eternity.

This life consists of a brief yesterday, a few short hours of today, and a few moments tomorrow. The oldest men among us scarcely live longer than a hundred years. But the life that is to be is forever. It will have no end. Men will rise from the grave and not die after. Life is eternal, unending; never after the resurrection will the children of our Father taste death. ("An Eternal Hope in Christ," General Conference Address, October 1, 1978.)

Modern Revelation

The World Needs Revelation. How this confused world of today *needs revelation* from God. With war and pestilence and famine, with poverty, desolation, with more and more graft, dishonesty, and immorality, certainly the people of this world need revelation from God as never before. How absurd it would be to think that the Lord would give to a small handful of people in Palestine and the Old World his precious direction through revelation and now, in our extremity, close the heavens. ("Revelation: The Word of the Lord to His Prophets," General Conference Address, April 3, 1977.)

The Iron Ceiling Was Shattered. In the meridian of time, the Son of God, the Light of the World, came and opened the curtains of heaven, and earth and heaven were again in communion.

But when the light of that century went out, the darkness was again impenetrable; the heavens were sealed and the "dark ages" moved in.

I bear witness to the world today that more than a century and a half ago the iron ceiling was shattered; *the heavens were once again opened*, and since that time revelations have been continuous.

That new day dawned when another soul with passionate yearning prayed for divine guidance. A spot of hidden solitude was found, knees were bent, a heart was humbled, pleadings were voiced, and a light brighter than the noonday sun illuminated the world—the curtain never to be closed again.

A young lad . . . Joseph Smith, of incomparable faith, broke the spell, shattered the "heavens of iron" and reestablished communication. Heaven kissed the earth, light dissipated the darkness, and God again spoke to man, revealing anew "his secret unto his servants the prophets." (Amos 3:7.) A new prophet was in the land and through him God set up his kingdom, never to be destroyed nor left to another people—a kingdom that will stand forever.

The foreverness of this kingdom and the revelations which it brought into existence are absolute realities. Never again will the sun go down; never again will all men prove totally unworthy of communication with their Maker. Never again will

God be hidden from his children on the earth. Revelation is here to remain. ("Revelation: The Word of the Lord to His Prophets," General Conference Address, April 3, 1977.)

The Truth of the Holy Scriptures

As Far As It Is Translated Correctly. We read of the unchangeable Lord in the holy scriptures. In the Bible, which we proclaim "to be the word of God as far as it is translated correctly" (Eighth Article of Faith), the Old Testament prophets from Adam to Malachi are testifying of the divinity of the Lord Jesus Christ and our Heavenly Father. Jesus Christ was the God of the Old Testament, and it was he who conversed with Abraham and Moses. It was he who inspired Isaiah and Jeremiah; it was he who foretold through those chosen men the happenings of the future, even to the latest day and hour.

And the New Testament is what it implies—a new, additional witness and testimony of the sonship of Jesus Christ and the fatherhood of the Father and divinity of this work, and the necessity of living the gospel, which he outlined and proclaimed. ("Revelation: The Word of the Lord to His Prophets," General Conference Address, April 3, 1977.)

You Have Reason to Believe. If you love the scriptures and are grateful, as most Christians should be, for all the several hundred pages of scriptures contained in the Old and the New Testaments, you have reason to believe that many additional books have been given. ("The Family Is Forever," Investigators Meeting, May 15, 1977.)

The Book of Mormon. By the power of God other books of scripture have come into being. Vital and priceless records of ancient America, with teachings of Christ, another testimony of his divinity, form the Book of Mormon, which we declare to be divine scripture, contemporary with and sustaining the Bible.

The Doctrine and Covenants, The Pearl of Great Price. Since that momentous day in 1820, additional scripture has continued to come, including the numerous and vital revelations flowing in a never-ending stream from God to his prophets on the earth. Many of these revelations are recorded in another scripture called the Doctrine and Covenants. Completing our

Latter-day Saint scriptures is the Pearl of Great Price, another record of revelation and translated writings of both ancient and modern prophets. ("Revelation: The Word of the Lord to His Prophets," General Conference Address, April 3, 1977.)

Darkness Came (Apostasy)

Spiritual Darkness Came. And so in the centuries following the ministry of the Lord Jesus Christ, gradually numerous changes came into the world program. *The great apostasy* from Christ's true way moved in upon the world.

The threatening storm with all the destructive elements shook the earth. The lights were extinguished and the spiritual darkness came.

Many councils were held of top leaders where they discussed God, disembodied him, convinced the people that God was a spirit only, that he had no flesh and bones, that the Father and the Son and the Holy Ghost were fused into one incomprehensible being. These and numerous other basic truths were changed and substituted and ordinances were changed as prophesied by the prophets. ("Investigators and Members," San Diego, California, May 3, 1975.)

Light Began to Pervade the Earth. The Dark Ages began to dispel in 1820 and light began to pervade the earth. It has been affirmed by students that inventive genius seemed to come to this earth almost simultaneously with the restoration of the gospel; that more material progress was made in the years following the great vision than in the many decades and centuries before. We know why.

In this encounter with Satan, he was temporarily vanquished. He had tried with all his power to prevent the coming of the light back. It was futile for the time had come; the day was at hand. The world was ready, the Father and the Son had waited long. This promised land had been discovered by Columbus and others; this choice country had been freed from overseas domination. The Constitution had been written. A humble boy who for centuries had been already predicted and was foreordained for the leadership now in 1820 came on the scene with strength and courage. He knelt in a grove and prayed for light.

And suddenly the heavens were opened and the isolation had ended, and God, the Father, and God, the Son, came again to the earth where they had previously been in each generation when properly welcomed by a sincere belief and faith.

The little wood where the boy kneeled is incidental. It could have been any clump of trees. The morning it happened was incidental. It could have been any of numerous lovely spring mornings. The scripture the boy read was incidental, for there are numerous ones which could have been a springboard for this inquiry. (Special Missionary Program, A.S.U., Tempe, Arizona, June 7, 1974.)

The Importance of Family Life

An Eternal Unit. From the beginning, The Church of Jesus Christ of Latter-day Saints has emphasized family life. We have always understood that the foundations of the family, as an eternal unit, were laid even before this earth was created! Society without basic family life is without foundation and will disintegrate into nothingness. ("Families Can Be Eternal," General Conference Address, October 4, 1980.)

Honesty and Integrity

We Believe in Being Honest, True. Today is the day to preach honesty and integrity. Many people have seemingly lost their concept of the God-given law of honesty. Joseph Smith led us in saying, "We believe in being honest, true, chaste, benevolent, virtuous, and in doing good to all men." (Thirteenth Article of Faith.)

Our Creator said in the carved message of Sinai, "Thou shalt not steal." Again it is reiterated in the basis of the Restoration. "Thou shalt not steal." (D&C 59:6.)

In public office and private lives, the word of the Lord thunders: "Thou shalt not steal; . . . nor do anything like unto it." (D&C 59:6.)

We find ourselves rationalizing in all forms of dishonesty, including shoplifting, which is a mean, low act indulged in by millions who claim to be honorable decent people.

Dishonesty comes in many other forms: in hijacking; in playing upon private love and emotions for filthy lucre; in robbing money tills or stealing commodities of employers; in falsifying accounts; in taking advantage of other taxpaying people by misuse of government or private loans without intent to repay;

in declaring unjust, improper bankruptcies to avoid repayment of loans; in robbing on the street or in the home money and other precious possessions; in stealing time, giving less than a full day of honest labor for a full day's compensation without paying the fare; and all forms of dishonesty in all places and in all conditions. ("A Report and a Challenge," General Conference Address, October 1, 1976.)

Summary of the Gospel Message

The Church of Jesus Christ of Latter-day Saints was organized 150 years ago today. On this sesquicentennial anniversary we issue to the world a proclamation concerning its progress, its doctrine, its mission, and its message.

On *April 6, 1830,* a small group assembled in the farmhouse of Peter Whitmer in Fayette Township in the state of New York. Six men participated in the formal organization procedures, with Joseph Smith as their leader. From that modest beginning in a rural area, this work has grown consistently and broadly, as men and women in many lands have embraced baptism. There are now almost four and a half million members, and the Church is stronger and growing more rapidly than at any time in its history. Congregations of Latter-day Saints are found throughout North, Central, and South America; in the nations of Europe; in Asia; in Africa; in Australia and the islands of the South Pacific; and in other areas of the world. The gospel restored through the instrumentality of Joseph Smith is presently taught in forty-six languages and in eighty-one nations. From that small meeting held in a farmhouse a century and a half ago, the Church has grown until today it includes nearly twelve thousand organized congregations.

We testify that this restored gospel was introduced into the world by the marvelous appearance of God the Eternal Father and his Son, the resurrected Lord Jesus Christ. That most glorious manifestation marked the beginning of the fulfillment of the promise of Peter, who prophesied of the times of restitution of all things, which God hath spoken by the mouth of all his holy prophets since the world began, this in preparation for the coming of the Lord to reign personally upon the earth. (Acts 3:21.)

We solemnly affirm that The Church of Jesus Christ of Latter-day Saints is in fact a restoration of the Church established by the Son of God, when in mortality he organized his work upon the earth; that it carries his sacred name, even the name of Jesus Christ; that it is built upon a foundation of Apostles and prophets, he being the chief cornerstone; that its priesthood, in both the Aaronic and Melchizedek orders, was restored under the hands of those who held it anciently: John the Baptist, in the case of the Aaronic; and Peter, James, and John in the case of the Melchizedek.

We declare that the *Book of Mormon was brought forth by the gift and power of God and that it stands beside the Bible as another witness of Jesus the Christ, the Savior and Redeemer of mankind.* Together they testify of his divine sonship.

We give our witness that the doctrines and practices of the Church encompass salvation and exaltation not only for those who are living, but also for the dead, and that in sacred temples built for this purpose a great vicarious work is going forward in behalf of those who have died, so that all men and women of all generations may become the beneficiaries of the saving ordinances of the gospel of the Master. This great, selfless labor is one of the distinguishing features of this restored Church of Jesus Christ.

We affirm the sanctity of the family as a divine creation and declare that God our Eternal Father will hold parents accountable to rear their children in light and truth, teaching them "to pray, and to walk uprightly before the Lord" (D&C 68:28). We teach that the most sacred of all relationships, those family associations of husbands and wives and parents and children, may be continued eternally when marriage is solemnized under the authority of the holy priesthood exercised in temples dedicated for these divinely authorized purposes.

We bear witness that all men and women are sons and daughters of God, each accountable to him; that our lives here on earth are part of an eternal plan; that death is not the end, but rather a transition from this to another sphere of purposeful activity made possible through the Atonement of the Redeemer of the world; and that we shall there have the opportunity of working and growing toward perfection.

We testify that the spirit of prophecy and revelation is among us. "We believe all that God has revealed, all that He does now reveal, and we believe that He will yet reveal many great and important things pertaining to the Kingdom of God." (Articles of Faith 1:9.) The heavens are not sealed; God continues to speak to his children through a prophet empowered to declare his word, now as he did anciently.

The mission of the Church today, as it has been from the beginning, is to teach the gospel of Christ to all the world in obedience to the commandment given by the Savior prior to his ascension and repeated in modern revelation: "Go ye into all the world, preach the gospel to every creature, acting in the authority which I have given you, baptizing in the name of the Father, and of the Son, and of the Holy Ghost." (D&C 68:8.)

. . . *It is our obligation, therefore, to teach faith in the Lord Jesus Christ,* to plead with the people of the earth for individual repentance, to administer the sacred ordinances of baptism by immersion for the remission of sins and the laying on of hands for the gift of the Holy Ghost—all of this under the authority of the priesthood of God.

It is our responsibility to espouse and follow an inspired program of instruction and activity, and to build and maintain appropriate facilities for the accomplishment of this, that all who will hear and accept may grow in understanding of doctrine and develop in principles of Christian service to their fellowmen.

As we stand today on the summit of 150 years of progress, we contemplate humbly and gratefully the sacrifices of those who have gone before us, many of whom gave their lives in testimony of this truth. We are thankful for their faith, for their example, for their mighty labors and willing consecrations for this cause which they considered more precious than life itself. They have passed to us a remarkable heritage. We are resolved to build on that heritage for the blessing and benefit of those who follow, who will constitute ever enlarging numbers of faithful men and women throughout the earth.

This is God's work. It is his kingdom we are building. Anciently the prophet Daniel spoke of it as a stone cut out of the mountain without hands, which was to roll forth to fill the whole earth. (See Daniel 2:31-45.) We invite the honest in heart everywhere to listen to the teachings of our missionaries who are sent forth as messengers of eternal truth, to study and learn, and to ask God, our Eternal Father, in the name of his Son, the Lord Jesus Christ, if these things are true. "And if ye shall ask with a sincere heart, with real intent, having faith in Christ, he will manifest the truth of it unto you, by the power of the Holy Ghost. And by the power of the Holy Ghost ye may know the truth of all things." (Moroni 10:4-5.)

We call upon all men and women to forsake evil and turn to God; to work together to build that brotherhood which must be recognized when we truly come to know that God is our Father and we are his children; and to worship him and his Son, the Lord Jesus Christ, the Savior of mankind. In the authority of the Holy Priesthood in us vested, we bless the seekers of truth wherever they may be and invoke the favor of the Almighty upon all men and nations whose God is the Lord, in the name of Jesus Christ, amen. (The First Presidency and the Quorum of the Twelve Apostles, "Proclamation," General Conference Address, April 6, 1980.)

A Voice of Warning

To Raise a Voice of Warning. I feel impressed, my brothers and sisters, to raise a voice of warning this morning. We are living in perilous times. Our only safety and our only hope and salvation is to live close to the Lord and keep his command-ments—not just some of them, but all of them—to the very best of our ability. We must ever strive for perfection. If we have sins or imperfections, let us change our lives, repent, and do better. The Lord says, "By this ye may know if a man repenteth of his sins—behold, he will confess them and forsake them." (D&C 58:43.)

Pursuing Personal Righteousness. We who are here, and mankind throughout the world, are faced with many challenges and many difficult problems, some of them seemingly impos-sible of solution. Peace and happiness are so much desired and sought after, and yet to most men seem so elusive.

In our search for peace, personal fulfillment, and social justice, many ignore the commandments of God, and pornog-raphy, abortion, sexual permissiveness, living together without marriage, drug abuse, child abuse, and a host of other problems grow each year.

For those who seek to resolve such complex and divisive problems, the prophets have clarified the issues and offered remarkably simple, yet highly effective solutions. They have proclaimed that only by pursuing personal righteousness, unselfishness, and obedience to the Lord's will can mankind find true happiness and stability.

Will We Change? Jesus Christ our Lord is under no obliga-tion to save us, except insofar as we repent. We have ignored him, disbelieved him, and failed to follow him. We have changed the laws and broken the everlasting covenants. We stand at his mercy, which will be extended only if we repent. But to what extent have we repented? Another prophet said, "We call evil good and good evil." (See Isaiah 5:20.)

We have rationalized ourselves into thinking we are "not so bad." We see evil in our enemies, but none in ourselves. Are we fully ripe? Has the rot of age and flabbiness set in? Will we change?

Repent of Your Sin. Apparently we would rather do things the devil's way than the Lord's way. It seems, for instance, that we would rather tax ourselves into slavery than pay our tithing; rather build shelters and missiles and bombs than drop to our knees with our families in solemn prayer, night and morning, to our God who would give us protection.

It seems that, rather than fast and pray, we prefer to gorge ourselves at the banquet tables and drink cocktails. Instead of disciplining ourselves, we yield to physical urges and carnal desires. Instead of investing in building our bodies and beautifying our souls, we spend billions of dollars on liquor and tobacco, and drugs, and other body-destroying, soul-stultifying concoctions.

Too many of our wives and mothers prefer the added luxuries of two incomes to the satisfactions of seeing children grow up in the fear and love of God. We golf and boat and hunt and fish and watch sports rather than solemnize the Sabbath. Total morality is found neither among the people nor among the leaders of states and nations. Personal interests and ulterior motives block the way. Old man "rationalization" with his long beard is ever present to tell us that we are justified in these deviations, and because we are not bad enough to be confined in penitentiaries we rationalize that we are not failing to measure up. The masses of the people are perhaps much like those who escaped destruction in the ancient days of this continent. The Lord said to them: "O all ye that are spared because ye were more righteous than they [the slain ones], will ye not now return unto me, and repent of your sins, and be converted, that I may heal you?" (3 Nephi 9:13.)

"Experience keeps a dear school," said Benjamin Franklin, "but fools will learn in no other."

Why Should There Be Spiritual Blindness? We live riotously, and divorce and marry in cycles, like the seasons. While leaders quarrel and editors write and authorities analyze and prognosticate, we break all the laws in God's catalog.

If only we would believe the prophets! For they have warned that if the inhabitants of this land are ever brought down into captivity and enslaved, "it shall be because of iniquity; for if iniquity shall abound, cursed be the land." (2 Nephi 1:7.)

O that men would listen! Why should there be spiritual blindness in the day of brightest scientific and technological vision? Why must men rely on physical fortifications and armaments when the God of heaven yearns to bless them? One stroke of his omnipotent hand could make powerless all nations who oppose, and save a world even when in its death throes, yet men shun God and put their trust in weapons of war, in the "arm of flesh." All this despite lessons of history.

Will We Ever Turn Wholly to God? Will we ever turn wholly to God? Fear envelops the world which could be at ease and peace. In God is protection, peace, safety. He has said, "I will fight your battles." But this commitment is on condition of our faithfulness. ("The Stone Cut Without Hands," General Conference Address, April 3, 1976.)

If We Fail to Serve Him? Who can doubt that God would be willing to do the same for us as for ancient Israel? But, conversely, should we not expect the same punishments promised Israel if we fail to serve him?

The land will be barren.

The trees will be without fruit and the fields without verdure.

There will be rationing and scarcity of food, and sore hunger.

There will be pestilence uncontrollable.

He will give no protection against enemies.

There will be faintness of heart, and the sound of a shaken leaf shall chase you into flight, and you will flee when none pursue.

Your power—your supremacy—your pride in superiority—will be broken.

Your heaven shall be as iron and your earth as brass. Heaven will not hear your pleadings nor earth bring forth its harvest.

Your strength will be spent in vain as you plow and plant and cultivate.

Your cities will be shambles; your churches in ruins.

The Israelites failed to heed the warning. They ignored the prophets. They suffered in fulfillment of every dire prophecy.

Do we twentieth-century people have reason to think that we can be immune from the same tragic consequence of sin and debauchery if we ignore the same divine laws as they did?

The outlook is bleak, but the impending tragedy can be averted. Nations like individuals must "repent or suffer." There is only one cure for the earth's sick condition. That infallible cure is simply righteous obedience, godliness, honor, integrity. Nothing else will suffice. (Area Conference Address, Lakeland, Florida, June 29, 1980.)

The Gospel Without Price. We give these truths to you, not in arrogance or worldly pride, but with a deep sincerity and a kindly offer—the gospel without price, the gospel of truth, the gospel of salvation and exaltation.

I know it is true. I know it is divine. I know it is the little stone that was cut out of the mountain without hands. I know it will fill the earth as prophesied and commanded by the Savior Jesus Christ when, in his last moments on earth, he said to his eleven apostles, "Go ye into all the world, and preach the gospel to every creature"—to every nation, kindred, tongue and people. (See Mark 16:15.) I know it is true from the birth of Adam to the days of Daniel to the days of Joseph Smith and to this day. I know it is true and divine. We offer it to you without price. We promise to you life eternal if you will follow its precepts strictly. ("The Stone Cut Without Hands," General Conference Address, April 3, 1976.)

CHAPTER TEN

Their Sins Are Forgiven Them

A promise direct from the Lord that their sins are forgiven gives them power and strength and should give them ability and success.

Your Sins Are Forgiven

Their Sins Are Forgiven Them. And there are still other great promises that come to missionaries. If there were no other blessings, this would be enough. Listen to the Lord in his promises to forgive sin:

> Behold, and hearken, O ye elders of my church, saith the Lord your God, even Jesus Christ, your advocate, who knoweth the weakness of man and how to succor them who are tempted.
>
> And verily mine eyes are upon those who have not as yet gone up to the land of Zion; wherefore your mission is not yet full.
>
> Nevertheless, ye are blessed, for the testimony which ye have borne is recorded in heaven for the angels to look upon; and they rejoice over you, and your sins are forgiven you. (D&C 62:1-3.)

This is addressed to the elders of the Lord's church by Christ himself. Their sins are forgiven them, assuming, of course, their total repentance. We are assuming that the young missionaries, if they had sins, that they have confessed them and adjusted them and recovered from them, but to have a promise direct from the Lord that their sins are forgiven gives them power and strength and should give them ability and success. (Regional Representatives Seminar, October 3, 1974.)

Spiritual Miracles Occur. The Lord has promised great blessings to us in proportion to how well we share the gospel.

We will receive help from the other side of the veil as the spiritual miracles occur. "Whoso receiveth you, there I will be also, for I will go before [you]. . . . I will be on your right hand and on your left, and my Spirit shall be in your hearts, and mine angels . . . about you." (D&C 84:88.)

The Lord has told us that our sins will be forgiven more readily as we bring souls unto Christ and remain steadfast in bearing testimony to the world, and surely every one of us is looking for additional help in being forgiven of our sins. (See D&C 84:61.) In one of the greatest of missionary scriptures, section 4 of the Doctrine and Covenants, we are told that if we serve the Lord in missionary service "with all [our] heart, might, mind and strength, [then we may] stand blameless before God at the last day." (D&C 4:2.)

I Will Forgive You of Your Sins. Here was the Prophet Joseph Smith and his associates going in a boat down the river with tens of thousands of people on either side of the river, waiting, hoping for the gospel. "For I will forgive you of your sins," the Lord said, "with this commandment—that you remain steadfast in your minds in solemnity and the spirit of prayer, in bearing testimony to all the world of those things which are communicated unto you." (D&C 84:61.) (New Mission Presidents Seminar, June 25, 1976.)

CHAPTER ELEVEN

The Gathering of Israel

*The Lord commanded, "Go ye into all the world,
and preach the gospel to every creature." (Mark
16:15.) That is this gathering of Israel.*

The Gathering of Israel

Go Ye into All the World. Now brothers and sisters, we are
in an era of great growth and expansion. It was necessary in
early days for us to gather in as large a group as we could for
our own protection. We are now a world church. We are not a
Utah church nor an American church. We are not a Japanese
church or a Polynesian church. We are not Chilean, Argentine, Uruguayan, or Paraguayan. We are the Church of Jesus
Christ, and it is a world church.

In the early days of this church, in the Restoration, Moses
came back to the earth and appeared to Joseph Smith and
Oliver Cowdery and gave the keys of the gathering of Israel.

I suppose the greatest scattering began at the tower of
Babel, when people went in all directions. And then Israel was
divided between Judah and Israel. The Jaredites brought
people to America. The Nephites later came and established a
great people in this land. This was the home of this earth and
its beginnings. At the time of the great flood, apparently Noah
landed on the other continent. And now we are scattered all
over the world.

As we have said, the Lord commanded, "Go ye into all the
world, and preach the gospel to every creature" (Mark 16:15).
That is this gathering of Israel. In the early days of the
Church, in the Restoration, the people from Europe came in

over a hundred ships. For fifty years they came in large numbers. They were authorized and encouraged to come to Zion so that they might be with the members of the Church. There were no stakes in Europe or South America or anywhere in the world. Few missions, no temples; and travel was very difficult. And so the world got scattered; but now we have begun the great process of gathering. So we send our missionaries all over the world, and when they have brought people into the Church, they have attended to the gathering. (Area Conference Address, Luna Park, Buenos Aires, Argentina, March 8, 1975.)

We Believe in the Literal Gathering of Israel. All of the nations of the world are being gathered. As Brother McConkie said in Mexico, all of the Saints are being gathered, and this is the effort of gathering. (See *Conference Report*, Mexico City, Mexico, Area Conference, 1972, pp. 41-46.) Every time you send one of your boys on a mission, he becomes an important part of the gathering of Israel. Whether he goes to Copenhagen, or to South Africa, or to Japan, he is helping with the gathering of Israel. (Area Conference Address, Samoa, February 15-18, 1976.)

Korea Is the Gathering Place for Koreans. Now I wish to say a word about another matter. Early in the history of this world there was the great scattering of Israel, but today we have the gathering of Israel. In sixty-five countries we are now bringing the gospel by these fine young men who are among you. What are they doing? They are gathering Israel. Now, in the early days of the Church we used to preach for the people to come to Utah as the gathering process largely because that was the only place in the whole world where there was a temple. Now we have sixteen temples, and two more that have been approved, scattered throughout the world. So it is no longer necessary that we bring the people all to Salt Lake City. Our missionaries preach baptism and confirmation. And then we come to you with conferences and to organize stakes. So we say again, stay in Korea. This is a beautiful land. In this land you can teach your children just as well as you could in Salt Lake City. Stay in Korea where you can teach the gospel to millions of people.

And so the gathering is taking place. Korea is the gathering place for Koreans, Australia for the Australians, Brazil for the Brazilians, England for the English. And so we move forward toward the confirmation of this great program the Lord has established for us. (Area Conference Address, Korea, August 15-17, 1975.)

The Gathering of Israel Is . . . Missionary Service. Now we are concerned with the gathering of Israel. This gathering shall continue until the righteous are assembled in the congregations of the Saints in the nations of the world. This reminds us of the tenth Article of Faith wherein the Prophet Joseph Smith said to his inquirer, "We believe in the literal gathering of Israel and in the restoration of the Ten Tribes; that Zion (the new Jerusalem) will be built upon the American continent; that Christ will reign personally upon the earth; and, that the earth will be renewed and receive its paradisiacal glory."

The gathering of Israel is then this great missionary service, wherein our missionaries go to the nations of the world. It is a matter of inviting scattered Israel to return to the Lord their God and to live his commandments.

Of this glorious day of gathering, the Nephite prophet Jacob had this to say: "The Lord . . . has covenanted with all the house of Israel . . . that they shall be restored to the true church and fold of God." (2 Nephi 9:1-2.)

And Nephi himself saw in vision this gathering that in the last days the covenant people of the Lord were scattered upon all the face of the land and that the church of the Lamb and the Saints of God were to be among the nations of the earth and the world's people.

Now the gathering of Israel consists of joining the true church and their coming to a knowledge of the true God. Note that these revealed words speak of the fold or the organization of the Church. Any person, therefore, who has accepted the restored gospel and who now seeks to worship the Lord in his own tongue and with the Saints in the nation where he lives, has complied with the law of the gathering of Israel and is heir to all of the blessings promised the Saints in these last days.

The Book of Mormon teaches that there is one God and one shepherd over all the earth. And the time cometh when he shall manifest himself unto all nations. (Area Conference Address, Honolulu, Hawaii, June 18, 1978.)

Israel to Be Gathered by Missionary Work

Millions More Will Join the Church. The gathering of Israel is now in progress. Hundreds of thousands of people have been baptized into the Church. Millions more will join the Church. And this is the way that we will gather Israel. The English people will gather in England. The Japanese people will gather in the Orient. The Brazilian people will gather in Brazil. So that important element of the world history is already being accomplished.

It is to be done by missionary work. It is your responsibility to attend to this missionary work. I believe that the last report showed that from all the missions in South America we had only ninety-two local missionaries. I believe there were about 3,500 of the missionaries from the northern continent. Now, brothers and sisters, this is your work. We expect that you will grow from 92 to 920 and perhaps sometime you will have 9,000. In other words, we expect you to do the missionary work for South America—you and the other nations of this part of the world. (Area Conference Address, São Paulo, Brazil, March 1, 1975.)

We Don't Need to Wait. We must remember that many of the Indians are illiterate. Many of the people of the other countries are illiterate. We are told that in developing nations, 40% of the people cannot read or write. Imagine for one moment that 40% of the population of any industrialized and developed country could neither read or write and that among these, that 40% that lived in the capital city spoke a dialect that could not be understood in the next largest town. Imagine, also, that there were about twenty different and distinct dialects, few with written equivalents in use throughout the country. Then you'd have a situation similar to that in a number of developing countries.

But our program must go to the illiterate. We don't need to wait until they've reached our educational standards. We've proven that we can learn their languages. We can use the inventions of man. We cannot wait to educate them to our standards. We must give them the blessings and let the Church programs bless them. (New Mission Presidents Seminar, June 27, 1974.)

Israel Is the Pure in Heart

Come to Zion. We sang "Come to Zion, Come to Zion." We sang that in Great Britain last week in every meeting, I think, and I felt to say to them, Zion is one of those words that has many definitions. In one sense Zion is all of America, North and South, and there are many people who think of their own home town as being Zion. Then there are "the pure in heart," and I told them to sing that song now with the thought that they were the pure in heart and that the people should assemble and come to Zion, to that Zion. We used to sing that song throughout the last hundred years and urge the people to come to America. (New Mission Presidents Seminar, June 25, 1976.)

A Little Zion. If I figured right, there were 170,000 who came to America during that [pioneer] period. They came to Zion, but now we have other Zions, little Zions all over the world, and we hope that every one of you will develop in your own mission a little Zion, the home of the pure in heart. (New Mission Presidents Seminar, June 25, 1976.)

I Have Never Met the People Who Would Not Be Blessed. As I have traveled in dozens of countries in the world for many years, brothers and sisters, I have never met people who would not be blessed and ennobled by hearing, accepting, and applying the gospel of Jesus Christ. I have never been in any country that could not become a veritable Eden, if its citizens would, to use the words of Alma, "give place" in their lives for the application of the gospel of Jesus Christ. The First Presidency and the Twelve see great wisdom in the multiple-Zions, many gathering places where the Saints within their own culture and nation can act as a leaven in the building of the Kingdom—a Kingdom which seeks no earthly rewards or treasures. (Commencement Address, Church College of Hawaii, April 13, 1974.)

CHAPTER TWELVE

The Work Among the Lamanites

The work among the Lamanites must not be postponed.

The Lord Loves the Lamanites So Much

The Lord Loves the Lamanites. There is a scripture in the Book of Mormon that I have thought of many times that pertains to you Lamanites. In 3 Nephi, the fifteenth chapter, verses 22-24, the Lord says:

> And they understood me not, for they supposed it had been the Gentiles [he was talking about]; for they understood not that the Gentiles should be converted through their preaching.

> And they understood me not that I said they shall hear my voice; and they understood me not that the Gentiles should not at any time hear my voice—that I should not manifest myself unto them save it were by the Holy Ghost.

> But behold, ye [Lamanites and Nephites] have both heard my voice, and seen me; and ye are my sheep, and ye are numbered among those whom the Father hath given me.

Doesn't that make you tingle and happy with joy that the Lord loves the Lamanites so much that he will permit them to hear his voice and see his face? Now in my many years of working with the Lamanites, I have seen many Lamanites who have had spiritual manifestations, and it is in keeping with what the Lord says in the 93rd section of the Doctrine and Covenants, verse 1: "Verily, thus saith the Lord: It shall come to pass that every soul [that means you and you and you—*every* soul] who forsaketh his sins and cometh unto me, and calleth on my name, and obeyeth my voice, and keepeth my commandments, shall see my face and know that I am."

What a promise! What a promise! And that is to *everyone*, and especially to the Lamanites. Sometimes Lamanites are a little ashamed that they are Lamanites. I have seen some who would say, "I am not Lamanite, I am a Nephite, or a Zoramite, or a Josephite," or something else. But I want to tell you it is *something* important to be a Lamanite—not just your fathers and mothers, but *you* are very, very special! The Lord calls you his own. I have a feeling about those people who say, "Well, he is only a Lamanite." I think the term is a glorious appellation. I hope you are always proud to be a Lamanite. The Lord is proud of you, too. . . .

We love you and the Lord loves you. How he loves you! And how he loves to do things for you! He would like to give you a gift, not wrapped up in fancy paper with ribbons, but a gift that is worth everything in the world: Life eternal, the privilege of going on with your loved ones forever. (Lamanite Conference Address, San Diego California North Stake, May 3, 1975.)

He Came Here to This Hemisphere. After the crucifixion and the ascension of the Savior, when he came here to this hemisphere to see the people here, he came to a temple which the people had built here. These people were known as Nephites, but there was a great mixture and all through these years there were Lamanites who accepted the theories of the Nephites; there were Nephites who accepted the Lamanites and so there was a mixture, and this Book of Mormon talks frequently about a mixture of our seed. (Indian Week Address, BYU, February 25, 1975.)

The Children of the First Covenant

Let Us Make a Special Effort with Them. Now I hope we shall never forget the Lamanites, "the children of the first covenant." Because of their fathers, they have waited long. Let us make a special effort with them. They have the promise of association with the Master. They are beginning to awaken. They are lovable people. It is our opportunity and responsibility as the Gentiles to bring the gospel to them. They will receive it gladly. They are a precious people. (Regional Representatives Seminar, April 5, 1976.)

There are numerous missions in South America, Central America, Mexico, and even the United States and the islands of the sea where tens of millions of Lamanites are found. We have made considerable progress in South America. They are called "the people of the First Covenant." The Lord calls them "our brethren, our people, my people." He sent angels to them. He visited them himself. The Lord seems to favor them. We must not bypass them nor ignore them.

Now, presidents, we are not giving them special priority, but wherever they are found they should be given their opportunities to hear the gospel and they will be found in most of your missions in large or smaller numbers.

Remember that the Gentiles shall bring Lamanite sons in their arms and Lamanite daughters upon their shoulders and kings shall be nursing fathers and queens their nursing mothers. (See 1 Nephi 21:22-23.) And we must teach them the gospel. (New Mission Presidents Seminar, June 20, 1975.)

Children of Great Promise. Of immense importance to this work of gathering the scattered branches of the house of Israel is the work of carrying the blessings of the restored gospel of Jesus Christ to the Lamanites, for the Lord's work in these latter days can in no wise be complete until these children of great promise are brought back into the fold. The Lord said through his prophet Lehi, "Behold, I say unto you, Yea; they shall be remembered again among the house of Israel; they shall be grafted in, being a natural branch of the olive tree, into the true olive tree." (1 Nephi 15:16.) ("Our Paths Have Met Again," *Ensign,* December 1975.)

You Who Are Lamanites. You who are Lamanites remember this: Your Lamanite ancestors were no more rebellious than any of the other branches of the house of Israel. All the seed of Israel fell into apostasy and suffered the long night of spiritual darkness, and only through the mercy of God have any of the branches been saved from utter destruction—the Gentile-Ephraimite mixture first, and then the Lamanite remainder of Joseph, that the saying might be fulfilled, "the last shall be first, and the first last." (Matthew 20:16.) You who are Lamanites remember: In your past are men such as the Nephi and his brother Lehi who, cast into prison while in the service of the Lord as missionaries, were so righteous and full of faith that though they were encircled by fire they could not be burned; whose faces shone like that of Moses when he descended from the mount; whose persecutors asked, "Who is it with whom these men do converse?" And the reply came: "They do converse with the angels of God." (Helaman 5:38, 39.) You are a chosen people; you have a brilliant future. You might possess all of the wealth of this earth, but you would be nothing compared to what you can be in this Church. You might rule over many nations, but you would have nothing compared to what you can have, through the holy priesthood, as a king or a queen unto the Most High God.

The Conveyance of This Land Was a Conditional One. Now the Lord gave you this choice land. He gave you beautiful bodies, bright minds, black shiny hair, sweet spirits, but remember the conveyance of this land was a conditional one, a gift that has to be earned and it has to continue to [be] earned, for it is not "as long as the grass shall grow and the water shall run"; it's as long as the possessors of the land shall occupy it with honor and distinction and cleanliness and worthiness. As long as that occurs, then it is yours and ours. (Indian Week Address, BYU, February 25, 1975.)

A Prophet of the Lord Began to Preach to the Lamanites. And so Joseph Smith, with his associates, came, restored the gospel, restored the Church, restored the priesthood, the power to do the things, and then hardly had Joseph Smith gotten the Church organized until he himself, a prophet of the Lord, went out into the plains and began to preach to the Lamanites, to the Indian people who were there in Kansas and Missouri and Iowa and the nearby areas. He preached the gospel, and on the side he was receiving revelations from the Lord, and the Lord was talking to him and he gave him revelation which gave him leadership and gave him the incentive to go forth.

Now, the Indian people that he met were not very friendly, but it was something new to them. They were used to riding the plains, killing the buffalo. They were used to doing the things that they had been doing for hundreds of years. It was hard to make the change in them, but it had to come and it came slowly and now is beginning to spread over the earth. (Indian Week Address, BYU, February 25, 1975.)

My Patriarchal Blessing Has Been Fulfilled. One of the outstanding things the patriarch told me was that I would be blessed to go on a mission to the Lamanites, or Indians, that I would have great success with them, and that I would see them grow into a mighty people. I have read the patriarchal blessing thousands of times: I didn't know how it would come to pass.

My first mission, I was called to the Swiss German Mission. There are no Indians there. Then the war broke out, and I was called to the Central States. There are some Indians there, but in all my two and a half years I was never called to the Indians. I wondered what the Lord was saying to me. I waited and waited. I was never called to go to the Indians, though I was in many positions in the ward and stake. And I wondered, is the Lord not going to fulfill this blessing? When I was forty-five years old I was called to be a member of the Council of the Twelve. But when I came into the Council of the Twelve Apostles, the President of the Church made me a member of the committee for the Indian program in all the world.

Since that day I have realized that my patriarchal blessing has been fulfilled. I have been all over the world where Indians live, in the isles of the sea, in South America, North America, and in many other places. I have been greatly blessed with the seeing of Indian people in this conference. I expect there will be a great deal of growth and development among them. We have seen these wonderful men and women in this conference. Let me speak to you. (Area Conference Address, La Paz, Bolivia, March 2, 1977.)

Andrew Kimball Was an Indian Missionary. My father, Andrew Kimball, was an Indian missionary. Soon after he and my mother were married and long before I was born, he went on a mission to the Indian Territory which was a territory of the United States at that time and later became part of Oklahoma.

My father was the mission president at a time when they didn't have all of the advantages that they do these days. There was no mission home, no mission cars, not even a mission horse. Father would travel with his missionaries without purse or scrip, and when he ran out of the wherewithal, he would go back to Salt Lake for a little while and get a job and work for a few months and save his money, then he would go back to the mission field and give leadership to his missionaries.

He loved the Indians and he used to sing the chants and the songs of the Cherokees and the other groups that were down there, and when we children wanted a home evening, we would always say, "Papa, come and sing for us the Indian chants and the Indian songs." (Indian Week Address, BYU, February 25, 1975.)

Will You Take Over the Work of the Lamanite People? One day I was called to be an Apostle, and I went to Salt Lake City and there I became acquainted with the President of the Church. He died soon after, and another President came along, Brother George Albert Smith, and soon after his appointment, he called me into his office and said, "Brother Kimball, I am just too busy now to look after all these details. Will you take over the work of the Lamanite people?" Frightened, I accepted, of course, and thanked him and then for many years, of course, I have enjoyed serving with the Lamanite people. I have been with the Lamanites in their wickiups and their hogans and their pueblo homes and their communities; I have gathered with them around campfires, joined with them in chants and dances; I have broken bread with them in their homes. I have found them to be a good people, and the longer I serve with them, the more I realize that they respond to the same teachings and kindness and love as others. They have the same emotions. When they are taught the gospel truths, they are, for the most part, faithful and possess powerful testimonies of the truth. Faith is a basic element in their lives. Mostly it is a rather simple, pure, and un-adulterated faith. (Indian Week Address, BYU, February 25, 1975.)

Can We Not Exercise Our Faith?

To Expand This Work Even Further? And can we not exercise our faith to expand this work even further? Enos prayed a prayer of mighty faith and secured a promise from the Lord that the Lamanite would be preserved. How glorious it would be if a million Latter-day Saint families were on their knees daily asking in faith that the work among these their brethren would be hastened, that the doors might be opened. ("Our Paths Have Met Again," *Ensign*, December 1975.)

The Day of the Lamanite Has Arrived. Certainly the day of the Lamanite has arrived. And now is our time to deliver the Lamanites from their bondage. No longer can we be satisfied to see them labor and struggle in their poverty and in their bondage. They must be educated, trained and brought out of obscurity into the light. ("The Lamanite," Regional Representatives Seminar, April 1, 1977.)

I Bring to You a Multitude. May I repeat a paragraph I wrote years ago:

I bring to you a multitude who have asked for bread and have received a stone, and who have asked for fish and have been given a serpent; a people who asked not for your distant, far-away sympathy, your haughty disdain, your supercilious pennythrowing, your turned-up nose, your superior snobbery, nor your cold, calculating tolerance.

It is a people who, unable to raise themselves by their own bootstraps, call for assistance and are asking you for boots with straps. They are calling for assistance from those who can push and lift and open doors. It is a people who pray for mercy, for forgiveness and beg for membership in the kingdom with its opportunities to learn and do. ("The Lamanite," Regional Representatives Seminar, April 1,1977.)

Nursing Fathers and Nursing Mothers. Our Lamanite work has been going forward. The American Indians and others of the Lamanites—sixty million more of them in South and Central America and Mexico and the islands, are accepting the gospel.

The placement program goes forward wherein thousands of Indian children enjoy the benefits of excellent schools and well-ordered homes. Many continue on in university training.

We are told that there are some thirty-six missions directed largely toward the Lamanite people. There are sixty stakes with more being organized which have large Lamanite memberships. There was a recent count of Church members among those stakes and missions exceeding tens of thousands.

Engineers, chemical researchers, medical doctors, lawyers, and many other professional people are coming from among the Lamanites.

The Book of Mormon prophecy which promises "nursing fathers and nursing mothers" for the Lamanite is being fulfilled. Some 10,000 or 15,000 Indian students are being taught in the seminaries and other instructional institutions of religion, and hundreds of the more mature students are receiving their degrees from Brigham Young University, probably the greatest benefactor of Lamanite students among all higher learning institutions. They may then go into teaching, surveying, organizing, banking, and other services. We are very proud of our Lamanites. We hope all of our people will be loving and kind and helpful to all of the minority people who come into the Church. ("A Report and a Challenge," General Conference Address, October 1, 1976.)

Because of Their Easiness and Willingness. The Lord has a comprehensive plan, and I have a firm conviction that the blueprint he worked out many millennia ago will be carried out through the programs of the Church. Even now the Church is bringing to bear its resources to educate the Lamanites, to improve their living conditions and their health, to bring them to a knowledge of the gospel of their Redeemer. I have asked for increased effort in the missionary work among the Lamanites, and I have been most gratified by the response. The missions in the Lamanite areas are in the most active and most productive of all, with many more converts per missionary than in any of the other missions. It is as in days of old: "And thus we see that the Lord began to pour out his Spirit upon the Lamanites, because of their easiness and willingness to believe in his words." (Helaman 6:36.) We have many Lamanite missionaries in the field now, and there will be many, many more, I am sure. ("Our Paths Have Met Again," *Ensign*, December 1975.)

The Work of the Lord Among the Lamanites Must Not Be Postponed

If We Desire to Retain the Approval of God. Our work among the Lamanites now moves forward.

President John Taylor warned: "The work of the Lord among the Lamanites must not be postponed, if we desire to retain the approval of God. Thus far we have been content simply to baptize them but this must continue no longer; the same organization of priesthood must be introduced and maintained among the house of Lehi as amongst those of Israel gathered from gentile nations." (Regional Representatives Seminar, March 30, 1979.)

Take Heed to Yourselves! You non-Lamanites who, looking at these your brethren and sisters, can only see that which is "dark and loathsome," take heed to yourselves! Look into your own past—any of our pasts—and you find centuries of loathsomeness and unrighteousness. And then look to the scriptures and discover the Lord's opinion of his chosen people, among whom the Lamanites are numbered. You who "pass by on the other side" when you meet one of these who have, as one may say, gone down from Jerusalem to Jericho and fallen among thieves and been stripped and beaten; in the words of the Prophet Joseph Smith, "you know no more concerning the destinies of this Church and Kingdom than a babe upon its mother's lap. You don't comprehend it." (Wilford Woodruff, General Conference Report, April 8, 1898. p. 57.) If you had been with me recently to witness a chorus of small Lamanite children singing "I Am a Child of God," you would have begun to see a vision of what the Lord has in mind for these, his people. ("Our Paths Have Met Again," *Ensign*, December 1975.)

I Will Soften the Hearts of the Gentiles

They Will Develop. Have you ever noticed how the less fortunate people develop so rapidly after they have joined the Church? I remember an old Indian down in the southwest who finally was baptized. When he came to the little lake in which he was baptized, his hair was awry, his shirt had never been pressed, his pants were baggy and he was barefooted. He was baptized. Just the next Sunday, when he came to Church, his shirt was ironed, his pants were ironed, his shoes were on his feet and his hair was combed. They will develop when the gospel begins to touch them. (New Mission Presidents Seminar, June 27, 1974.)

No Longer Merely Teach and Preach to Them. Brethren, many challenges face all of us as we fellowship and teach the gospel to the cultural and minority groups living in our midst. When special attention of some kind is not provided for these people, we lose them.

In April of 1977 as I was speaking to you about the Lamanites, I said that we could "no longer merely teach and preach to them, but we must establish the Church among them." This statement applies to all other cultures as well. (Regional Representatives Seminar, October 3, 1980.)

An Aymara District President. In Bogota, Colombia, a week or two ago, there sat near me a man, a district president. He was much shorter than I. He was typical of the hundreds who were in attendance from Ecuador and Peru. These people were named "Indians" by Columbus when he came, but more especially and for a long period of time as "Lamanites" by the Lord, whose people they were. His calloused feet were in sandals. He was dressed in white pants, broad at the bottom and about ankle length. On his upper body he had a poncho, with his arms through the slits, and this was covered by a dark blanket; his hair carefully braided extended to the middle of his back. He was speaking almost no English, very little Spanish, but he was communicating in his own language, Aymara. He and his group sang for the thousands of those people attending the conference in Bogota. They sang, "I Am a Child of God." They believed it; they felt it; they were not estranged; they felt they were part of this great program.

This is not new to you, but it is very vital, and it is time we began to emphasize this part of the work. ("The Lamanite," Regional Representatives Seminar, April 1, 1977.)

Stability and Progress. As more of the missionaries come from the less developed countries, we may need to ask for more financial contributions from more of the brethren who are prospering in the States.

I am concerned with the proselyting of the Lamanites through the Americas and the islands, for I realize that some of them have very limited education, understanding, and financing, but I am convinced fully that all of the people of the world need the gospel and that the gospel will dissipate their many limitations in education and understanding, their superstitions, their class systems and all of the things which hamper them. *The Church will bring to them stability and progress.* (Regional Representatives Seminar, April 3, 1975.)

I Could See You Children of Lehi. When I was in Mexico in 1946, I was dreaming for the people of Mexico. I had a dream of your progress and development. Now, this is precisely what I dreamed; this was my vision for the people of the Lamanites. I got up from my bed and wrote my dream. Maybe it was a vision rather than a dream. This is what I wrote:

As I looked into the future, I saw the Lamanites from the isles of the sea and the Americas rise to a great destiny. I saw great numbers of Lamanites and Nephites in beautiful homes that have all the comforts that science can afford.

I could see you children of Lehi with your herds and flocks on a thousand hills, and instead of working for others I could see you getting the management of the positions of responsibility. I saw you the owners of many farms and ranches and homes and gardens. In my dream I no longer saw you the servants of other people. I saw you the employers. I saw you the masters, owners of banks and businesses.

I saw the people of Lehi as engineers and builders, building lofty bridges and great edifices. I saw you in great political positions and functioning as administrators over the land. I saw many of you as heads of governments and of the counties and states and cities. I saw you in legislative positions, where as legislators and good Latter-day Saint citizens you were able to help make the best laws for your brethren and sisters.

I saw many of your sons becoming attorneys and helping solve the world's problems. I saw your people as owners of industries and factories, producing automobiles and machinery, canning fruits and vegetables. I saw your young people training to become administrators of the schools and universities and to gradually move into your positions on the faculties.

I saw doctors as well as the lawyers looking after the health of your people. I saw young Mexican men and women becoming great lecturers, owners of newspapers with their influence on public affairs. I saw great artists among you and students that will go into the laboratories to learn much for the benefit of mankind.

Many of your people I saw were writing books and magazine articles and continuing to have a powerful influence on the thought of the country. I saw you in the movie industry, writing great plays, and especially plays of the Book of Mormon, perhaps, and of the story in history of the Lamanite people in this area for the last thousand years.

I saw you in pageants and in ceremonies. I saw you last night in such a program. You have already arrived, in many respects, to make my dream come true. I see your people in their homes on Monday nights with their children around them, teaching them the truths of the everlasting gospel. I see your boys particularly, and some girls, on missions—not only hundreds of them, but thousands of them.

I saw the Church growing with rapid strides, and I saw them organized in wards and stakes. (I think there was not a single stake or ward in all of Mexico when I dreamed this dream.) I saw a temple of God and expect to see it filled with men and women and young people. . . .

Now, brothers and sisters, all this dream can come true. Much of it has already come true in the years that have passed.

The Lord said this concerning our growth: "And as all have not faith, seek ye diligently and teach one another words of wisdom; yea, seek ye out of the best books words of wisdom; seek learning, even by study and also by faith." (D&C 88:118.)

This means that you can reach all the heights that are now in your dreams. It will mean many sacrifices on the part of parents to be sure that children are taught right in the home, to see that your children have the opportunities to go to school and learn all of the things of the world. I know this is going to be difficult, but it comes through sacrifices on the part of parents.

Now, this dream is over thirty years old. In thirty years you have done marvelously well. You can close your eyes and begin to dream again. I can see you in your automobiles, in your beautiful homes that are clean and well kept. I can see you travel to the far corners of the earth. I can see things that are almost unbelievable that will happen to you and your children.

Now, that was my dream. Maybe it was a vision. Maybe the Lord was showing to me what this great people would accomplish. So I look forward to another thirty years of tremendous progress. I think I see stakes by the hundreds in Mexico, missionaries by the thousands, all the people who are at home becoming missionaries at home.

The Lord is kind. His heart is full. He wants to bless you, and as we close this glorious conference, we leave our blessings, the blessings of the leadership of the Church, with you.

Many hundreds of you are converts. If you are living all the commandments you have been taught, you are making no mistake, for this is truly the Lord's kingdom upon the earth. This I know. I know the Lord loves you, and he will bless you if you merit it. Until we come again, God bless you, and may our love cover you like a blanket. (Area Conference Address, Mexico City, Mexico, February 17, 1977.)

"I Am Proud to Be a Lamanite." One of the things that impressed me most as I heard the testimonies was the large number that said, "I am proud to be a Lamanite! I am proud to be a member of the Church!" What more could anyone wish, to be blessed to be a member of The Church of Jesus Christ and also to be a Lamanite! We have Lamanites from New Zealand, Tonga, Samoa, Tahiti, Hawaii, and Fiji, as well as the more local ones. We have Lamanites from all over North America, and from one tip to the other in South America. We have about 60,000,000 Lamanites, and I pray that one day all 60,000,000 of them will be able to say, "I am grateful to be a Lamanite, but I am even more grateful to be a member of The Church of Jesus Christ of Latter-day Saints." (Lamanite Conference Address, San Diego California North Stake, May 3, 1975.)

The Lamanites Must Rise Again. The Lamanites must rise again in dignity and strength to fully join their brethren and sisters of the household of God in carrying forth his work in preparation for that day when the Lord Jesus Christ will return to lead his people, when the Millennium will be ushered in, when the earth will be renewed and receive its paradisiacal glory and its land be united and become one land. For the prophets have said, "The remnant of the house of Joseph shall be built upon this land; and it shall be a land of their inheritance; and they shall build up a holy city unto the Lord, like unto the Jerusalem of old; and they shall no more be confounded, until the end come when the earth shall pass away." (Ether 13:8.)

In this I have great faith. ("Our Paths Have Met Again," *Ensign*, December, 1975.)

PART TWO

Teach by the Spirit

Consequently we have a double responsibility: we must testify of the things we know, feel, and have felt, and we must live so the Holy Ghost can be with us and convey our words in power to the heart of the investigator.

CHAPTER THIRTEEN

More Worthy Missionaries

We hope all of our missionaries are qualified missionaries, clean and worthy. We hope they are better prepared and more devoted and consecrated to their work.

And so we repeat it: Every LDS male who is worthy and able should fill a mission.

The Lord's Command

The Opportunity Is Given to Every Boy. The Lord expects every boy to become a missionary. He said that in the scriptures. It is not forced upon anyone, but the opportunity is given to every boy. So, we hope that every little boy will be building toward his mission all through these years of growing up. As soon as a little boy is born and in his mother's arms, the parents can start saving money for his mission nineteen years ahead, so that every boy would be indoctrinated to prepare for his mission.

Now, all of my sons have filled missions, and my grandsons are filling missions. We have many great-grandsons who are already planning for their missions. I ask you, are there any reasons why my grandsons should go on missions if your son does not go on a mission? This is one way that every boy can partly repay the obligation that he owes to the Lord.

Not only the boys, but some girls and some couples of older people may go on missions. And besides that, every member of the Church should be a missionary. Each person cannot give up his work to go on a full-time mission, but he can do missionary work in between working hours. Already we have some very fine young men from this country who are now missionaries. And within two or three years there should be hundreds of boys on missions from this country. This is the message of the gospel. We receive blessings, and then we go out and give blessings. There are nearly four billion people in the world. They all need the gospel. The gospel will make new people out of them. It changes and transforms their lives if they live it. People who receive the gospel deeply in their hearts are not the same. They change. (Area Conference Address, Taiwan, August 13-14, 1975.)

Every Boy in the Church to Go on a Mission. We are asking every boy in the Church—every boy in the Church to be worthy of a mission. That's the important thing—the worthiness. Yet, if there is any boy who has already had a difficult time, he should see his bishop immediately and get it cleared up as soon as he can, and make himself available for a mission. (Youth Fireside of the Woods Cross Region, Bountiful, Utah, August 28, 1977.)

Every LDS Male Who Is Worthy and Able Should Fill a Mission. This means that since Adam the Lord has taught us correct doctrines and we may accept or reject them, but the responsibility is ours. It means that, having the Holy Ghost which we receive at baptism time, we all know good from evil. The conscience whispers to us what is right and what is wrong. We cannot blame others or circumstances. We know what is right.

Every person has free agency. He may steal or curse or drink; he may defile himself with pornographic material; he may lazy away his life, fail to do his duty, commit sexual sins, or even take life. There is no force, but he must know that sin brings its proper punishment, sooner or later and in total, so that one is stupid indeed to choose to do the wrong things.

Every person can fail to attend his meetings, fail to pay his tithing, fail to fill a mission, ignore his temple obligations and privileges, but if he is smart, he must know that he is the deprived one.

Again the Lord answers the question: "And that every man should take righteousness in his hands and faithfulness upon his loins, and lift a warning voice unto the inhabitants of the earth; and declare both by word and by flight that desolation shall come upon the wicked." (D&C 63:37.)

Did you note that said "every man," and every boy that is becoming a man? Of course, we do not send a young man steeped in uncleanness and sexual or other sins. Certainly such a one would need to be cleansed by deep repentance before he could be considered. And so we repeat it: *Every LDS male who is worthy and able should fill a mission.* ("Planning for a Full and Abundant Life," General Conference Address, April 6, 1974.)

Train Our Missionaries Better. When I ask for more missionaries, I am not asking for more scrubs or mentally disturbed missionaries, or more testimony-barren missionaries, or more immoral missionaries. I am asking that we start earlier and train our missionaries better in every branch and every ward in the world. That is another challenge—that the young people will understand that it is a great privilege to go on a mission and that they must be physically well, mentally well, spiritually well, and that "*the Lord cannot look upon sin with the least degree of allowance.*" (Regional Representatives Seminar, April 4, 1974.)

A Mission—Education—Marriage and Family. As I visit with young people like you, I remind them of their many goals in life: a mission—education—marriage and family. By careful planning you can have all of these, if you take "first things first.".

We expect and the Lord expects that every normal young man should fill a mission for him. You have got to accept opportunities when you are here, and you are here to make progress. Everything with which to progress, young man, you got from the Lord. You had very little to do with it yourself. He gave you sight and vision; he gave you brains; he gave you all the blessings you have. He gave you these privileges and then he said, "Send them out into the world and give everybody else an opportunity." It is not a matter of going out into the mission field to develop myself, but to go out and see how much good I can do for others, how many people that I can bring into the kingdom of God. . . .

Now, my brothers and sisters, may I conclude by saying this: Every young man will begin when he is an infant, at his mother's knee, to prepare for his mission, saving his money, preparing his thoughts and plans. He will return from his mission, do his normal courting as he goes on with his education, and when it is completed, then he will conclude the marriage and then will go forward with his family after he has his life's work. ("Marriage and the College Student," Tri-Stake Fireside, Ricks College, February 5, 1978.)

Many Leaders Never Filled a Mission. In the calling of missionaries, I have interviewed many people in my organizing of stakes in the past 30 years, and I have been surprised to find the number of good men who are now in stake presidencies, high councils, and bishoprics who are middle-aged, yet have never filled a mission. I have frequently in my surprise asked them why not and far too often they have said that they were never invited to go on a mission. Many of them had hoped for a call, but were never invited by their bishop and felt they were not to call themselves. I hope that you Regional Representatives and General Authorities will make it clear to every bishop that he must give opportunity to every boy in his ward. Let them prepare themselves with a mission in mind, and when they are sufficiently cleansed and purified and ready, then they can be called into the mission field. Let the bishops understand it is not their right to stand off at a distance and decide whether a boy could go on a mission or should stay home and go to school or whether his mother could support him or whether his parents need his help, but let the boy make his own decisions, and the bishop will give every boy his opportunity. ("Lengthening Our Stride," Regional Representatives Seminar, October 3, 1974.)

Through the Family and the Organizations of the Church. I am asking for missionaries who have been carefully indoctrinated and trained through the family and the organizations of the Church, and who come to the mission with a great desire. I am asking for better interviews, more searching interviews, more sympathetic and understanding interviews, but especially that we train prospective missionaries much better, much earlier, and much longer, so that each anticipates his mission with great joy. (Regional Representatives Seminar, April 4, 1974.)

Three Areas of Preparation. [A missionary's] preparation consists largely of effort in three areas:
1. Keeping his life clean and worthy and remaining free from all sins of the world. (The Lord has provided that forgiveness can be had if there is total repentance. If there have been problems, there must be a total transformation of life, a change in one's life, if he is to be forgiven.)
2. Preparing the mind and the spirit—to know the truth. To arrive at mission age and be illiterate in the gospel, or otherwise, would be most unfortunate indeed. Certainly by the time a

young man reaches his nineteenth birthday, he should be prepared to step from his conventional role at home into the important role of the missionary without a total reorganization of his life, his standards, or his training.

3. Preparing to finance his own mission so it may be his own contribution, so far as possible. How wonderful it would be if each future missionary could have saved for his mission from birth. How wonderful it would be if every boy could totally or largely finance his own mission and thereby receive most of the blessings coming from his missionary labors. ("President Kimball Speaks Out on Being a Missionary," *New Era*, May 1981.)

Youth Should Seek to Gain Testimonies. President Woodruff was born March 1, 1807; he was baptized December 31, 1833, when he was twenty-six years old, and was ordained a teacher on January 25, 1834.

What we learn from this experience is that he prayed in his childhood to know the truth, and in his young manhood he spent many nights calling upon the Lord. We learn that he desired to preach the gospel, that his heart was right, and that he immediately believed the gospel when he heard it preached.

Young people should seek to gain testimonies and should desire to go on missions. We appreciated what was said about the missions this afternoon by President Ezra Taft Benson. All young men in the Church should be very eager to go on a mission, and they should also assist their parents to fill missions after the families are raised. ("Preparing for Service in the Church," General Conference Address, March 31, 1979.)

Parents to Prepare Children for Missions

Every Child Should Be Watched As He Grows. Now I would like to mention another matter, the priesthood. I have noticed sometimes in missions that it has slowed down and that all the brethren are not coming to priesthood as their age and experience would indicate. Every child should be watched as he grows in the Church from babyhood to eight years of age. And *every child should be baptized on or near his eighth birthday.*

Branch presidents should be watchful to be sure that when that little boy becomes twelve years of age, he is ordained a deacon in the Church. It is a tremendous development for a little boy to have this responsibility and to grow in power. Then he soon becomes fourteen years of age, and after being a faithful deacon for two years, he becomes a teacher. Branch presidents and parents should be sure that their little boys are given this opportunity.

And then at sixteen he becomes a priest. Think of sixteen-year-old boys being made priests in the Lord's kingdom; they are given the privilege every week of breaking the bread and blessing the bread and water for the sacrament.

Now during all of these years these little boys will have been indoctrinated by their parents, and by the branch officers, and by the branch presidents to anticipate serving missions. And when these young men are approximately nineteen, they are called on missions. And then, after the missions, they return home to their education, to their courtships, to their marriages, to their families, and to other facets of life. (Area Conference Address, Hong Kong, August 13-14, 1975.)

Good Enough for a Son of God? One young man, when called on a mission, replied that he didn't have much talent for that kind of thing. What he was good at was keeping his powerful new automobile in top condition. He enjoyed the sense of power and acceleration, and when he was driving, the continual motion gave him the illusion that he was really getting somewhere.

All along, his father had been content with saying, "He likes to do things with his hands. That's good enough for him."

Good enough for a son of God? This young man didn't realize that the power of his automobile is infinitesimally small in comparison with the power of the sea, or of the sun: and there are many suns, all controlled by law and by priesthood, ultimately—a priesthood power that he could have been developing in the service of the Lord. He settled for a pitiful god, a composite of steel and rubber and shiny chrome. ("The False Gods We Worship," *Ensign*, June 1976.)

This Challenge Should Sink Deep into Your Hearts. When a boy thinks about being ordained an elder, he thinks about being made a missionary. What could be more important than to be a missionary? Every convert boy should eventually become a missionary. That's every boy—if he retains his worthiness. The Lord requires this. The Lord gave us our bodies; he gave us our minds, our strength, everything we possess. All he requires in return is just a small part of our total time and energy. So we all should go on missions. Sometimes, even older men can go; But certainly every nineteen-year-old son ought to look forward to a mission. Now, I said before we are serious about this. It isn't just a matter of, "Oh, it would be nice if our boy could go on a mission." But rather, "It is very important that my boy go on a mission." This challenge should sink deep into your hearts brethren, that from today on there will never be a boy born into this Church who isn't baptized and later ordained a deacon, a teacher, a priest, and an elder. Now, that's pretty well the parents' responsibility. After that, the boy's activities become more and more to be the responsibility of the boy, of the individual himself. (Area Conference Address, Papeete, Tahiti, March 1, 1976.)

In Every Home Evening. Now, there's another part to that too. In every home evening the father and mother are teaching that boy and girl to live the commandments of the Lord. It doesn't matter how much money he has; he cannot go on a mission if his life is not righteous. So the parents are teaching the children all those years to keep their lives clean.

Before we get to the mission, we talk about them becoming a teacher. For two years we are teaching every boy, "You are going to be a teacher in the priesthood"; and then for two more years you are teaching him that he is going to be a priest. I think it is terrible for a father to let his boy grow up without anticipating these glorious privileges. When he's a priest, then he begins to think about being an elder, and his parents stir his thinking. Then they begin to talk about what? A mission. *Every boy should fulfill a mission; but first he must keep his life clean, and then he goes on his mission.* The degree of growth and progress for these boys is remarkable. I think every father can be very proud of his sons. (Area Conference Address, Mexico City, Mexico, February 17, 1977.)

Communicate with Your Families. We urge you as leaders, fathers, husbands, and sons to develop even more your capacity to communicate with each other in your families, in your quorums, in your wards, and in your communities. Accept the reality that personal improvement on the part of each priesthood holder is expected by our Father in Heaven. We should be growing and we should be developing constantly. If we do, others will sense the seriousness of our discipleship and can then more easily forgive us our frailties which we sometimes show in the way in which we lead and manage. ("Boys Need Heroes Close By," General Conference Address, April 3, 1976.)

You Must Teach Your Boys and Girls on Monday Nights. You brethren are responsible for this! You can bypass it if you want because you have your free agency. The Lord said, before the world was formed, "I decided to give every man his free agency. He can do as he pleases." But you know as well as I that you don't evade the responsibility. You may commit murder, you may commit adultery, or you may drink, or you may do anything you want to, but you can't avoid the responsibility and the penalties that come as a result of it. These things we must keep in mind.

Now, my brethren, that is how you get your boys on missions. You start before they are deacons, and you continue on until they are nineteen years of age and have received their calls. That is how you get your boys and girls to go to the temple. You put a picture, perhaps, of the London Temple in the bedroom of your boys and girls, and then you call it to their attention frequently. "See that temple, isn't it beautiful? Inside the temple are numerous great blessings for you."

Brethren, *you can't just sit and let things slide. You must take your responsibilities seriously. You must teach your boys and girls on Monday nights;* it is a good time to do it. There should never be anything that is vulgar or immoral in your lives. There should never be any petting for the girls and boys, and parents don't let them date early in their lives. They need to have a little more maturity, so that they will be solid and firm.

Recently, when we had some outbreaks of immorality in the United States, the Church sent forth a statement to all the world reaffirming our standards that we keep clean in this Church. We are moral and worthy, and we have a good family life, and men really love their wives, and the wives really love their husbands.

Brethren, this is the gospel of Christ. We must go to work at it now, and not merely play at it. We actually work at it to be sure that all these lessons are properly learned by our children; for, after all, that is the responsibility of parenthood. (Area Conference Address, Glasgow, Scotland, June 21, 1976.)

We Don't Just Feed It and Clothe It. Now as I said to the women, there are no bad boys and no bad girls at eight years of age. They may be misguided; they may not always act as they should. But that is your fault and my fault if we are their parents, because we can train them to be beautiful characters all through those younger years. If they are sassy or if they are rebellious, then we look at ourselves and say, "We must not have fully done the job that the Lord gave to us."

You see, we don't bring children into the world just to have fun with them and play with them and to be proud of them. We bring children into the world because the Lord, after he created this great world of ours, wanted it peopled by a righteous people who could go to other worlds and be the leaders there. So when a child is born, we have a tremendous responsibility. We don't just feed it and clothe it. We don't just give it housing. We have to do much more. What would a parent be like who would let his child go to school with holes in the bottoms of his shoes and without a coat and without proper clothing, if he could afford them? What would he be like? Yet, there are many, many parents who let their children go to school or to seminary without family prayer, so they are not prepared for the experiences that come to them.

One day in Salt Lake City I went into a school to visit a seminary class of young people. It was seven o'clock in the morning. I happened to think about it, and said to them, "Boys and girls, before you came from home this morning, did you have prayer? How many of you had prayers?" There were thirty-five boys and girls in this congregation, and thirty-three of them had come without any family prayer in the morning.

Think of a father or a mother who would get up early and leave, and fail to have a family prayer for these boys and girls who are going out among a lot of Gentiles, who are going to be taught and trained with a great many false notions. Think of parents that would not protect their child. They would give him a coat of course; they might give him some breakfast; but they would not prepare him to meet the world. (Area Conference Address, Manchester, England, June 19-20, 1976.)

Righteous Pride. May I suggest you drive down North Temple and see the parade of people coming to the mission home. There they are—the father helping to carry the luggage, the mother beaming with pride and trying to keep up with the tall, handsome young man in a fresh new suit, carrying his luggage. And there is a pretty little girl hanging on to him. It may be but puppy dog love, but they both think it's real. She has on her best. She thinks she is making the great sacrifice.

There is a sister in mid-teens, proud as anything, and there are four younger boys, about 16 and 14, and 12 and 10, not quite so carefully groomed. Their clothes are neither new nor in accordance with missionary standards, but they are tagging along, trying to keep up, and the whole family is approaching the door of the mission home.

Behind them come another family and another and another and another, and approximately 200 or 300 families have passed you up, not even knowing who you are, not caring much, for they have a messenger they are sending out to take a message to the world.

And then drop in the barber shop and see the family there, watching the missionary son get his hair trimmed to missionary standards, and then they go through their purses as he comes out of the chair neat and clean and sweet and smiling. They are not through yet. Now they are fumbling with their purses to see if they have another $1.75. All the time they are encouraging the sixteen-year-old boy to get in the chair, and under their kindly, gentle persuasion his locks are trimmed and he and his younger, red-headed brothers go back to the mission home to get one more glimpse of their missionary brother once more before he goes into the classwork. They are filled with righteous pride.

The picture changes. Here they are at the airport, about four days later, and they are exchanging best wishes with their contemporary families from Oregon and Arizona and elsewhere. The mothers' tears are draining fast and fathers bite their tongues as they say goodbye. The newly furbished missionary goes down through the electric testing machine and into the plane and the family with exultant pride leaves their missionary boy and returns to their Idaho home. (Regional Representatives Seminar, October 3, 1974.)

· Keep Your Life Clean and Unspotted

Every Boy Will Keep Himself Worthy. I just want you folks all to praise with me this fine young man who is filling his mission today. Every young man goes on a mission. Every young man in this Church. *He is expected to by the Lord, he is expected by the Presidency of the Church. He is expected by every bishop and every stake president. Every boy fills a mission.* He can, if he will. He will if he will change his life and put it in total order and let it come first, the gospel and its program first. So now we have large numbers but at least half of them are still not in the mission field and we hope that the day will come, very soon, when every boy will keep himself worthy from the time he is born until his mission day so that he can state to his stake president and his bishop, "I am worthy, I love the Lord, the gospel is true. I want to go out and further the work of the Lord." (Missionary Farewell, Scottsdale, Arizona, May 14, 1978.)

I Hereby Pledge to My Lord. We hesitate to speak to youth about these serious matters, but we are told that youth already know more than we do about them. They do not lack information. Youth lacks maturity and determination and judgment, and so we repeat, if we are pledging our lives, one of the first pledges should be, "I will keep my life clean and unspotted from the sins of the world. I will never under any circumstances or any series of temptations yield to the temptation to commit adultery or immorality of any kind or to change my life or imperil it. *I hereby pledge to my Lord and to my Church that I can be depended upon to save my chastity and my worthiness. I will not defile myself. I can be depended upon throughout my life to keep myself pure and unspotted from the sins of the world.*" ("The Trends of the Times," Utah State University Address, April 30, 1978.)

My Responsibility to Warn Young Men and Young Women. And as a leader of the Church, I feel that it is my responsibility to warn young men and young women of the shoals ahead. They are young, they have not had such wide experience, they may not recognize the clever way that the evil one has to destroy people. Once destroyed, it is very, very difficult to get back on course, but to you, the lucky, who go straight forward, you will not have any special difficulties. (Murfreesboro, Tennessee, July 26, 1975.)

It Is Not an Outworn Garment. That the Church's stand on morality may be understood, we declare firmly and unalterably it is not an outworn garment, faded, old-fashioned, or threadbare. God is the same yesterday, today, and forever, and his covenants and doctrines are immutable. When the sun grows cold and the stars no longer shine, the law of chastity will still be basic in God's world and in the Lord's church. Old values are upheld by the Church, not because they are old, but rather because through the ages they have proved right.

Sometimes one says, "That's your opinion, and this is mine." And I say to those, "Your opinion is as good as mine, except that mine about these things is bolstered by thousands of years of prophets all of whom have seen the same direction and have been revealed to and inspired by the same God."

When your grandparents and your great-grandparents were on this earth, remember that the law was the same; and when you are grandparents and great-grandparents, the law will still be the same, there will be no deviation in the order of life in the Church of Jesus Christ, because it is basically sound and will always be the law in the Church.

Illicit sex is a selfish act, a betrayal, and is dishonest. To be unwilling to accept responsibility is cowardly and disloyal. Marriage, as you know, is for time and for all eternity. Find the right person, you marry in the temple, and are sealed by a servant of the Lord who has delegated to him the authority from the President of the Church, and then you are married forever, through all eternity. (Murfreesboro, Tennessee, July 26, 1975.)

It Is the Most Serious Thing in This Life Next to Murder. As I looked at the boy, looked into his eyes, I said, "No, my boy, you were not expressing love when you took her virtue." And I said to her, "No, you were not expressing real love in your heart when you robbed this fine boy of his chastity. It was lust that brought you together, and it is the most serious thing in this life next to murder."

I continued, "If you really love one another, one would rather die for that person than to injure him or her. At the hour of indulgence, pure love is pushed out one door while evil sneaks in the other. Your affection has been replaced with biological materialism and uncontrolled passion. You have accepted the doctrine which the devil is so eager to establish—that the sex relation is justified on the grounds that it is a pleasant experience."

"When the unmarried yield to the lust which induces intimacies and indulgence, it is called fornication; when the married person does the same, it is called adultery, and as stated before it's the worst sin in the world until you get to murder, which is unforgivable." (Murfreesboro, Tennessee, July 26, 1975.)

I, the Lord, Remember Them No More. While we cannot tolerate sin, and we exercise Church discipline against those who sin, we must help the transgressor with love and understanding, to work his or her way back to full fellowship in the Church. Let us help each toward the blessings of lasting repentance.

The Lord has said to us: "He who has repented of his sins, the same is forgiven, and I, the Lord, remember them no more." (D&C 58:42.)

But we must remember that there can be no forgiveness of these serious sins without total repentance, and there can be no total repentance without much suffering. ("The Trends of the Times," Utah State University Address, April 30, 1978.)

Begin Early Saving for That Mission (Financial Preparation)

The Financing of Missionaries. Another area which we must consider . . . is the financing of missionaries. As the number of missionaries from foreign lands increases, there will be more and more demand for financing outside of home. This we must take care of in two ways. First, we must watch the grants more carefully. It must be obvious that a boy from a deprived country who has been used to pennies all his life and then he is given all at once $125 a month to spend, he will feel that is the best he has ever had it; missionary work isn't so bad, doesn't demand so much, so we can reduce that, perhaps, and let them sacrifice; sacrifice brings forth the blessing of heaven. And when we get away from sacrifice in all of our Church work, in our service and in the organizations and the subsidiaries, I tell you, when we get away from the sacrifice, we have slipped a cog.

Here is another great dividend to come to us from having every boy in the less prosperous countries fill a mission, for when all the boys from Tonga or Mexico or Central America or from any other area are carrying on the work largely themselves, then they can reduce the mission costs down to a figure commensurate with incomes in that particular country and not have them set it by American standards.

Secondly, whenever you go into the stakes and missions, indoctrinate the bishops and the families that they should start at the birth of a male child and begin to put away money and help him save for his mission so that at nineteen years when he is of age, that he would have a reasonable mission fund. Every boy should have saved much toward his mission. I think it's sad that many boys count on their parents totally, many people here in our own communities. If he was born in the Church or if he has been converted in later years, he still has that responsibility. It's his mission; it's his opportunity and responsibility. Remember that pennies make dollars and sacrifices for a just cause make character. (Regional Representatives Seminar, October 3, 1974.)

Navajo Rugs Woven by His Mother. Recently there came to my office an Indian boy. He was ready for his mission. He brought with him three Navajo rugs which had been woven by his mother. He will sell them in order to help sustain him on his mission. No doubt she will continue to weave in order to support him.

Just yesterday a stake president whose stake includes part of an Indian reservation called to tell me another interesting story:

The father of the family is not a member of the Church. The mother and eight children are. Recently the ten-year-old boy went to his father and told him he wanted to go on a mission as soon as he was old enough. His father said he didn't mind him going on a mission, but there was no money so he couldn't see how it would be possible. The boy said, "Father, you are an artist; paint me a picture and I will make copies and sell them to build up a missionary fund."

The father painted the picture entitled "A Family Is Forever" and the picture has now been copyrighted and copies made to be sold to help build up a missionary fund. This afternoon that stake president is bringing this little boy to my office to present the original of his father's picture.

In my mind these Indian boys exemplify a new generation of Lamanites emerging in the Church. A generation ago I would have marveled at one or two prepared for missionary service. But now we have over two thousand of them. (Regional Representatives Seminar, March 30, 1979.)

Saving Money. The second thing is the psychology of it. If that boy is saving money when he is three and five and seven and twelve and fifteen, he is going on a mission because he would long since have given up his savings if he is not going to think about going on a mission. So keep them worthy and then see that every boy has an opportunity. (Spokane, Washington, July 24, 1974.)

Begin Early Saving for That Mission. There is no reason why any boy in this Church needs to forfeit his mission because of lack of funds if he and his family will begin early saving for that mission. When he is of mission age and worthy, he should first do all that he can, and then the family should do all they can, to prepare financially for the mission. If he still lacks funds, he can then talk to his bishop or branch president. The mission presidents and stake presidents will do all they can, then they can call upon us. We have a fund to which many generous people contribute in order to help missionary work. We will need much more in this fund as hundreds and even thousands of young men call upon us, especially from the less developed countries. (Regional Representatives Seminar, April 3, 1975.)

Do the Best You Can. Of course, if the boy is a convert in his teens, his years of saving are limited. If he lives in a country where the economic standards are low and opportunities are severely limited, he can still be governed by this policy so far as possible and do the best he can. ("President Kimball Speaks Out on Being a Missionary," *New Era*, May 1981.)

A Substantial Check. We received a substantial check recently from a mother whose son had saved up his missionary money, then was the victim of a highway accident and lost his life: "I just didn't feel I had the right to use this money for myself as my son had been saving it to go on a mission. He and his father were killed three years ago at the age of 17. It was a terrible accident. . . . They were all going elk hunting and a large oil tanker going very fast in their lane of traffic hit them." (Regional Representatives Seminar, March 31, 1978.)

Stretch Their Souls in Service

Provide Continually Significant Opportunities. We are concerned, brethren, with our need to provide continually significant opportunities for our young men to stretch their souls in

service. Young men do not usually become inactive in the
Church because they are given too many significant things to
do. No young man who has really witnessed for himself that the
gospel works in the lives of the people will walk away from his
duties in the kingdom and leave them undone. We hope our
bishoprics, who have a special stewardship in this regard, will
see to it they have effective quorum activities and active youth
committees. As our young men learn quorum management,
they are not only blessing the Aaronic Priesthood youth in those
quorums, but they are preparing themselves as future fathers
and future leaders for the Melchizedek Priesthood quorums.
They need some experience in leadership, some experience in
service projects, some experience in speaking, some experience
in conducting meetings, and some experience in how to build
proper relationships with young people. ("Boys Need Heroes
Close By," General Conference Address, April 3, 1976.)

He Should Be Ordained. One-third of all the males from ages
twelve to nineteen hold the Aaronic Priesthood—only one-third.
Now that is pathetic if only one-third of the boys from twelve to
nineteen hold the Aaronic Priesthood. That is the privilege of
every boy, and he should be ordained a deacon at twelve, not at
fourteen or sixteen or eighteen. He should be ordained, and
shame on a father who doesn't have his twelve-year-old boy
ordained a deacon. There are a few bad boys at twelve, but most
twelve-year-old boys are quite submissive to their fathers. At
nineteen or twenty they may be rebellious but not very likely,
not if the father has been training his boys all through the years.
So for twelve years you talk deaconhood. "Why, my boy,
you're going to be a deacon in just six more years; in just five
more years—four, three, two, one. Next Sunday you are going to
be ordained a deacon, and the bishop has already spoken to
you." *This is a responsibility of the father and the mother, but
it is also a responsibility of the bishop, of course, who will
follow through.* The bishop or branch president will follow
through always and never think of letting a boy just vegetate
and grow up without the priesthood and without the opportunities. Doesn't that strike you as being sad indeed, to have
two-thirds of the possible boys not ordained to the priesthood?
(Area Conference Address, Manchester, England, June 19-20,
1976.)

Then the Ordained Teacher. Then the ordained teacher will look forward to the day when he is made a priest, and there is his wonderful opportunity to perform baptisms and to bless the bread and water and, through the deacons, have it passed— these sacred emblems—to the congregation. ("Magnify the Priesthood," Area Conference Address, Tokyo, Japan, October 30, 1980.)

Seminary and Institute Buildings Will Be Crowded. Can you imagine what would happen to the seminary and institute programs for these delightful young men who have been planning for missions since birth until seminary days? Seminary and institute buildings will be crowded with a new kind of maturity and seriousness that will give the Church a new image. The morality of the youth will greatly increase. They will be taught cleanliness and righteousness in a way that they have never been taught before through example and family life. ("Lengthening Our Stride," Regional Representatives Seminar, October 3, 1974.)

We Must Do Our Work Better and Sooner. We are rearing a royal generation—thousands of whom sit with us here tonight— who have special things to do. We need to provide them with special experiences in studying scriptures, in serving their neighbors, and in being contributing and loving members of their families. All of this requires, of course, time for planning and time to implement—anything but the casualness we sometimes see on the part of some fathers and adult leaders. We have reasons to believe, brethren, that the impact of the world on our LDS youth is not only greater than it has ever been, but that it comes sooner than it has come in the past. Thus, we must do our work better and sooner! ("Boys Need Heroes Close By," General Conference Address, April 3, 1976.)

The Responsibilities of the Women of the Church

Well, Maybe We Had Better Wait. I remember when I was in Australia, one of the finest of missionaries there told me his story. He was going to college and nearing graduation. He found a very beautiful young woman and she seemed to like him really well too. One night he said, "I would like you to be my wife."

And she said, "I would like you to be my husband, but where did you fill your mission?"

And he said, "Well, I have been too busy to go on a mission. The other fellows can do that. I have got to get my education."

And she just quieted down a little and said, "Well, maybe we had better wait."

And so he was in one of the next companies going to Australia. And when he told me about his return home, he said, "She was waiting for me, and we were married in the temple, and we are the happiest couple in all the world."

Do you young women realize how much power you have? If there was an army here telling them they had to go, it would not be as powerful as you would be. When one of these boys falls in love with you, you have the controls. You can just say what you want to say, but you could say, "Oh, let's wait until you get back from your mission." It is that important.

Do not fail this mission. And tell your little brothers who are very small that they are going on missions. Help them to get their money ready for it. (Area Conference Address, Luna Park, Buenos Aires, Argentina, March 8, 1975.)

All Will Be Highly Useful in the Kingdom. Some girls may be called on full-time missions, and all will have the opportunity to be highly useful in the kingdom of God if they prepare themselves. It has been said that "when you educate a man, you educate an individual; but when you educate a woman, you educate a whole family." (Dr. Charles D. McIver.) We want our women to be well educated, for children may not recover from the ignorance of their mothers. ("The Greatest Personage Was the Most Perfect Teacher," Assembly Hall, Temple Square, September 12, 1975.)

Responsibilities of Married Couples

We Need Many Older Couples. We have many places in the world today where we could send some older couples who are young enough to carry forward missionary work, and it would be a glorious opportunity for many people, when they are retired sometimes, if they retire early. (Fireside Address, Orlando, Florida, December 19, 1976.)

Their Experience and Work and Leadership Were Sorely Needed. An older couple retired from the world of work and also, in effect, from the Church. They purchased a pick-up truck and camper and, separating themselves from all obligations, set out to see the world and simply enjoy what little they had accumulated the rest of their days. They had no time for the temple, were too busy for genealogical research and for missionary service. He lost contact with his high priests quorum and was not home enough to work on his personal history. Their experience and leadership were sorely needed in their branch, but, unable to "endure to the end," they were not available. ("The False Gods We Worship," *Ensign*, June 1976.)

Find Men and Their Wives Who Are Young Enough. We should keep alert to find men and their wives who are young enough and yet who are free enough and capable enough to possibly precede young missionaries into new fields. Sometimes people with greater maturity may do an unbelievable work in opening up the program. There are many people in the Church who are ready for sacrifice. (Regional Representatives Seminar, October 3, 1974.)

CHAPTER FOURTEEN

Missionaries from the Nations

It calls for an "all-out" effort. This appeal is not for the rich or the poor, the successful or the intelligentsia, but to every heart and mind in the world—to every corner of the earth. We are still far from our goal.

It Calls for an All-Out Effort

We Still Have Too Few Missionaries. In obedience to our invitation, our people are sending their young men into the mission field to preach the gospel. We are still urging that every young man have the privilege of a mission to give him a rounded-out life and also to teach the gospel to a dying world. We are still pressing our young men, our bishops, our stake and mission leaders, and we are anxious for more missionaries, better and stronger missionaries, more capable and better trained missionaries.

We are remembering that the Lord of heaven and earth, whose program it is and who has created and peopled this earth —he is anxious. He commanded that we continue and increase our efforts to reach the people. We continue to read his earnest statements that the gospel must go to all the world, to every creature, every clime, every people, every soul. It calls for an "all-out" effort. This appeal is not for the rich or the poor, the successful or the intelligentsia, but to every heart and mind in the world—to every corner of the earth. We are still far from our goal. Though we have made some excellent advances, we are still far from the mark. We still look at the seeming millions in the many lands with which we have to do. We still see numerous nations without a knowledge of their Savior, their Redeemer, without the gospel and its saving and exalting principles. We still see nations who have closed doors and limited visas, greatly limited opportunities for us to enter and teach the gospel.

We still have too few missionaries. Especially do we have too few local missionaries from the areas across the seas and in the distant lands, those who speak the language and know the culture of the people. (Regional Representatives Seminar, October 2, 1975.)

Every Community Should Furnish Its Own Missionaries (in Samoa). We used to think that the missionaries should come from America, but now every community furnishes its own missionaries. And they go to many other countries in the world.

If the records are right, you have fifty-eight missionaries from this stake. But I am looking for the day when you will have two or three or five hundred missionaries from this area. When we think of all the Lord has given to us—our parents, our homes our families, all the things we enjoy—certainly every boy child can plan to give two years back to the Lord as a missionary. This same record says there are 502 young men, unmarried, who are nineteen to twenty-six years of age and who have not yet filled missions. They are the ones who should be going on missions by the scores at this time.

We may not be able to get those that are twenty-six years old, but we can get the little boys that are now six years old and six months old. And so *every young mother*, when she cuddles her baby in her arms will look upon him and think, "This is going to be one of the greatest missionaries that the Church has ever had."

That is part of your heritage and my heritage.

Our daughter had five sons. The fifth son is just now going to Guatemala to fill his mission. The other four have already served. When your first son goes into the mission field, then it is easy to train all the others so that they will not fail to go. Another way to guarantee this matter is to start when they are little, tiny children to put in a little savings bank some pennies, nickels, and dimes. And every time that child receives a gift of money you say, "Well, what are you going to do with it now, Te'o? That would be good to go in your mission fund." As he grows up to maturity, his mission fund also grows and is available. Keep it before him all his life. Get a picture of the New Zealand Temple and a picture maybe of the Hawaiian Temple, and put them in his bedroom where he will see them every night when he goes to bed and every morning when he gets up. Then frequently remind him in home evenings, and at other times, of his obligation. These little boys are precious. And someday, some of them will be General Authorities of the Church, perhaps. They will be political leaders in your own communities. And they will bring you much joy and credit for all the effort you spend while they are little tiny fellows growing toward this. (Area Conference Address, Samoa, February 15-18, 1976.)

Every Boy Who Is Born in a Latter-day Saint Home (in Guatemala). I must not pass without saying a word about the missionaries. Do you know how many missionaries we have from this country and from all the other countries? We have some twenty-three hundred local missionaries. But we have twenty-six thousand from America. Now, it is not proper to depend upon the American boys to preach the gospel. Many of these mission presidents say that the local boys, the Guatemalans and Mexicans, the Japanese, the Germans, are better missionaries almost than the ones who come from the States. Now, it is very important that we furnish local missionaries. Every boy who is born in a Latter-day Saint home should anticipate a mission. (Area Conference Address, Guatemala City, Guatemala, February 21, 1977.)

Why Don't You Use British Boys?

It Is Not an American Job (in England). The other day when the press interviewed us, one young man said to me, "President Kimball, why do you send American missionaries here to England? We have a lot of fine boys here. Why don't you use British boys for your missionaries?" And of course that pleased me very much. And then I said, "It is because we didn't have the British missionaries that we sent the American missionaries, but now we have turned the corner. From today on we are going to have many, many missionaries in this area." There are many young people who have thought they were not obligated to go on a mission, that that was an American job. We would like to emphasize very strongly at this time that it is not an American job. It is a British job, and it is a Norwegian job, and a Brazilian job. Wherever there are members of the Church, the young men will furnish the missionaries, of course.

We are hoping for the day when the British missionaries will not only supply enough missionaries to take care of all missionary work in Britain, but they will build a bridge across the channel and take the gospel to *Spain* and to *Portugal* and to *Italy* and to *France* and to *Holland*, that they will be able to do much of the work in the world. (Area Conference Address, London, England, June 20, 1976.)

When You Find a Frenchman, Send Him to France. Now, we return to the statement of Joseph Smith. "When you find a Frenchman," he said, "send him to France." I looked at a map of France and though they were hard to count, like the stars in the heavens, it seemed to me that there were more than 100 departments or counties in France.

Returning from Munich last year, we drove through a part of France. The distances were great and the counties were many and the cities were all along the way and yet we have only 545 missionaries in France. Why can we not have missionaries in every county and city and district in that great land. We seem to have in France and Belgium and Switzerland some 633 missionaries. With over fifty million people in these areas, do we have enough missionaries? Are the ones we have just covering the waterfront or are they really proselyting the countries? Why do we have so few converts in that part of the world? We note in those three areas we have only 37 local missionaries. Even 1 percent of 17,000 members could be 170 full-term missionaries. We have 37. Surely we shall see a great growth in numbers, but more especially in leadership and efficiency when our French boys are teaching French people. Then we could expect many local and stake missionaries to add luster and strength. These countries are probably some of the ten toes of the image which Daniel saw and which were to be broken in pieces and absorbed by the great kingdom of God. Have we made as much progress as we might have made? (New Mission Presidents Seminar, June 27, l974.)

When You Find an Italian, Send Him to Italy. Again we return to Joseph Smith's statement, "And when you find an Italian, send him to Italy." We're making some headway there, but most of the missionaries in Italy are from the United States. We have two missions there and how happy I shall be when we have a thriving stake in Italy, and especially in Rome. A Rome stake! Oh, glorious will be that day!

We have opened up Italy. We have 413 missionaries there. We have some 300 members, but only 5 missionaries from Italy, the balance of the 413 from America. Of course we could say that they are new and we cannot expect so much. But brethren, I believe that Italian boys are the ones who can convert the Italians. The Prophet Joseph seemed to think so. They will convert members and after their missions are over, they will be branch presidents, bishops, stake presidencies, mission presidencies in the stakes and missions in that land. There is no stake there now. We've been doing business, our Father's business, there for about five years. Why don't we build the tressel while the house is in the building? Why don't we pull in the dirt crane and lift the stones and metal into place while we're sealing them with the cement in the trowel? I hail the day when we have a stake in Rome. It must come true. It's a beautiful dream.

I seem to remember the Italians as the Romans of yesteryear. I've thought of them as big men, powerful men, men with a will, men of power, men of destiny. Maybe they would still have been ruling the world if they had not gone to pieces in immorality and evil and degeneracy, when they had their giants perform in their circuses with the gladiators, when they marched against nations and brought back the spoils and wealth and glory and slaves. Does some of the same kind of blood still run in the veins of the Italians as it did in the old Roman days? Now is our chance to see. We call upon the missionary people with you other folks to help to find that better way to greater success. (New Mission Presidents Seminar, June 27, 1974.)

When You Meet with an Arab, Send Him to Arabia. The Prophet again continues. "And when you meet with an Arab, send him to Arabia." Maybe we've thought this out of the realm of possibility. Again, let us apply the formula to the Arabians. Last week I met an Arab. He's a youthful seventeen. He's clean cut, handsome, sparkling dark eyes, well groomed. He wants to serve the God of this universe. (New Mission Presidents Seminar, June 27, 1974.)

Germany Must Be Part of the Gospel. This was done and many Germans and Americans have knocked upon German doors for 140 years and today we have four missions, five stakes, and 23,000 membership of the Church. I was told one day that there were 150 cities in Germany, each with over 100,000 population in whom there had never been missionaries. I cannot vouch for the truth of that statement, but if it is true, it is to our shame. The Germans are strong, vigorous, powerful people. Joseph Smith is said to have called the Germans an exalted people. Germany must be part of the gospel of Jesus Christ. (New Mission Presidents Seminar, June 27, 1974.)

We Need Your Boys

You Will All Send Your Sons on Missions. We have as full-time missionaries in this total area about 1,767. These missionaries are largely from Utah and America. We believe that the Japanese people, as well as the English and the Brazilians and all others, should do their full part in the proselyting to the world. With over one hundred million people in Japan and other millions of people in China and elsewhere in Asia, it is evident that we need your boys. There is no more reason why any of these men should send their sons and grandsons on missions than there is for you.

I remember a few years ago when I went first to Europe. I began to talk missionary work. The brethren there who thought that the gospel was well established decided that the missionaries should come from America. They said, "We can't send our boys. They have to get to school, and they must do this and that. We can't send our boys. Let the American boys do the proselyting."

We have not found that attitude here. We are very proud of the young men who are already in the mission field from Japan. But we expect and hope that you will all send your sons on missions. You will have little difficulty getting your boys in the mission field if you pray with them night and morning and always pray for the missionaries. (Area General Conference Address, Tokyo, Japan, August 9, 1975.)

Converts of Many Countries Should Also Fill Missions. I wondered a great deal about the matter of convincing these converts of many countries that they should also fill missions. When I saw a likely young boy growing up I thought I would plant the seed and so I gave him a small coin and said, "This is for your mission, to start to plan for your mission and when you are nineteen you will fill a mission." Then I conceived the idea of teaching their parents also. As an example, I looked forward to the stake conference in London. When my turn came to speak I said to the congregation, "I would like every boy that's twelve or thirteen years of age to come up to the front." There was a rustle and a bustle and soon a large line of young men twelve and thirteen years of age were on the stand in a long line. When they were ready, I interviewed each of them before the congregation. I asked him his name, his age, his priesthood, and what he was going to do when he was about nineteen, and if his parents were members of the Church and if they were present at this special conference. Next I said to him, "What are you going to do when you're about nineteen?" He answered, "I don't know." I said, "Oh, yes, you do. You're going on a mission." And his answer was, "Am I?" And then I talked about the obligation of every boy to his Maker, from the brains and the other blessings that he had received and his opportunities. Then I opened my purse and took out a ten shilling note and gave it to him and said, "Now, this is yours. This is to be the seed money for your mission. Now I want you to go back and sit with your folks down there in the congregation and you whisper to them and tell them that you are planning now to go on a mission." With a happy face, he found his parents and relayed the message.

We then had each one of the twenty-five or thirty boys come up to the pulpit and took them also through a similar kind of interview. There were parents listening all over through the congregation. When I asked one of the boys the special question and especially about his priesthood, he said, "I haven't any." And it turned out that he wasn't even a member of the Church. But he had come with one of his friends and I told him that he also could fill a mission if he would place his life in order and make himself ready. Now I gave to each one of these boys ten shillings which I saw they treasured, and they took them back to their seat with their parents. When I said, "If I have one left I will give it to you," to the last boy, all the brethren reached in their purses to get ten shillings out of it. They all seemed to be interested in following as closely as they could, but I found one more and had enough. I didn't know how many boys were coming up to the front.

I Taught Them Their Duty. A similar program I've carried forward in Denmark and Sweden and Norway. I taught them their duty and obligation toward the missionary work in Finland and Germany and Holland. In Holland they'd baptized more than 2,000 people as I remember, in the past certain time and they were still no more members than there were those many many years ago because of the rapid migration to this land. In France and Austria I also found the same situation prevailing, children being born, reared, married, and carrying forth with their life's work though never giving a thought to missionary work. Many hundreds of thousands have caught their inspiration in my lifetime since I have carried forward some such program in Japan and Korea and the islands of the sea and Australia and New Zealand and elsewhere. Sometimes there was half a promise from the boy, but I was sure that in most cases it had sunk deeply and would bear fruit.

The Sons and Daughters in Other Lands Would Fill Missions. I went to Latin America and there I found that relatively few of the new members, either the parents or the sons and daughters, had any idea of filling a mission. In the United States I gave a silver dollar and soon I was receiving some help from some of the brethren. One stake president created a little wood box that held exactly forty dollars and he sent the total forty silver dollars in it for this special purpose. Many hundreds of thousands have got their inspiration in this effort to make the gospel teaching universal. I know that all the other brethren have been working on this equally as strongly and trying to develop this program whereby the sons and daughters in other lands would fill missions.

There Should Be Many, Many More. And now today we have two or three thousand or more local missionaries. There should be many, many more who speak the language, German, Japanese, Indian languages, Finnish, and all other languages, and they're growing to maturity with a testimony of the gospel and a training that is indispensable to them. Now, this has been going on for years and already there are bishops and high counselors in the newly organized stakes in the world who have sons who are ready now to go on missions and they will receive that training and now we have the work going forward. Now we still have American missionaries, but we also have missionaries from practically every nation where the gospel is preached as evidenced by the reading of the roll of the presidents of these new missions. We are very proud of them and already we're beginning to send boys of the second generation, the sons of former missionaries. Perhaps the Lord has found even better ways than that that but he will reveal them to us as we prepare for them. (New Mission Presidents Seminar, June 1977.)

A Few Boys from South America. As to the missionary work, we have only a few boys from South America who are in the mission field. In each of these youth meetings and in the other meetings, we note many handsome young men. President Tuttle has told you we need you.

We remember that the Lord Jesus Christ created the earth, and he organized the program for the earth. And he said to send people all over the world to preach the gospel. To the eleven Apostles who were left after Judas committed his crime, the Lord said, "Go ye unto all the world, and preach the gospel to every creature." (Mark 16:15.)

Now, we saw as we came over from the other building, that the streets were crowded with people tonight, with thousands of young people your ages. And I said, as we came through the crowds, "I wish they were all going to be in the theater. I am sure they need what we could give them." They need what you can give them, for most of you have been born and reared in the Church, and you know the program. You know that nobody can ever reach the heights of happiness unless he lives the commandments of the Lord. The world needs the gospel. (Area Conference Address, Luna Park, Buenos Aires, Argentina, March 8, 1975.)

It Is Your Responsibility to Convert These Nations

It Is Your Responsibility to Convert These Nations. Now, brethren, there is much to do. You are the leaders to do it. We have conferred upon you, as you know, all the priesthood you need to carry on the work in Brazil. You will always work under the Presidency of the Church, and the Council of the Twelve, and the General Authorities, of course, but the detail work is for you to do. It is your responsibility to convert these nations, Argentina, Uruguay, and all the other nations. That's your responsibility. We're helping you. Right now we're sending to you many missionaries and have been for a quarter century or more. And we are willing to continue if we can. But we have problems. We have difficulties getting visas to get into Brazil for as many missionaries as we would be willing to send you. Now what are you going to do if and when the day comes when the government does not see fit to give us visas? Shall we discontinue the missionary work or are you ready and willing to pick it up and go forward with it?

Now you have wonderful boys here. We saw this building filled with them last night, young men and young women. Mostly we are talking about young boys for missionaries, though we do send some lady missionaries, of course. But this building is filled with them. It will be filled with them this morning. Look around you and see all these wonderful young men. Now they are not inferior. Your boys are not inferior; they are superior young men. They can pick up this program and carry it forward, but you must initiate it: you, the leaders; you, the bishops; you, the branch presidents; you, the mission president. Don't let any boy grow to maturity without having been interviewed for a mission. Now some of them may not be worthy. Some of them may have been immoral. Some of them may not care, and maybe they will not repent. But most of your boys, if you start very young with them when they are just little boys, will stay clean. And they'll save their money. They'll be expecting a mission, they'll go on missions, and they'll bring into this Church millions of people through the years.

They'll do something else. While they are in the mission field they'll grow and develop like a blossoming plant. You've seen it and we've seen it. We've seen it with our boys. They grow and they prosper. They learn. They change lives. They become great leaders. Some of these young missionaries just thrill us. They just amaze us with the growth and the strength that comes to them while they have been in Brazil these two years. Now that can happen to every one of your boys.

Every Brazilian boy, every Argentine, every Uruguayan—*every boy should fill a mission.* Now we do not want him to fill a mission unless he is worthy. So that's the reason you will start when he is eight years old or before.

You fathers, of course, will have been training your little boys from the time they are born. As soon as they can talk, as soon as they begin to understand, you begin to tell them about a mission for themselves.

When they are eight years old, you bishops and branch presidents always call them in and interview them for baptism. You might say, "Well, why would we interview them? We know they are not wicked boys." Of course they're not. But this is the chance to teach them what they are going to do. They're going to be righteous and clean living and clean thinking. That's at eight years of age when they are baptized and confirmed. And by the way, don't let weeks or months pass. You must have in every ward and branch a list of all your children, all your boys. One of your counselors maybe could watch that list. And he says, "Bishop, next week Johnny will be eight years old." So then he gets an interview as do all the others. (Area Conference Address, São Paulo, Brazil, March 1, 1975.)

To Save Wons *for the Little Boy (in Korea).* Now, the gathering cannot be accomplished unless we have missionaries. There are some 20,000 boys and mostly young men coming from America to all the parts of the world. For this past century, most missionaries have come from America. But we know that there is no reason why they shouldn't come from Korea and Japan and the Philippines and elsewhere. Your sons are sons of God, the same as my sons are. So we think your boys, and a few of your girls, should fill missions to pay to the Lord a little bit of the obligation they owe him for their existence. No person here organized his own brains. No one gave himself his eyes nor his ears nor his mouth. Nobody gave himself his arms and his legs and his strength. Someone must have done it for us—our parents, our heavenly parents and our earthly parents. So we are asking you to send your boys on missions. *Every boy should go on a mission, if he is worthy, and we expect you parents to teach them so they will be worthy.*

We hope to a great extent that your children can save their own money so that they can pay their own way into the mission field. While we are getting started with this program, there are some funds that can be given to assist those who are not able to do it themselves. Brothers and sisters, will you keep that in mind? Will you put it in your book? Will you think about it every day? That is the only way that we can ever gather Israel. And it is a natural way, and the Lord has given it to us.

For every little boy that is born and placed in his mother's arms, the mother could begin to think, "Someday this will be a missionary and maybe a great leader in the Church." And you could begin to save *wons* for the little boy and help him to gather funds for his mission.

If you will do this, I promise that this country will grow and prosper. You who are poor and have suffered with poverty will be blessed financially. You will dress better and live in better homes because the Lord never requires a blessing he doesn't make provisions for. And the missionary work, like the tithing, will pour out blessings, as Malachi said, so many blessings that there'll hardly be room enough to receive them. (See Malachi 3:10.) (Area Conference Address, Korea, August 15-17, 1975.)

Through Migrant Workers. One of the ways in which the Lord may choose to take the gospel to the far reaches of the earth will be through migrant workers, who come for a time where we have members and/or missionaries, who could, in some cases, take the gospel back later with them to their homeland. Some nations permit freedom of religion, but not proselyting. The advantages of having such individuals accept the gospel are twofold: First, they, for instance, would have no language barrier when they return to their homelands; and, second, they understand their culture, their own people, and the policies of their government better than "outsiders" might. (Regional Representatives Seminar, October 3, 1974.)

If Only One Percent of the Church Population Was on Missions. Last September, I gave you information showing the number of Church members, their location around the world, the number of missionaries serving in the various countries and the percentages. Let me give you a few comparisons for the past six-month period.

Six months ago, South America had 1,522 missionaries or .68 percent of the Church population of 223,000. They now have 243,000 members and 1,443 missionaries or .59 percent. Canada had 1.06 percent of their members on missions. They now have .98 percent. The United States had 1.0 percent last September and now have only .89 percent—25,026 missionaries then and 22,959 now. With a total Church population of 4,160,000, we have 27,699 missionaries, or .67 percent, compared with a .65 percent six months ago, a slight increase. But I repeat what I said last time: if we only just had one percent of the Church population, we would have over 41,000 missionaries. (Regional Representatives Seminar, March 30, 1979.)

They Will Always Be Good Ambassadors

Oh, How We Need Your Help. I have been all over the world
. . . , and I've preached the gospel to a great many people. I've
been among the Indians in the Southwest; I have been among
the Indians in India. I have been all over the country, and I have
preached the gospel and borne my testimony to people all over
the world.

I remember when we had only six or eight hundred missionaries in all the world. Now we have twenty-three thousand,
approximately. I remember when my people who were
approached to go on missions would say, "Oh, I can't go, I've got
so many cows, I've got so many acres. I've got so much to do."

I know and I am finding out that where there is a will there is
a way, and the Lord can help us find the ways to teach. Now it is
quite obvious that twenty-three thousand missionaries is
nothing. It is just a drop in the bucket when we talk about four
billion people. Even if we talk about only the people of Sydney, if
we had all our missionaries right here in Sydney, we would
probably not get around to all the people here.

Now I hope to see the day when a great army of Australian
boys go across the Pacific and go down into South America. I am
looking forward to the day when a great army of your sons may
cross the Indian Ocean and go to India and Burma and the other
nations in that area. It is not easy, because of their doctrines,
because of their way of life. It isn't easy.

We are going to have to have a lot of help and I am convinced
since the Lord is the one who said you have to go and do it, he
will be able to open the gates for us. To that end we have asked
all the people of the whole world to include in their family
prayers and in their morning prayers and in their evening
prayers and in their Church prayers always to ask the Lord to
open the gates, open the doors so that the people can be proselyted and taught the gospel of Jesus Christ.

Now unfortunately that is what we are up against. If you
have faith, if I have faith, faith enough to keep asking the Lord, I
am positive the day will come when the gates will be opened.
They will say, "Here, here are a lot of visas, take them and use
them."

Whenever I visit a foreign country and talk to the people
there who are in charge of the government, I always mention to
them, "You know, these missionaries are the best ambassadors

that you have ever had or ever will have. These young men who come to Australia, these young men who go to New Zealand, these who go to Japan—they are the best people for the country, the very, very best. They will always be good ambassadors." Have you ever noticed a group of missionaries talking about their missionary service? They talk about Sister so-and-so being baptized and Brother so-and-so joining the Church, and they always say good things about the nation. . . .

I don't see any reason why we couldn't send Australian boys all over the East. I don't see why we couldn't send them all over the south, South America. However, the South Americans are doing a tremendous job there, turning in a great many missionaries.

Now that is what we are asking you to do. Will you brethren pledge with yourself tonight that you just will not have any more prayers without this suggestion in them to the Lord: "*Oh, how we need your help.* Help us to find the way to get to these people. Help us to convince these people. But above all, help us to open the doors and get into these nations that are far, far away." (Area Conference Address, Sydney, Australia, February 28, 1976.)

CHAPTER FIFTEEN

Missionary Preparation: A Family Responsibility

Teach your boys that they should fill honorable missions.

Father's and Mother's Responsibility

It Is the Divine Role of Parents to Teach the Truths. It is the divine role of parents to teach the truths of the gospel to their children. Consequently, we recently asked that this statement be read in all our sacrament meetings:

> The First Presidency frequently emphasizes the importance of weekly family home evenings as a prime opportunity for parents to teach and strengthen their families. In addition to family gospel study on Sundays, Monday nights are reserved for family home evening, which may include instruction in gospel principles, love, and harmony, and may include other family activities.

> We ask that parents and leaders give this theme powerful emphasis, for closeness to our Father in Heaven and a constant spirituality in our lives is our greatest need as individuals and as a people. A true Latter-day Saint home is a haven against the storms and struggles of life. Spirituality is born and nurtured by daily prayer, scripture study, home gospel discussions and related activities, home evenings, family councils, working and playing together, serving each other, and sharing the gospel with those around us. Spirituality is also nurtured in our actions of patience, kindness, and forgiveness toward each other and in our applying gospel principles in the family circle. Home is where we become experts and scholars in gospel righteousness, learning and living gospel truths together.

As a youth, and with my wife and children in our own home, I remember our beloved family activities. Heaven was in our home. When each person did something, whether it was sing a song, lead a game, recite an article of faith, tell a story, share a talent, or perform an assignment, there was growth and good feeling. ("Therefore I Was Taught," *Ensign*, January 1982.)

It Isn't Enough Just to Bear Children. If we do nothing else during this whole conference, we want to stimulate you folks so that you will begin to train your little boys as soon as they are born, while they are still in your arms and nursing, and to start teaching them the gospel. Oh, of course, this training will be done in quite a different way. They will grow up knowing that you always kneel in your family prayers, and they will come to realize that you always pray for your bishop and your stake president and for the First Presidency of the Church and the other brethren. They will come to realize these things. Don't wait until they are teenagers to train them in the truths of the gospel. Teach them when they are one and two and three and four years old.

In the sixty-eighth section of the Doctrine and Covenants, the Lord says, "And they (parents) shall also teach their children to pray, and to walk uprightly before the Lord." (D&C 68:28.) It isn't enough just to bear children; it isn't enough just to provide them a home; it isn't enough just to give them their clothes. They must have training; they must have the gospel and the Spirit in their lives. While that is happening, they will be learning all about missionary work. If, in every home, there were a picture of the temple then the boy and girl, from infancy, would learn to think of that as a part of their lives. Of course, they will marry in the temple, but after they have filled their missions. (Area Conference Address, Manchester, England, June 19-20, 1976.)

We Cannot Just Take It for Granted. Brothers and sisters, this gospel is real. We cannot just take it for granted. We cannot just live in a house and let the rest of the world go by. Each of us must be participating in the activities of the Church. There are things to do. The Lord has said we should attend our meetings. Do you know that less than half of us go to sacrament meetings? Less than half of us, in general. Some wards and stakes exceed that, of course, but that is terrifying, when we think of boys and

girls growing up in a home where their parents don't take them
to the meetings from the time they are infants until they are
grown, or make up their own minds. That is the responsibility
of parents—the father and the mother. "Parents who have
children in Zion"—you remember the scripture. And so we
expect that of the parents. Whether you want to or whether you
don't, you go to meetings yourself, and take your children with
you and teach them the practice. (Dedication, Fair Oaks, California, October 9, 1976.)

The Parents Had Ignored All of the Spiritual Things. One
day I had a woman come into my office to be interviewed about a
problem in her family. As we discussed the family problems, I
found that both she and her husband had come from families in
which there were eight children. They both lived in the same
community before their marriage, and she had seven brothers
and sisters, all of whom were faithful in the Church. He had
seven brothers and sisters, none of whom were faithful in the
Church. This caused me to wonder what was the difference.
They both lived in the same community, went to the same
school, had the same teachers, and yet here was one group of
youth who were almost failures. They were failures; they failed
to live up to the commandments; while on the other side, all of
them had been faithful and true to the teachings of the parents.

As I investigated further, I found that the difference was in
the parents. In the one case, the parents had ignored all of the
spiritual things, whereas in the other family, they had been
faithful in everything: home evenings, family prayer, tithing,
and all of the things required of Latter-day Saints. (Area Conference Address, Japan, August 8-10, 1975.)

Hold Family Home Evening

You Train Them. There is no reason why one cannot hold
Family Home Evening, because there are no meetings, no other
situations that would keep our families from getting together.
And think what a father and mother can do when they take
these little tots that are only one and two and three years old and
train them. Those are the days. It isn't eighteen and twenty and
twenty-one that you train your children. That is a little too late.
You train them when they are little tots on your lap, in your arm,

and it is amazing how much those children learn and hold in their minds and their hearts. (Fireside Address, Orlando, Florida, December 19, 1976.)

Every Monday. I hope that every family will *hold home evening every Monday night without fail.* Missionary work will be one of the strong points that will be brought before it; and the father and the mother and the children in their turns will offer prayers which will be centered around this very important element—that the doors of the nations might be opened to us and then, secondly, that the missionaries, the young men and women of the Church, may be anxious to fill those missions and bring people into the Church. ("Fundamental Principles to Ponder and Live By," General Conference Address, September 30, 1978.)

We are highly oriented in the family program. We ask that *every Monday evening the family will get together* as father, mother, children, and have a good family evening; whereby the father and the mother teach the children all of the things that they should know about the growing-up years of their lives— how faithful they should be, how clean they should be, how truthful and honest. Is there any family in this total area that is not holding family evening? Is there any one of the fathers or mothers here who misses the family evening? You need not raise your hand. Just answer this question in your own heart. You cannot rear your family as they should be reared without this important program. (Area Conference Address, La Paz, Bolivia, March 2, 1977.)

There are many other things that the father is responsible for. It is his responsibility *to have this home evening every Monday night.* We saw hundreds of people going to the show tonight; that's all right if it's a good show. But no shows on Monday night; that's the night when the father and mother and all the children are together, and then they never fail. The father is the head of the family, and the mother assists the father, and they have an assignment. When you have a little girl or a little boy doing the best he can in presenting a program, you have a growing spirit; such children will grow up to be righteous, worthy men and women. There will be very few exceptions to this rule. (Area Conference Address, Lima, Peru, February 25, 1977.)

The Panacea for the Ailments of the World. Home life, home teaching, parental guidance, father in leadership—these are the panacea for the ailments of the world, a cure for spiritual and emotional diseases, a remedy for problems. Parents should therefore not leave the training of children to school teachers or to the Primary or the Relief Society or the Sunday School or Mutual. The father and the mother must undertake this great responsibility, using the Church programs to assist them. Herein is the success the Lord wants to be achieved in the family home evening which He has established. ("Train Up a Child," *Ensign,* April 1978.)

Let Me Go Back to the Home Evening. Brethren, there are so many things to do to bring up our children in righteousness. *Let me go back to the home evening. Every Monday night, as sure as the sun comes up—every Monday night, we have a home evening.* And the father and the mother and all of the children—the teenagers and the little folks—get together. They follow a program that they have conceived and worked out. They sing and they pray and they take turns in looking after the details of this program. It isn't good enough to take your sons and daughters to the movie. In the first place, in our country, the movies are hardly worth going to. But even if they are entertaining and good, they are not equal to a home evening that is conducted by the family. Brethren, will you follow this very, very carefully. And remember this again, "Why call ye me Lord, Lord, and do not the things which I say?" (Luke 6:46.) (Area Conference Address, Montevideo, Uruguay, October 27, 1978.)

We All Participate Together. If there is to be a contribution to the building fund or the Red Cross or a Saturday morning spent helping the elders quorum, make sure the children are aware of it and, if possible, let them prepare and work in it. All of the family could attend the baptism and confirmation of every child. And all of the family could root for the son who is playing a game in athletics. But particularly the home evening is the time when we all participate together. (Area Conference Address, Buenos Aires, Argentina, October 29, 1978.)

Family Meetings and Councils. We encourage fathers and mothers to take up in their family meetings and councils the major family activities of missionary work, genealogical work, and welfare work. Fathers and mothers should train their sons to want to be missionaries, and later, if health and other conditions permit, parents can look to the day when they, too, may serve a mission. ("Therefore I Was Taught," *Ensign*, January 1982.)

The Sabbath: Time for Our Family to Be Together. We encourage a thoughtful and prayerful review of the suggestions the Brethren have felt to approve for your consideration in planning Sabbath, home evening, and other weekday activities in our homes:

"As we *plan our Sunday activities*, we may want to set aside time for our family to be together, for personal study and meditation and for service to others. We might want to read the scriptures, conference reports, and Church publications; study the lives and teachings of the prophets; prepare church lessons and other church assignments; write in journals; pray and meditate; write to missionaries; enjoy uplifting music; have family gospel instruction; hold family council meetings; build husband-wife relationships; read with a child; do genealogical research, including the four-generation program and family or personal histories; sing Church hymns; read uplifting literature; develop our appreciation for the cultural arts; plan family home evening study and activities; plan other family activities; friendship nonmembers; fellowship neighbors; visit the sick, the aged, and the lonely; hold interviews with family members. . . .

"Monday evening activities might include any of the activities suggested for Sundays; lessons from family home evening manual; family games; cultural events; family service projects; sharing talents with family members; home beautification projects; gardening; inventory of year's supply; other food storage projects; home production projects; planning for vacations and special activities; family council meetings; planning or participating in a physical fitness program; fellowshipping nonmember friends; recreational activities." ("Our Family," Salt Lake City: The Church of Jesus Christ of Latter-day Saints, 1980, pp. 2-3.) ("Therefore I Was Taught," *Ensign*, January 1982.)

The Family Prayer

If There Isn't Any Prayer. We have mentioned the home evening, the family prayer. I remember the little program of the

Indian student placement program which has become quite important in the Western States. I remember hearing about one little girl who had come from a Latter-day Saint home. She had come to this home of an official of the government in Utah. They had been to meet her to bring her to their home. And they sat around and soon the dinner was ready, and the father, who was an official of the community pulled up his chair and started to eat. And the little girl sat there, and he said, "What's the matter, darling, can't you eat anything?"

She replied, "We haven't had the blessing on the food." Never again would he forget that. He knew that was important, very important—*the family prayer*. ("Do It!" Area Conference Address, Honolulu, Hawaii, June 18, 1978.)

Family Prayer Is Needed. Never hesitate to gather your family around you for your prayers, especially in those times when more than morning and evening family prayer is needed. Extra needs require extra prayers.

Your little ones will learn how to talk to their Father in Heaven by listening to you as parents. They will soon see how heartfelt and honest your prayers are. If your prayers are a hurried and thoughtless ritual, they will see this too.

Difficult as it seems, I have found when praying, other than in private and in secret, that it is better to be concerned with communicating tenderly and honestly with God, rather than worrying over what the listeners may be thinking. The echoing of "Amen" by the listeners is evidence of their accord and approval. Of course, the setting of prayers needs to be taken into account. This is one reason why public prayers, or even family prayers, cannot be the whole of our praying. ("We Need a Listening Ear," General Conference Address, October 6, 1979.)

Never a Meal Without a Blessing. Let there never be a meal without a blessing on the bread or on the food. Let there never be a day without your calling them all together and offering a *prayer of thanksgiving* that you all got out safely; *a prayer of appreciation* for all of the blessings that you have; for the health and strength that you have. Let that be a constant prayer in your life. (Special Flood Conference, Rexburg, Idaho, June 13, 1976.)

Let the Children Take Their Turn in Prayer. We have much to say about this because it is about the most important thing there is before our nation, isn't it? The nation is going to pieces unless we can stop the trends and get the people to come home and leave the bars and the social functions and all other things that would distract them and draw them away from the serious things of life. Every Monday, and oftener if you want to, you get your children together around you and see that they pray. *Let the children take their turn in prayer* as you have already done in the morning when you get up, you all get up early enough that you can plan your day so that the father does not grab a piece of toast or something and go off to his work. So that the children don't grab a piece of bread to take care of them in their school work but that the family meets with some degree of order. They have their prayer and the father prays and the mother prays and the children pray, all in their turn. It is amazing how small children can be and catch the spirit of it and they pray before they can talk fully and well. If they pray for their bishop, for their stake president, you know they are never going to talk against them. They are never going to find fault with them. If they pray for the Presidency of the Church, you know they are going to love them. If they pray for the missionaries, you know they are going to want to be a missionary. There will be an exception now and then, but they will want to be a missionary and the time goes and they reach their objectives if they are properly taught. (Fireside Address, Orlando, Florida, December 19, 1976.)

It Is Not Enough Just to Pray. The home should be a place where reliance on the Lord is a matter of common experience, not something saved for special occasions. One thing is to have established a regularity of family prayer. It is not enough just to pray. *It is essential that we really speak to the Lord,* having faith that he will reveal to us as parents what we need to know and do for the welfare of our families. It has been said of some men that when they pray one of the children is likely to open his eyes to see if the Lord is actually there. A child leaving to go away to school or on a mission, or a wife suffering from stress, a family member being married or desiring guidance in making an important decision—all of these situations which the father is in charge of will be blessed by their participation. (Area Conference Address, Buenos Aires, Argentina, October 29, 1978.)

The Home Is the Teaching Situation

Every Father Should Talk to His Son, Every Mother to Her Daughter. The home is the teaching situation. Every father should talk to his son, every mother to her daughter. Then it would leave them totally without excuses should they ignore the counsel they have received. ("God Will Not Be Mocked," General Conference Address, October 4, 1974.)

To Fortify Our Homes and Families. We need continually to fortify our homes and families and defend them against the onslaught of evils such as divorce, broken families, brutality and abuse, especially of wives and children. We need to constantly guard against immorality, pornography, and sexual permissiveness that would destroy the purity of the family members, young and old. ("Fortify Your Homes Against Evil," General Conference Address, March 31, 1979.)

The Home Is Our Peculiarity. My brothers and sisters, the home is our peculiarity. The home and the family are our base. This we have heard much about and will continue to hear more about in the talks of the Church leaders. Family life, home life, children and parents, loving each other and depending upon each other—that's the way the Lord has planned for us to live. The currents he wants us to follow will resist the adverse forces and carry us back into the presence of the Lord. (Area Conference Address, Buenos Aires, Argentina, October 29, 1978.)

Be Kind One to Another. In such homes, where we are "kind one to another, tenderhearted, forgiving one another" (Ephesians 4:32), where we are holding our family meetings, discussions, and councils, where we are praying, working, and playing with love as our chief motive, where we are trying to share the gospel with others and fulfill the other purposes of the Lord—in those homes there will dwell a powerful spirituality and unity that will be a lifelong strength to all family members.

We earnestly encourage all individuals and all family units throughout the Church to evaluate anew their progress in living these truths. Their applications will be your shield and protection against the evils of our time and will bring you individually and collectively great and abundant joy now and hereafter. ("Therefore I Was Taught," *Ensign*, January 1982.)

Father's Role in Missionary Preparation

Fathers, Train Your Sons. Righteous, anxious fathers produce good sons generally. And so it is important that you plan
your life very carefully. You're home every Monday night. You
teach your children how to pray and walk uprightly before the
Lord. That means that they will be taught they should never
steal, should never take anything that does not belong to them.
You remember Moses received that commandment from the
Lord: "Thou shalt not steal" (Exodus 20:15).

But that's only one of the commandments you are teaching
your children. And you live to see a happy day, to see your
children following your righteous example. (Area Conference
Address, Lima, Peru, February 25, 1977.)

Children Mimic Fathers. We are told by many who have
made a study of the matter that the child gets much of his training in his very early years—not when he is eighteen or twenty or
sixteen or fourteen—but when he is six months old, or when he
is a year or two years or three years old. He watches his father,
and while he doesn't understand fully he is mimicking his
father, and if you wait until it is too late to rear your children, my
brethren, you may lose some of them. What you say, what you
do, and how you act are all acted out and mimicked by your boy.
When you love your little child and become a companion to him,
and when you sit in the family home evening every Monday
night and teach him, he is looking at you with an admiration.
Remember that the mother is not the only one to totally look
after the child. The fathers and mothers rear their children
together and give them experiences and training that they
deserve. (Area Conference Address, Rochester, New York, April
12, 1980.)

The Cycles of Inactivity. The cycles of inactivity and indifference are recurring cycles from father to son. The Church must
now break that cycle at two points simultaneously: We must
reach out and hold many more of our young men of the Aaronic
Priesthood to keep them faithful, to help them to be worthy to go
on missions, and to be married in the holy temple; we must, at
the same time, reach and hold more of the fathers and the prospective holders of the Melchizedek Priesthood! One of the consequences of this cycle of indifference and inactivity in fathers

and young men is the swelling sisterhood of the Church, among whom are many gallant and faithful sisters. (New Mission Presidents Seminar, June 20, 1975.)

Mother, You Take Care of It. We are talking about home evening. That means at home. That does not mean going to shows, although that could be done occasionally, of course. That means in your own house, your own home, and the father does not say, "Mother, you take care of it." The father is in charge of the home, every week. A possible exception could come, of course, in an emergency. And the children take their turns in this home evening. (Fireside Address, Orlando, Florida, December 19, 1976.)

My Father Baptized Me. The scripture says that parents shall teach their children to pray and walk uprightly before the Lord. And if they haven't taught their children the law of baptism and confirmation, and to do right by the time they are eight years of age, then the sin will be upon the heads of the parents. (D&C 68:25-28.) Now that does not say parents start to teach the child at eight years of age. By then the child should have received many of the concepts that will be an important part of his life. So you will already have had your child taught and trained in honesty, uprightness, integrity, and cleanliness; in the love of the Lord and his fellowmen; and in all the things that a grown person should know. He should know much of it before he is eight. Then when he is eight, he is clean, he is sweet, he is free from immorality or sins of any kind; and the father leads him to the baptismal font, perhaps, or baptizes him himself. My father baptized me. I baptized all my children, with the permission of the bishop, who has the responsibility, of course. We don't go and do it ourselves without authority. So the father looks after that. (Area General Conference Address, Glasgow, Scotland, June 21, 1976.)

Father's Blessings. I was down in Toquepala, Peru. We were dedicating a chapel. Many of the men who were employed in that mining town were Americans. After the dedication they had a dinner at one of the homes. As we moved around in the home, a young boy came to me and said, "Brother Kimball, I'm thinking about a mission. Would you give me a blessing?"

I said, "Why, of course. I'd be very happy to give you a blessing, but isn't that your father I met in the other room?"

He said, "Yes, that's Dad."

I said, "Well, why don't you ask him to give you your blessing?"

"Oh," he said, "Dad wouldn't want to give a blessing."

So I excused myself. In time I ran into the father and I said, "You have a wonderful boy there. I think he would like to have a blessing from his father. Wouldn't you like to give him a blessing?"

He said, "Oh, I don't think my boy would want me to give him a blessing."

But as I mingled among these people I saw the father and son a little later, close together. I could understand that they had come together in their thoughts and that the boy was proud to have his father bless him, and the father was delighted to be asked.

I hope you boys in this audience will keep that in mind. You have the best dad in the world, you know. He holds the priesthood; he would be delighted to give you a blessing. He would like you to indicate it, and we would like you fathers to remember that your boys are a little timid maybe. They know you are the best men in the world, but probably if you just made the advance, there would be some glorious moments for you. ("Planning for a Full and Abundant Life," General Conference Address, April 6, 1974.)

Mother's Role in Missionary Preparation

A Mother Has Great Influence. A mother has far greater influence on her children than anyone else, and she must realize that every word that she speaks, every act, every response, her attitude, even her appearance, has an effect on the young people who grow up under her watchcare. The attitudes and the hopes and the beliefs of the child are pretty well determined by what happens with the mother of the family. She is a co-partner with God in bringing his spirit children into the world. Sometimes we think of the husband as being the other part to this co-partnership, but that isn't entirely true. There could not possibly be children, there could not be offspring, if we depended wholly upon fathers. The Lord had to make the program and give power to the seed that it might develop and bring forth children. No greater honor could be given to a woman than to assist in this divine plan. I wish to say without equivocation that a woman will find no greater satisfaction and joy and peace and make no greater contribution to mankind than being a wise and worthy woman and raising good children.

She Can Keep Them Close to the Lord. I remember a distant woman relative who had a very large family. One day she was talking about her family and said, "As I nursed my little boy child, I decided that surely he would be the president of the nation or the President of the Church." But she said, "When he got up in his teens I began to wonder if I could even keep him out of prison." Of course this was partly a joke, but she was saying a great truth. A mother can keep her boys out of prison. She can keep them close to the Lord. There may be an exception but the great majority of mothers can keep their sons and daughters faithful to the truth. They are with them much more definitely than the fathers, and they have much influence upon their children.

I'm wondering if we're doing all we can toward the training of our children. The home evening is most eminent. You do not need to push or force your children, but the power of suggestion is always most valued. I'm thinking, wasn't it Hannah who said to the Lord as she prayed, "If you will give me a son, I will give him back to you" (see 1 Samuel 1:11), and every mother would want her son to be faithful enough to go back and serve her Heavenly Father. She was very serious and meant what she said. When he was older he became the prophet of the Lord. (Area Conference Address, La Paz, Bolivia, March 2, 1977.)

There Are Two Ways of Spreading Light. There are two ways of spreading light—to be the candle or to be the mirror that reflects it. Parents can be both. A child will carry into his own life much that he sees in his family home life. If he sees his parents going to the temple frequently, he will begin to plan a temple life. If he is taught to pray for the missionaries, the mind and heart will be pointed toward the missionary program, and he will plan from his earliest youth to save and prepare for a mission call. ("Train Up a Child," *Ensign*, April 1978.)

Teaching Basic Virtues

Honor and Integrity and Honesty. We urge you to teach your children *honor* and *integrity* and *honesty.* Is it possible that some of our children do not know how sinful it is to steal? It is unbelievable—the extent of vandalism, thievery, robbery, stealing. Protect your family against it by proper teaching. ("God Will Not Be Mocked," General Conference Address, October 4, 1974.)

Teach Honor and Discipline and Family Life. I would like to mention a few specific things. Your attendance at your sacrament meetings is excellent; and at the other meetings, likewise. About 70 percent of you have your home evenings, and that is excellent. Here is the basis for your growth and development. We want our friends to know that we teach honor and discipline and family life. Our reading of history reveals the fact that those countries which forgot their family life lost their civilization. (Area Conference Address, Samoa, February 15-18, 1976.)

Train Up Your Children in the Proper Way. I was inspired by these fine young people who sang and danced last night, and the thought came to me: All those thousands of young people—does every one of those boys hold the priesthood? Does every one of the boys and girls go to Sunday School every week? Do the *niños* go to Primary, and do your wives and the older girls go to Relief Society? And do you go every week to your priesthood meeting and to your sacrament meeting? That is for everybody, and so the father takes his entire family, little ones and medium-sized ones and all, to the sacrament meeting every Sabbath. He will see them grow and prosper.

Brethren, we probably do not think of these things always as being vital. One of the old prophets said, "Train up a child in the way he should go: and when he is old, he will not depart from it." (Proverbs 22:6.)

That is a prophetic promise to every one of you men. You just be certain that you and your wife train up your children in the proper way. Then you may have great promises for the future. (Area Conference Address, Santiago, Chile, March 1, 1977.)

To Honor Our Fathers and Mothers. The Lord's fifth commandment—to honor our fathers and mothers. The family is the basic unit of society. Strong, loving and unified families are essential for local, national, and world solidarity. ("Conserving Our Heritage," World Conference on Records, August 12, 1980.)

Children, Obey Your Parents in the Lord. Sometimes we get a little bit independent, don't we, when we get twelve or fourteen or sixteen or eighteen and think we know more than our parents and we know what we want to do and we have freedom to do it. Remember that that is a bad situation when we begin to take that independent spirit because we will go many, many years from today before we will know more than our parents do because they have had much experience.

One thing that we can do to protect ourselves in the first place against evil is to be faithful to our parents. There is seldom ever a parent that would even suggest to his children to do wrong. Sometimes parents give wrong examples, sometimes they do not do all they could to keep children in the right way, but remember that parents are generally good and wholesome and interested and very, very anxious *to give the example* and to teach in righteousness. (Layton Region Youth Conference Address, May 5, 1974.)

It Is Not Enough to Honor. It is not enough to honor our parents in some narrow way. If we truly honor them we will seek to emulate their best characteristics and to fulfill their highest aspirations for us. No gift purchased from a store can begin to match in value to parents some simple, sincere words of appreciation. Nothing we could give them would be more prized than righteous living for each youngster. Even where parents have not great strength of testimony, they will take pride in the strength and conviction of their children, if the relationship between them is a tolerant, loving, supporting one. (Dedicatory Address and Prayer, Independence Missouri Stake Center, September 3, 1978.)

Teach Sacrifice

We are hoping that the regional representatives who are here and mission presidents and the stake presidencies and the bishoprics will really go to work now and find the young men of this nation who can fill missions.

Yes, we know it is somewhat of a sacrifice because our boys have gone. We have five grandsons who have filled their missions already. All our own sons have filled missions. We know it is a sacrifice, but we know sacrifice brings forth the blessings of heaven. We expect and hope that every mother and every father will begin to train that little boy from the time he is born, to look forward to a mission for himself and then to a temple marriage for himself, and to work out his program of education and other things in between. That is a part of the sacrifice that is asked of us. (Area Conference Address, London, England, June 20, 1976.)

Sacrifice Brings Forth the Blessings of Heaven. Teach your children these basic principles in your family councils. Our pioneer forebears used to sing those lyrics about how "sacrifice brings forth the blessings of heaven." (*Hymns*, no. 27.) It still does, my brothers and sisters! Let us not forget the uses of adversity. ("Follow the Fundamentals," General Conference Address, April 4, 1981.)

Teach Chastity and Cleanliness

The Lord said, "Be ye clean, that bear the vessels of the Lord" (Isaiah 52:11). And we must state and restate and call to the attention of our children and their children that chastity and cleanliness are basic in the Church. Parents should teach their children in their home evenings and in all their activities as they rear them that unchastity is a terrible sin, always has been, always will be and that no rationalization by any number of people will ever change it. As long as the stars shine in the heavens and the sun brings warmth to the earth and so long as men and women live upon this earth, there must be this holy standard of chastity and virtue.

Our Children Must Be Taught. Our children must be taught from infancy that sex outside of proper marriage is an abomination in the eyes of the Lord and that boys and girls must keep themselves clean and unspotted from the world and free from all sexual impurity. They must learn that there must never be sexual improprieties of any kind in the premarriage days and that every boy and girl should bring to the marriage altar a clean body and an unpolluted mind. (Area General Conference Address, Stockholm, Sweden, August 17, 1974.)

Plant the Seed of Missionary Service

You Will Make a Great Missionary, Won't You? I have noticed in recent years nearly every time I see a little boy, I say, "You will make a great missionary, won't you?" You plant into his mind a seed. It is just like plants and other vegetation. It grows and grows, and if a father and a mother talk to their little boys, particularly, and their little girls, about going on a mission when they are infants almost, that little seed will grow and grow and they won't need to say anything about missionaries when they get a little older. The boys plan it. We have evidence of that. (Fireside Address, Orlando, Florida, December 19, 1976.)

There Is Where Father Was. I have mentioned a time or two that a woman in England had a husband who was a seafaring man. He spent all of his time on the ocean. They had three sons, and as she saw those beautiful little spirits growing into maturity, she said, "I will never have my sons go on the ocean. I will never let them be seafaring men." One day her husband did not return to his home after one of his voyages. He was a victim of the sea. After his burial, she got a great picture and put it on the mantle wall in her living room. The picture was of a big ship in full sail on the water. These three little boys grew up with that in mind. "There is where father was." He was their ideal. That little seed grew in their system and in their minds. All three of her sons went to sea. I have used that to say that if in every bedroom in Zion, if there were a little picture of a temple, a temple of your choice, where the boys and girls would see that temple every time they went into the room, they would none of them go to sea. Her children went to sea because that is what they were taught. The mother was training them all those years unintentionally to go to sea and that is where they went. And so it will be with the parents, the fathers and mothers, if they train their boys and girls, if they talk about it, if they pray about it, if they thank the Lord when their sons and daughters do these things and if they will keep it before them constantly by a picture in the living room or in the bedroom, somewhere, then their sons and daughters will be married in the temple and they will keep themselves clean so they can. They will keep their lives in order and that, of course, is the purpose of all our teachings and training. (Fireside Address, Orlando, Florida, December 19, 1976.)

Give Them Experience. It is well for parents to start preparing their sons to save money early in their lives. Let them have the spirit of saving. Let them also have the spirit of studying and praying about the gospel, of seeing for themselves how the gospel works in their own lives and in the lives of those around them. Let them have the spirit of service throughout their growing years and the experience of helping others discuss the joys of the gospel message in their lives. Let them use their seminary and institute classes and experiences as a training ground for acquiring spiritual knowledge of great value to themselves and others. Let them prepare by keeping their lives clean and worthy and by wanting with all their heart to help the Lord take the gospel to those who are ready for it.

If we prepare in this manner, our preparations will bring many blessings and spiritual rewards, and soon our preparations will become our regular life-style. As with a person and a family, so with a quorum, ward, or branch. Almost nothing can have such a powerful effect on a priesthood quorum or Church group than that which comes by being a vital part of friendship-ping, and fellowshipping and making someone an important part of the Church. The joy and fellowship and love among all concerned increases many times over. ("Are We Doing All We Can?" *Ensign*, February 1983.)

When a Child Is Eight Years of Age

Then we have this program of preparation of boys. I referred to it slightly last night, these fine little fellows that were singing for us last night. They have something to do. That isn't the end of their service when they sing a song. That's just a part of the preparation for it, for every child is baptized when he is eight years of age. The Lord gave us that by revelation. He said, "When a child is eight years of age or approximately, that child should be so well trained he should understand why he's baptized and what the blessings are that can come to him, that the Holy Ghost is given to him." Of course, they don't understand it all fully, totally, as they will at a later date, but if all parents will teach their children to pray and to walk uprightly before the Lord, they will pay great dividends for the child at eight; it is amazing how much the child knows in general about life itself. (Dedication of Chattanooga First and Second Wards, July 26, 1975.)

Grow Up Without Baptism? How can a mother and a father who love their children ever permit them to grow up without baptism? . . . That is something that is difficult to understand. With the right kind of training in our homes, every nine-year-old boy ought to be subservient to his parents. What parents should do is plan that from each child's infancy until his baptism date, for his first eight years, the child will be right under his mother's care and his father's. Surely every boy who is eight years of age can be brought into the waters of baptism properly. We ask the bishoprics to watch that very carefully too, and to keep this date before them constantly.

Perhaps a thousand times during those eight years the parents will remind the child, "Now on such a date you are going to be eight years of age; would you like Daddy to baptize you, or what is your pleasure?" There may be mischievous boys, but there are not bad boys at eight years of age or nine or ten.

I know many families who make a very great celebration on this particular day when a child, boy or girl, becomes eight years of age. It is far more important than a birthday party, and so it is planned weeks and months and years ahead.

After the Child Has Been Baptized? After the child has been baptized, the next thing to look forward to is his twelfth birthday. (The girls will have comparable opportunities.) According to the record, there are 124 boys here who are deacon age but haven't been ordained. Will you parents make a mental note and a written note if you have a son that isn't baptized to date or isn't ordained a deacon in his proper time? See that another week doesn't pass during which your boys are not honored with the priesthood, having been baptized at the right time.

Now a word about the missionary work before the time is gone. The boy moves up gradually and is fully converted with each step he takes, of baptism, deacon, teacher, priest, elder, and missionary. Will you pledge with me this night that you will go back to your wards and your homes and check up on all the boys and all the girls to see if they are active and receiving the blessings to which they are entitled? (Area Conference Address, Samoa, February 15-18, 1976.)

You Are Going to Be a Deacon. Now, a boy hardly gets over the time of his baptism when he starts talking about becoming a deacon in four years. All four years that little boy receives teachings about his preparation for the priesthood. We teach this little boy, "You are going to be a deacon. You are going to be a good deacon. You are going to be at priesthood meeting every week. You are going to pass the sacrament and that is a great honor." Every boy will anticipate with gladness the day when he can pass the sacrament, and he will think this is a sacred time of his life. These boys will never laugh or scuffle with each other while they are having the sacrament or passing it. The boys will always think to themselves, "This is a sacred covenant; I must do it righteously, and I must act temperate and properly. I must behave while I am performing these ordinances that are the Savior's."

Then the boy begins to think about becoming a teacher because the time has been established as fourteen years when he should become a teacher. Shame on the bishop or other leader who fails to have the boys properly ordained and taught and trained for this special privilege that they will have.

So we give the office of teacher to these young men, if they are clean and worthy and ready. Then they go forward doing other duties. Now the boy will go home teaching. What a tremendous responsibility. There are many patriarchs and members of the stake presidencies and bishoprics who are home teachers. And this is one responsibility of these young men, these new teachers.

Then the ordained teacher will look forward to the day when he will be made a priest, and there is his wonderful opportunity to bless the bread and the water and then, through the deacons, pass these sacred emblems to the congregation. Now, the boy becomes a priest, and he blesses the sacrament and he performs other duties, whatever his leaders ask him to do, but he looks forward to the time when he will be ordained an elder. And just think of the blessings that will come to him from that. Do you know, brethren, that every man in the world—millions of them— would be anxious to hold this priesthood that you hold, if only they just knew what it means. It makes me very sad when I realize that millions of men who live in our world today would like what you have, which many men among us do not take advantage of. (Area Conference Address, Pasadena, California, May 17, 1980.)

Teach Journal-keeping

I promise you that if you will keep your journals and records, they will indeed be a source of great inspiration to your families, to your children, your grandchildren, and others, on through the generations. Each of us is important to those who are near and dear to us—and as our posterity read of our life's experiences, they, too, will come to know and love us. And in that glorious day when our families are together in the eternities, we will already be acquainted.

While It Is Fresh. You should continue on in this important work of recording the things you do, the things you say, the things you think, to be in accordance with the instructions of the Lord. Your story should be written now while it is fresh and while the true details are available. ("President Kimball Speaks Out on Personal Journals," *New Era*, December 1980.)

To Write Their Personal Records. So we urge all our multitudes of people to write their personal records and biographies and their genealogies and all be prepared for the days when the temples are made available and can be used by all. This is a program long followed by members of this Church, but today there are numerous friends—Catholics, Protestants, Jews, and others—who are filling our genealogical rooms with their preparation of their family lines. ("The Lord Expects His Saints to Follow the Commandments," General Conference Address, April 2, 1977.)

Teach Scripture Study

No father, no son, no mother, no daughter should get so busy that he or she does not have time to study the scriptures and the words of modern prophets. None of us should get so busy that we crowd out contemplation and praying. None of us should become so busy in our formal Church assignments that there is no room left for quiet Christian service to our neighbors. ("Boys Need Heroes Close By," General Conference Address, April 3, 1976.)

Scripture study as individuals and as a family is most fundamental to learning the gospel. Daily reading of the scriptures and discussing them together has long been suggested as a powerful tool against ignorance and the temptations of Satan. This practice will produce great happiness and will help family members love the Lord and his goodness. ("Therefore I Was Taught," *Ensign*, January 1982.)

Every Boy Can Learn the Scriptures. Now, let me say a few things about the scriptures. One of the Brethren suggested you study the scriptures. Every boy can get scriptures. And every boy can learn the scriptures. You can learn them much easier when you are young than you can when you are old. (Area Conference Address, Monterrey, Mexico, February 19-20, 1977.)

CHAPTER SIXTEEN

Make Up Your Mind for a Mission

You can make up your mind this early that you will fill an honorable mission when you reach mission age, and to that end that you will now earn money and save it and invest it for your mission, that you will study and serve and use every opportunity to properly prepare your mind and heart and soul for that glorious period of your life.

Make Up Your Mind

I'm Going to Be Responsible. Now we are greatly concerned about the world in which we live. In the newspapers, all of the periodicals, all the radio and television and other media there are so many ugly things that are presented to us. It makes us realize that we must stand on our own feet or not stand at all. And so we hope that today everyone of you will make up your mind that, "I am going to be responsible for what I am; what I think; what I do with my life." We hope that that will be in your minds always. You don't need to think the things that are broadcast. You don't need to do the things that are suggested. You can do as you please, for God has given you your free agency in building your life. ("So Many Kinds of Voices," Long Beach, California, April 9, 1978.)

You Do It Today. Mrs. Kimball has said to make up your mind. Today, make up your mind. You don't wait until next Sunday to say, "Shall I go to priesthood meeting?" You do it today! Don't wait until you get a call from the Brethren to go on a mission. Start to save money. You start to save today and mark it "for my mission" and "for my college." You don't wait until marriage to make these decisions. You make your proposal and you decide on the date, and you decide upon where you are going to be married. That is always in your mind, from the time you are little boys. Only in the temple will I be married, in the holy temple of God, so that the marriage will be permanent. That is the decision. That is one of the newest decisions that we make. We make them today! Wouldn't it be a loss of a great deal of time and efforts if every Sunday morning we had to stop and say, "Shall I or shall I not go to priesthood meeting? Shall I or shall I not go to sacrament meeting today? Shall we or shall we not go?" What a lot of wasted effort . . . Settle it once and for all. "I *am* going on a mission, I *am* going to be worthy to go on a mission. I *am* going to get a degree as a start. I *am* going to live the commandments of the Lord and I am going to start." (Devotional—Expo '74, Spokane, Washington, July 24, 1974.)

Decide to Decide. Indecision and discouragement are climates in which the adversary loves to function, for he can inflict so many casualties among mankind in those settings. My young brothers, if you have not done so yet, decide to decide! ("Boys Need Heroes Close By," General Conference Address, April 3, 1976.)

Happiness Comes by Living the Commandments

You Will Pay the Cost! Now, brothers and sisters, this is very, very important. Just before you leave, make up your mind what you want to do. If you want to go out and shoot and kill, you can do anything you want to do, but you will pay the cost! And in these times of inflation, it looks pretty high! You will not want to do the things that will make you unhappy. Happiness comes by living the commandments, but unhappiness comes by not living the commandments. (Youth Fireside of the Woods Cross Region, Bountiful, Utah, August 28, 1977.)

It Is Not Enough to Acknowledge the Lord. It is not enough to acknowledge the Lord as supreme and refrain from worshipping idols; we should love the Lord with all our heart, might, mind and strength, realizing the great joy he has in the righteousness of his children.

It is not enough to refrain from profanity or blasphemy. We need to make important in our lives the name of the Lord. While we do not use the Lord's name lightly, we should not leave our friends or our neighbors or our children in any doubt as to where we stand. Let there be no doubt about our being followers of Jesus Christ.

It is not enough to refrain from movie-going, hunting, fishing, sports, and unnecessary labor on the Sabbath. Constructive use of the Sabbath day includes studying the scriptures, attending church meetings to learn and to worship, writing letters to absent loved ones, comforting the sorrowing, visiting the sick, and, in general, doing what the Lord would have us do on this, his holy day.

If we truly honor our parents as we are commanded to do, we will seek to emulate their best characteristics and to fulfill their highest aspirations for us. Nothing we could give them materially would be more prized than our righteous living.

It is not enough to refrain from killing. We are rather under solemn obligation to respect life and to foster it. Far from taking a life, we must be generous in helping others to enjoy the necessities of life. And when this has been accomplished, we seek to improve the mind and the spirit.

We refrain from taking harmful substances into our body. Through wisdom and moderation in all things, we seek good health and a sense of physical well-being.

It is not enough to refrain from adultery. We need to make the marriage relationship sacred, to sacrifice and work to maintain the warmth and respect which we enjoyed during courtship. God intended marriage to be eternal, sealed by the power of the priesthood, to last beyond the grave. Daily acts of courtesy and kindness, conscientiously and lovingly carried out, are part of what the Lord expects.

It is for us to keep our hearts and minds pure, as well as our actions.

"Thou shalt not steal," the Lord said on Sinai. (Exodus 20:15.) Thus it is for us to be honest in every way. We must be generous, the very opposite of selfishness. When money is needed, we give money. But often what is needed more is love and time and caring, which money cannot buy. When that is true, even being generous with our money is not enough.

Bearing false witness and coveting the belongings of others are further evidences of selfishness. "Love thy neighbor as thyself," Jesus taught. On this and on the love of God "hang all the law and the prophets." (Matthew 22:39-40.)

Kindness, helpfulness, love, concern, generosity—we could go on for the list of virtues is endless. The development of these traits is what the Lord asks of us. "If there is anything virtuous, lovely, or of good report or praiseworthy, we seek after these things." (Articles of Faith 1:13.) ("Hold Fast to the Iron Rod," General Conference Address, September 30, 1978.)

I Made Up My Mind

I Made up My Mind Definitely. I think if I've had any success it was because of what I am telling you to do. When I was a little boy, I made up my mind when we used to sing the Word of Wisdom song "In Our Lovely Deseret" in Primary: "Drink no liquor, and we eat but a very little meat," and so on (some of the older folks will remember it). But I made up my mind as young as I was: "I, Spencer Kimball, will never take tobacco, liquor, tea, or coffee into my mouth. Never will I do it!" You see, I made up my mind definitely, and so I never had to worry about it again! Because my mind was already made up. Along the years there were many temptations, but I never had to worry about taking one side or the other because I had made up my mind, and that was the end of that. And you can do the same, whether it be with the Word of Wisdom, or with tithing, with your temple marriage, with your missionary work, or whether with all of the doctrines of the Church, you make up your mind that this is it. This is it! I will not alter my life nor change it from what I have made up my mind to do! (Youth Fireside of the Woods Cross Region, Bountiful, Utah, August 28, 1977.)

To Keep the Promise to Myself and to My Heavenly Father. May I tell you another goal that I set when I was still a youngster.

I had heard all of my life about the Word of Wisdom and the blessings that could come into my life through living it. I had seen people chewing tobacco, and it was repulsive to me. I had seen men waste much time in "rolling their own" cigarettes. They would buy a sack of "Bull Durham" tobacco or some other brand and then some papers, and then they would stop numerous times in a day to fill the paper with tobacco and then roll it and then bend over the little end of it and smoke it. It seemed foolish to me and seemed such a waste of time and energy. Later when the practice became more sophisticated, they bought their cigarettes ready-made. I remember how repulsive it was to me when women began to smoke.

I remember as a boy going to the Fourth of July celebration on the streets of my little town and seeing some of the men as they took part in the horse racing as participator or as gambler, betting on the horses, and I noted that many of them had cigarettes in their lips and bottles in their pockets and some were ugly drunk and with their bleary eyes and coarse talk and cursing.

It took a little time to match the ponies and arrange the races, and almost invariably during this time there would be someone call out, "Fight! Fight!" and all the men and boys would gravitate to the fight area which was attended with blows and blood and curses and hatreds.

Again I was nauseated to think that men would so disgrace themselves, and again I made up my mind that while I would drink the pink lemonade on the Fourth of July and watch the horses run, that I never would drink liquor or swear or curse as did many of these fellows of this little town.

And I remember that without being pressured by anyone, I made up my mind while still a little boy that I would never break the Word of Wisdom. I knew where it was written and I knew in a general way what the Lord had said, and I knew that when the Lord said it, it was pleasing unto him for men to abstain from all these destructive elements and that the thing I wanted to do was to please my Heavenly Father. And so I made up my mind firmly and solidly that I would never touch those harmful things. Having made up my mind fully and unequivocally, I found it not too difficult to keep the promise to myself and to my Heavenly Father. ("Planning for a Full and Abundant Life," General Conference Address, April 6, 1974.)

The Matter of the Word of Wisdom. I mentioned the matter of the Word of Wisdom, that I made up my mind so definitely, certain that I would never fail. I went to a Rotary International Convention in Nice, France. Sister Kimball and I went back in 1935. We had an invitation to a special dinner, and in front of me there were seven goblets of wine. When men who were waiting on the tables came along with additional wine, ready to pour it, the thought came to my mind a second time: "I'm a long way from home; I am in France, and nobody would ever know if I drank a glass of wine, nobody will ever know." But I was wrong. Somebody would know. I would know. And the Lord would know, and he knew I had made up my mind when I was a child that I was going to follow this path. (Youth Fireside of the Woods Cross Region, Bountiful, Utah, August 28, 1977.)

CHAPTER SEVENTEEN

The Church and Missionary Preparation

Please be ever alert to the needs of the precious individuals and families who make up the membership of your wards and branches. You are the nurturing shepherds of our people.

It's a Priesthood Program

It's a Matter of Planning and Organizing. I notice a great many children here today, many of whom are boys. I wonder how many boys there are in this audience. Would all the boys that are under twenty-one please stand up—that's fine. Thank you very much.

I would just like to point out to this stake president that there is an army of missionaries, an army of missionaries, and I feel absolutely certain that all these boys can fill honorable missions if they will. It's a matter of planning and organizing and setting aside their funds, earning funds; work is glorious to be in the life of every person and every boy ought to be making money and saving his money for his mission. We send a few girls on missions; they are wonderful missionaries, but it's really a priesthood program, and we want to have a great many more missionaries tomorrow than we have today. The world needs us as it needs nothing else in all the world. The world of which you are a small part needs the gospel of Jesus Christ. Nothing else in existence could do it the good that the gospel would bring to the families of this earth who become so involved and so frustrated and so confused and without guidance and leadership. They get on the wrong paths. And so we need this missionary work. (Dedication, Granger Utah North Stake, April 28, 1974.)

Act Now. I plead with all stake presidents and Melchizedek Priesthood quorum presidents to inspire and train the fathers and men of the quorums to realize the importance of the calling of a father. *I plead with priesthood holders throughout the Church to return to their kingdoms—their homes—and with kindness and justice inspire their families to obey God.* I plead with mothers to follow their husbands in righteousness, to motivate their husbands to spiritual greatness.

Act now, before it is too late. Now is the time to chart the course of action you will follow tomorrow and next week and next year. Now is the time to commit yourself to be as Abraham, to follow the Lord, to refuse to procrastinate, to repent of those sins you have committed, to begin to keep those commandments you have been failing to live. Determine now to attend priesthood and sacrament meetings every Sabbath, pay your tithing faithfully, sustain in very deed the General Authorities of the Church, visit the temple often (or whenever possible if one is not near), give service in the organizations, and keep your actions constructive, your attitudes wholesome. ("The Example of Abraham," *Ensign*, June 1975.)

We Should Not Be Afraid to Ask. We should not be afraid to ask our youth to render service to their fellowmen or to sacrifice for the kingdom. Our youth have a sense of intrinsic idealism, and we need have no fear in appealing to that idealism when we call them to serve.

Our young men in the Church should be very eager to go on a mission, and they should also assist their parents to fill missions after the families are raised. Young people should study the gospel, prepare themselves for service in the Church, and keep the commandments as diligently as it is possible to do. ("President Kimball Speaks Out on Being a Missionary," *New Era*, May 1981.)

The Role of Youth Advisors and Teachers

I Wanted Them to Have Beautiful, Abundant Lives. I hoped these 152 years—and a possible eventual millennium for my posterity—of training that would supplement their parents' training, would bring out a beautiful normalcy in the lives of my posterity and of all others—a well-balanced approach to living.

Knowing the tendency for most young people to be hero-worshippers, I hoped you as their teachers would qualify for that admiration that is almost adoration. I wanted them to have beautiful, abundant lives patterned after the ideal image of an eternal family. This they would learn, a little from what you would tell them, but far more from what you would show them. Consequently, I hoped the picture which was impressed during these fifteen decades of learning would be near the ideal. This would lead me to expect honor, integrity, cleanliness, positiveness, and faith in our instructors of religion. I expected the teachers to appear before these young people as well-dressed, well-groomed, positive, happy people from homes where peace and love have left a warm, vibrant influence as their day with them began. I wanted them to feel sure that their teacher, that very morning, had walked out of a loving home where peace reigned and love was enthroned. This is still part of the challenge facing you marvelous men and women who labor in our weekday religious education program.

Lead Them with the Light of Your Own Testimonies. Stay close to the fundamentals so that what you teach will be true. Strengthen your lessons by making them simple. Love your students and lead them with the light of your own testimonies. Be humble and live the gospel in your own homes and your own lives, so that those whom you teach will do likewise. ("The Greatest Personage Was the Most Perfect Teacher," Assembly Hall, Temple Square, September 12, 1975.)

Talk Missionary Work to the Little Ones. Let the Primary and the Sunday School talk missionary work to the little ones. Let youth programs, including seminaries, talk missionary work to the growing up young men and women. Let parents make missionary work an important element in their family home evening so that their children may grow to maturity being frequently reminded of their duty. (New Mission Presidents Seminar, June 25, 1976.)

Just As We Keep Track of Our Bank Accounts. I am pleased to see so many young men here tonight, holders of the Aaronic Priesthood. I should like to speak of them especially. The point I wish to make is that every one who is a deacon is to become a teacher and a priest and an elder and a seventy and a high priest. Every one. I know of no reason why every boy should not have the higher priesthood and the high callings within that priesthood when he attains the proper age, and if he is worthy. We call on the leaders, the mission and stake presidencies, and the bishopric, to see that they do. We must keep track of these boys and men just as we keep track of our bank accounts. We watch their birthdays and their activities. No man can get the priesthood by himself. You could not buy it if you had all the money below the Mason-Dixon Line. You could not force it if you were a king. You just wait patiently and prove yourselves, and then the priesthood leaders call you to various positions.

So we say to you bishops and stake presidents, the responsibility is yours. (Area Conference Address, Lakeland, Florida, June 28, 1980.)

To the Greatest Extent Possible. Bishops and branch presidents, please be ever alert to the needs of the precious individuals and families who make up the membership of your wards and branches. You are the nurturing shepherds of our people. To the greatest extent possible, let your counselors and others who serve and work under your direction be the managers of programs. If you will pursue this emphasis, you will often be able to detect very early some of those members who have serious difficulties, while their challenges and problems are still small and manageable. Be conscious of the little tensions and problems you may see in families so that you can give the required attention, counsel, and love when it is most needed. An hour with a troubled boy or girl now may save him or her, and it is infinitely better than the hundreds of hours spent in their later lives in the reclamation of a boy or girl if they become inactive. ("Ministering to the Needs of Members," General Conference Address, October, 1980.)

The Role of the Priesthood Quorum

We Must Find a Way to Reach and to Hold. We must find ways to reach and to hold more of our Aaronic Priesthood youth, to prepare these young men to serve as full-time missionaries, as well as to prepare these young men who are the future fathers in the Church for that lofty role. We must find improved ways of vitalizing our Melchizedek Priesthood quorums, particularly in order to reach the prospective elders who are in so many cases the fathers of so many of our boys and girls and our young men and women. ("Lengthening Our Stride," Regional Representatives Seminar, October 3, 1974.)

Use Returned Missionaries. There is no reason why the hundreds of fine young men who are honorably released from their full-time missions cannot be used more adequately in the Kingdom, and this is very important, as I see it. So many of them are under-used now, and their spiritual strength ebbs away before our very eyes. Why cannot the elders quorums of the Church and the Melchizedek Priesthood MIA use these young men even more than now to reach and to teach some of the prospective elders in their wards? Why can't we find at least many of the full-time missionaries we need among the young men and women between the ages of nineteen and twenty-five who have not served on missions? Why can't we have our priesthood quorums so effectively taught, especially now that the scriptures are the course of study, so that inactive fathers who come, and are stirred to search the scriptures themselves, see clearly the obligations they have to the Kingdom and to their families? No sincere, conscientious father can read the Lord's charge to the Church to do missionary work and not want to have his son engaged in that service. (Regional Representatives Seminar, October 3, 1974.)

In His Full Capacity. Brethren, this is a wonderful kingdom. The Lord has spent a great deal of time indicating what we should do to magnify our callings as best we can. The Lord revealed the fact that twelve deacons make a quorum, and 24 teachers, and 48 priests and 96 elders. That's the way to get the work done, to get every man and boy active in his full capacity. It isn't enough just to be a casual member. The blessings—real blessings—can never come to us in that manner. (Area Conference Address, São Paulo, Brazil, November 4, 1978.)

The Roles of Seminary and Institute

I Wish Every Boy and Girl Could Go to Seminary. I wish every boy and girl could go to seminary, because that is where they learn many of the truths of the gospel. Seminary is where

184184184

many of them get their ideals settled in their minds about what they are going to do, and they go on missions. ("President Kimball Speaks Out on Being a Missionary," *New Era*, May 1981.)

To Take Charge of Your Lives. Indeed, the mission of all religious educators in the Church Education System is to assist parents in rearing their children to be righteous Latter-day Saints, willing and capable to serve effectively in the kingdom of God. This is your part. To do your part well, it is wise to remember with Oliver Wendell Holmes, that "to reach a port, we must sail, sometimes with the wind, and sometimes against it; but we must sail, and not drift, nor lie at anchor." You need to heed this admonition to take charge of your lives.

Teachers Must Carefully Pick up the Fallen Torch. We are constantly exerting ourselves to impress upon the parents of the Church that it is their primary responsibility to rear their children in faith and teach them correct principles of living. But we must be realistic, for many parents fail in varying degrees to train their children properly. Therefore, all other agencies dedicated to doing good must carefully pick up the fallen torch. Among the Church's most effective torch-bearers are those who teach in the seminaries and institutes and others who teach religion at our Church university and colleges. For many youngsters, you teachers and your lovely wives constitute one of the best models of proper home living. I hope that each of you is striving to be the perfect husband and father with proper control of self and with loving family relationships, so that your students see in you and your family the ideal after which to pattern their lives. ("The Greatest Personage Was the Most Perfect Teacher," Assembly Hall Temple Square, September 12, 1975.)

Role of the Missionary Training Center

Thousands of Young Men Will Be Trained. We have the Language Training School on the Brigham Young University campus where thousands of young men will be trained to speak Spanish and Portuguese and Scandinavian and Russian and Japanese and Korean and all the languages to which they are called, even in the Indian languages, Aymara and Quechua. Those languages are taught to the young men, and it is amazing that perhaps in all the world there are no communities as language motivated and interested and trained as in The Church of Jesus Christ of Latter-day Saints. You can go to almost any little town with a thousand people, maybe, and there you would find scores, if not hundreds of men, mature men, who have previously learned a language in some of the missions. (Fireside Address, Orlando, Florida, December 19, 1976.)

In His Own Tongue. It is written: "For it shall come to pass in that day, that every man shall hear the fulness of the gospel in his own tongue, and in his own language, through those who are ordained unto this power, by the administration of the Comforter, shed forth upon them for the revelation of Jesus Christ." (D&C 90:11.)

For many years we have approached the taking of the gospel to numerous people in their own tongue. Today, with our schools at the language training missions, we believe we have set a new pace for the whole world.

The ability of our missionaries to learn the various foreign tongues is exemplified by the experience we had in Finland.

As we sat in a conference with the ambassador to Finland, we discussed the very great difficulty of learning the Finnish language, and he said, "It has often been contended that only a Mormon elder or a new baby could ever learn the Finnish language."

All over the Church we now have maturing men, heads of families, who have, through their mission experience, learned the various languages.

We are very proud of this accomplishment and hope that all other nations in the world will respond with a comparable reaction. (Regional Representatives Seminar, April 5, 1976.)

CHAPTER EIGHTEEN

Teach by the Spirit

The Holy Ghost stirs our memory, as well as our understanding. . . . This is one of the reasons why we Latter-day Saints must live in a worthy manner so that we can have the influence of the Holy Ghost and have his constant companionship to guide us, to direct us. His guidance is far more important than the learning of techniques, although these can be helpful.

If Ye Receive Not the Spirit Ye Shall Not Teach

Teach the Principles. In the Doctrine and Covenants, the Lord has said, "And the Spirit shall be given unto you by the prayer of faith; and if ye receive not the Spirit ye shall not teach." (D&C 42:14.) Assuming that your work is closely allied to that of the priesthood, you shall "teach the principles of [the] gospel, which are in the Bible and the Book of Mormon, in the which is the fulness of the gospel" (D&C 42:12)—not mere ethics—and you always have the liberty to turn to them, and to interpret them, and bring them to the point where your inspiration leads you to give it to that particular sister—a different message to every person, a different approach to testimony. ("The Vision of Visiting Teaching," *Ensign*, June 1978.)

The Manner of the Workings of the Spirit. We have all felt the outpouring of the Spirit of the Lord as we have assembled in his name to worship and be instructed by the power of the Holy Ghost. This has always been the pattern of the meetings of the Saints, for we read in the Book of Mormon the words of Moroni, who said: "And their meetings were conducted by the church after the manner of the workings of the Spirit, and by the power of the Holy Ghost; for as the power of the Holy Ghost led them whether to preach, or to exhort, or to pray, or to supplicate, or to sing, even so it was done." (Moroni 6:9.) ("Revelation: The Word of the Lord to His Prophets," General Conference Address, April 3, 1977.)

Every Young Man Can Pray for the Spirit

He Was Going to Get It. Then, in 1820 the Lord came to the earth again with his Son and with his angels and they reestablished the gospel upon the earth. They did it through the instrumentality of Joseph Smith. Joseph was a prophet of God. He was a young boy—only fourteen years of age. . . . He knew that the gospel was in the Bible, much of it was. He was determined that if it was there he was going to get it, because he wanted the truth. He didn't want any false doctrine. So he went into this grove and knelt down in the woods and prayed. Oh, how he prayed! Few young men would ever pray as he had prayed, but every young man can pray in the same manner. (Area Conference Address, Suva, Fiji, February 23, 1976.)

With Study and Much Prayer

Study Is an Important Element. In the last chapter of the Book of Mormon we read this: "And when ye shall receive these things, I would exhort you that ye would ask God, the Eternal Father, in the name of Christ, if these things are not true; and if ye shall ask with a sincere heart, with real intent, having faith in Christ, he will manifest the truth of it unto you, *by the power of the Holy Ghost.*" (Moroni 10:4.)

That is no casual promise. It is a positive one, and every soul in this world may have a revelation, the same one that Peter had. That revelation will be a testimony, a knowledge that Christ lives, that Jesus Christ is the Redeemer of this world. Every soul may have this assurance, and when he gets this testimony, it will have come from God and not from study alone. Study is an important element, of course, but there must be associated with study much prayer and reaching, and then this revelation comes. ("President Kimball Speaks Out on Testimony," *New Era*, August 1981.)

We Must Live So the Holy Ghost Can Be with Us

Conversion Process. As a vital link in the conversion process, *we should bear our testimonies that the gospel is true*; our testimonies may well be the spark that ignites the conversion process. Consequently, we have a double responsibility: *we must testify of the things we know, feel, and have felt, and we must live so the Holy Ghost can be with us and convey our words in power to the heart of the investigator.* ("It Becometh Every Man," *Ensign*, October 1977.)

The Holy Ghost Stirs the Memory. So often, however, what we need by way of encouragement to keep the commandments and to serve others is to simply be stirred in our memory by the Spirit concerning the things we already know, rather than receiving new inspiration and revelation. It has been said that "memory is the stomach of the soul," in that it receives, digests, and nourishes us. *The Holy Ghost stirs our memory, as well as our understanding.* We must, then, do what we already know is right—the simple things, the straightforward things, and the specific things. This is one of the reasons why we, as Latter-day Saints, must live in a worthy manner so that we can have the influence of the Holy Ghost and have his constant companionship to guide us, to direct us. His guidance is far more important than the learning of techniques, although these can be helpful. ("Small Acts of Service," June Conference Address, June 21, 1974.)

The Spirit Teaches Right from Wrong. We know right from wrong. Every boy and girl does. The moment he is brought out of the water after his baptism at eight and receives the Holy Ghost the next day in sacrament meeting, he then has the Holy Ghost, which will lead him into righteousness. He will know whether it is wrong or whether it is right. Whether he understands all the details or not, he will feel it, for that is a part of the gospel of Christ. ("So Many Kinds of Voices," Long Beach, California, April 9, 1978.)

Testify by the Spirit

You Have a Testimony. You have a testimony! It needs building and lifting and enlarging, of course; and that is what you are doing. Every time you bear your testimony it becomes strengthened. I ask missionaries, "What think ye of Christ and the claims that are made?" And I hear inspiring testimonies from youth—sure testimonies, ringing with conviction. I am gratified at the replies saying, "He is the Christ, the Son of the living God." ("President Kimball Speaks Out on Testimony," *New Era*, August 1981.)

Testimony Is a Tremendous Thing. You know this testimony is a tremendous thing, a most important thing. Any minister or priest can quote scripture and present dialogues. But not every priest or minister can bear his testimony. Don't you sit there in your fast meeting and cheat yourself and say, "I guess I won't bear my testimony today. I guess that wouldn't be fair to these other members because I have had so many opportunities." You bear your testimony. And one minute is long enough to bear it.

With Some I Am Not Well Pleased. The Lord says in the 60th section of the Doctrine and Covenants, "With some I am not well pleased for they will not open their mouths." (D&C 60:2.) What does he mean? He says that if they do not use it, they will lose what he has given them. They lose their spirit. They lose their testimony. And this priceless thing that you have can slip right out of your life.

Every month the First Presidency and the Twelve meet with all the General Authorities in the temple. They bear testimony and they tell each other how they love one another just like all of you. Why do the General Authorities need a testimony meeting? The same reason that you need a testimony meeting. Do you think that you can go three, and six, and nine, and twelve months without bearing your testimony and still keep its full value?

Some of our good people get so terrified at triteness that they try to steer around and away from their testimonies by getting out on the fringes. Don't you ever worry about triteness in testimony. When the President of the Church bears his testimony, he says, "I know that Joseph Smith was called of God, a divine representative. I know that Jesus is the Christ, the Son of the living God." You see, the same thing every one of you says. That is a testimony. It never gets old, never gets old! Tell the Lord frequently how much you love him.

You Have to Keep Fighting. We often see this in the lives of members of the Church. One said to me in a stake I visited, "I assiduously avoid all testimony meetings. I can't take the sentimental and emotional statements that some of the people make. I can't accept these doctrines unless I can in an intellectual and rational way prove every step." I knew this type of man as I have met others like him. In no case had they gone all-out to live the commandments: little or no tithing, only occasional attendance at meetings, considerable criticism of the doctrines, the organizations, and the leaders, and we know well why they could have no testimony. Remember that the Lord said: "I, the Lord, am bound when ye do what I say; but when ye do not what I say, ye have no promise." (D&C 82:10.)

Such people have failed to do what he says, so, of course, they have no promise.

Testimony meetings are some of the best meetings in the ward in the whole month, if you have the spirit. If you are bored at a testimony meeting, there is something the matter with you, and not the other people. You can get up and bear your testimony and you think it is the best meeting in the month; but if you sit there and count the grammatical errors and laugh at the man who can't speak very well, you'll be bored, and on that "board" you'll slip right out of the Kingdom. Don't forget it! You have to fight for a testimony. You have to keep fighting!

I Know Without Question. I know without question that God lives and have a feeling of sorrow for those people in the world who live in the gray area of doubt, who do not have such an assurance.

I know that the Lord Jesus Christ is the Only Begotten Son of our Heavenly Father, and that he assisted in the creation of man and all that serves man, including the earth and all that is in the world. He was the Redeemer of mankind and the Savior of this world and the author of the plan of salvation for all men and the exaltation of all who live the laws he has given.

He it was who organized this vehicle—this true church—and called it after his name: The Church of Jesus Christ of Latter-day Saints. In it are all the saving graces.

I know that the Lord has contact with his prophets, and that he reveals the truth today to his servants as he did in the days of Adam and Abraham and Moses and Peter and Joseph and the numerous others throughout time. The countless testimonies of the Brethren throughout the ages are positive and uniform, uplifting and faith-building and hope-building, and they encourage worthiness. God's messages of light and truth are as surely given to man today as in any other dispensation.

I know this is true, and I bear this testimony to you, my beloved brothers and sisters and friends in all the world. ("President Kimball Speaks Out on Testimony," *New Era*, August 1981.)

You Will Receive the Light

I Promise You. I promise you faithfully that if you will study and pray, keeping your mind open, you will receive the light, and it will be to you as the dawning of a new day after having gone through the night of darkness. ("Absolute Truth," *Ensign*, September 1978.)

Open the Storehouse of Spiritual Knowledge. Almost without exception the missionaries have lived worthily, kept the commandments, and have been rewarded with a knowledge as promised by their Savior, in proportion to their faithfulness. It is not blind loyalty but faithful observance and turning of keys which open the storehouse of spiritual knowledge. The Lord will not discriminate between his children but delights to own and bless us all, if we will let him. And here he reveals another most important item—one must be free from sin to claim the blessing of an unwavering testimony. ("Absolute Truth," *Ensign*, September 1978.)

One Must Be in Tune with the Spirit. To acquire a testimony, then, *one must be in tune with the Spirit of the Lord, keep his commandments*, and be sincere. Because one does not receive this positive assurance is no reason why another cannot. To say that another person cannot see the light because you fail to comprehend it is to place unwarranted limitations on another's power. To say that no one can know of the doctrine because you do not is like saying that there is no germ or virus because it is not visible to you, and is to deny the word of God. Destructive criticism of the officers of the Church or its doctrines is sure to weaken and bring an eventual end to one's testimony if persisted in.

"If in this life only we have hope in Christ, we are of all men most miserable." (1 Corinthians 15:19.) And there are many miserable people in the world because they have no hope. But, when the gospel lights a life, then hope comes into it, and it gives a person something for which to live. Study if you will the philosophies of men which continue to change, but remember to appraise and evaluate such theories as of human origin. But anchor your faith, your hopes, your future to God who is unchangeable, for he is the same yesterday, today, and forever. If you cannot understand fully today, wait patiently and truth will unfold and light will come. Accept unreservedly the fact that God lives, that Jesus is the Christ, that life is eternal, and that the kind of life we live here will determine the degree of eternal joy and peace we shall have throughout eternity. ("President Kimball Speaks Out on Testimony," *New Era*, August 1981.)

The Testimonies of the Holy Prophets

They Help Us. The testimonies of the holy prophets of God have been written in the scriptures but also have often been written in red because these individuals are the Lord's prophets. They help us to see the end from the beginning. The prophets have always been free from the evil of their times, free to be divine auditors who will still call fraud, fraud; embezzlement, embezzlement; and adultery, adultery. ("Listen to the Prophets," General Conference Address, April 2, 1978.)

Your Missionaries Will Burn with Enthusiasm

The Church That Was on Fire. And I've often told the story of the Church that was on fire. When the cry went forward in the small town that Robinson Hall was burning, men came from every direction of town with their buckets. One stood at the canal and dipped the water and handed the bucket to his fellow who passed it up the line and the last one threw it on the flames. The fact that the hall burned down is not the point of our story, but as the last walls fell in and the futile effort had come to an end, one man put down his bucket and said, "Well, I never saw you at church before." And the other said, "Well, the church has never been on fire before." And so brethren of the regional and mission representatives in the mission presidencies, I doubt if your missionaries will *burn with enthusiasm* unless they catch it from you, an effervescent spark plug, always ahead of his missionaries and planning and thinking. (New Mission Presidents Seminar, June 27, 1974.)

My Heart Woke Up Today. Once in a missionary meeting in a South American mission a young missionary sat and absorbed the instructions and testimonies and finally bearing his own he said, "My heart woke up today. I'll be a missionary from today on. I've never been raised heavenward. I never left the earth before." (New Mission Presidents Seminar, June 27, 1974.)

Reach for Higher Things

The story is told of the hunchback prince who became straight and tall by standing each day before a statue of himself.

Change comes by substituting new habits for old. You mold your character and future by thoughts and acts.

You can change by changing your environment. Let go of lower things, and reach for higher. Surround yourself with the best in books, music, and art and we may say, people.

We generally like to think that deprived people are deprived through no fault of their own, but perhaps they might be.

Certainly we want all of our people to be happy but much depends on the person. Self-pity is destructive.

What to do.

Do all you can to right your own wrongs—all in reason. Make yourself attractive physically, well groomed, well dressed, attractive mentally, engaging. Do everything you can to achieve your proper ends. Then change yourself to accept what you cannot change. ("Small Acts of Service." June Conference Address, June 21, 1974.)

A Greater Vision. There is the old story you have heard so many times of the question asked of three builders of St. Paul's cathedral in London, "What are you doing here?" The first one answered, "I am working eight hours a day. I am putting in time. I am earning my living this way."

The second one said, "I am putting brick on brick and I am building a structure here." The third, when asked, raised himself to full stature and said, "I am building a great cathedral."

So it seems to me that visiting teachers who must go and do their teaching, who must get in their reports, who must answer to a call, who must do anything, are just time watchers, clock watchers. I guess there could be some of those, the clock watchers, in the Church. Then there are those who have a little better vision, "Why, it is part of the work of the Lord and, therefore, I guess I should set aside my own interests and go." ("The Vision of Visiting Teaching," *Ensign*, June 1978.)

Lock Your Hearts Against Distractions

Just Keep Your Hearts Locked. If missionaries will, when they leave Salt Lake City, the Mission Home—the day they are set apart—if they will just lock their hearts! If they've got a girl in there that's all right, lock her in! But if you haven't got one in, then lock it against all other girls of every description! And the same applies for young women, too. I am talking mainly to you Elders. You lock your heart and you leave the key at home. And you never open it here! It's impossible to fall in love with someone unless you open your heart! Your heart is the only organ that has any ability to get into love, you see, and when a missionary says, "I just fell in love with a girl!" well, that's as silly as it can be! Nobody falls in love unless they want to! Unless they're trying to! Nobody does, nobody ever did!

So we just don't fall in love unless we are fooling around. We never fall in a crater unless we are somewhere near the edge of it. I have been up to Vesuvius and on a number of craters and volcanoes and I know. Just keep your hearts locked! Lock them in Salt Lake when you leave the Mission Home and don't give a thought to it. But if you go around and say, "Well, she is kind of a pretty girl! She surely is a sweet little thing! She's a nice girl! I'd like to talk with her—I'd just like to visit with her!" well, you are in for trouble and that trouble can bring you a lifetime of trouble and a lifetime of regrets if you continue on with it.

So, can I impress that again? *Lock your hearts and leave the key at home!* Wherever you live, leave the key home with your folks. And your heart—it's only that part of it that deals with people generally that you open up. We just can't tolerate it, can we? We can't individually, we can't totally.

Someone said, "Well, is there any harm to marry a Mexican girl if you are working in Mexico?" No, that isn't any crime, but it proves that some missionary has had his heart open! He has unlocked it! Is it wrong to marry a German girl when you have been on a German mission? Why, no there is no crime in that, if you met her some other way. But when you meet her in the mission field and you have opened your heart, I tell you, it isn't right! And you have shortchanged your mission!

Just keep your hearts locked! Your whole thought should be missionary work. How can I make it more plain and more important than that! I'd like to because there is no reason whatever for any missionary to ever become involved, not even in a decent way, with any girl in the mission field. It isn't the place! You guaranteed, you promised! You went through the temple! You remember what you did in the temple? Remember you promised you'd do all the things the Brethren request of you, to live the commandments. That's one of the commandments when you go into the mission field — "Thou shalt not flirt! Thou shalt not associate with young women in the mission field or anyone else for that matter on any other basis than the proselyting basis." You promised and you would not want to break a promise you made before the Lord in the holy temple of the Lord. And when you wrote your letter [of acceptance] to President McKay that was implied in it. You knew, of course — every missionary knows — that he isn't going out to court, that he isn't going out to find a wife! He's got plenty of opportunity when he gets home, and the mission field isn't the place.

Sometimes we find a young man who has not been popular at home; he has been very, very backward at home and he hasn't had many dates. And so when he gets out into the mission field and somebody flatters him a little — some girl shows a lot of interest in him — why, he's flattered. He thinks all at once, "Well, that's whom I should marry!" Well, I say this once more by repetition and for emphasis, you lock your hearts at home, and if you haven't done so, do it now and send the key back! You will not permit any impression, no romantic thought or impression in your mind. For two years you have given yourself to the Lord, totally, to teach the gospel to the world. When you have done this perfectly for two years and then you go home, you are infinitely more attractive, more able, more dignified, more mature to make those important decisions for your life in the matter of personages to enjoy eternity with you. ("Lock Your Hearts," Mission Tour in Latin America, 1967 or 1968.)

Carelessly Picking Up Some Careless Thoughts. If we lie, it is charged against us. If we steal, we become responsible. If we are filthy in our thoughts or actions, then our own nature begins to show destructive elements in our lives. Sometimes our life sails along carelessly picking up some careless thoughts which become translated into careless actions and sometimes even defilement takes place, and as we approach the teen years and move along through those years, many times there are little and increasing defilements, early dates, increasing intimacies, physical contacts in what is generally referred to as "necking" or "petting." Sometimes they are indulged in and sometimes even to immorality, fornication or adultery. And our lives become damaged and defiled. Often these improprieties are increased until deep sin is the result and fornication or adultery has been committed. (Layton Region Youth Conference Address, May 5, 1974.)

CHAPTER NINETEEN

To Act as Representatives of the Lord

*As children of God, the second great commandment
—to love our neighbors as ourselves—ever reminds us
that our families—extended and immediate—living
and dead—are our neighbors.*

We Must Love Our Neighbors as Ourselves

To Love and to Serve. We must remember that those mortals we meet in parking lots, offices, elevators, and other meetings to come are that portion of mankind God has given us to *love* and to serve. It will do us little good to speak of the general brotherhood of man, if we cannot regard those who are all around us as our brothers and sisters. If our sample of humanity seems unglamorous or so very small, we need to remember the parable Jesus gave us in which he reminded us that greatness is not always a matter of size or scale but of the quality of one's life. If we do well with our talents and with the opportunities around us, this will not go unnoticed by God. And to those who do well with the opportunities given them, even more will be given! ("The Perfect Executive," Sun Valley, Idaho, January 17, 1977.)

Glorious Consequences. God does notice us, and he watches over us. But it is usually through another mortal that he meets our needs. Therefore, it is vital that we serve each other in the Kingdom. The people of the Church need each other's strength, support, and leadership in a community of believers as an enclave of disciples. In the Doctrine and Covenants we read about how important it is "to succor the weak, lift up the hands which hang down, and strengthen the feeble knees." So often, our acts of service consist of simple encouragement or of giving mundane help with mundane tasks—but what glorious consequences can flow from mundane acts and from small but deliberate deeds! (Opening Address, June Conference, June 21, 1974.)

We Must Pray for Spiritual Power

Prayer Keeps Us in Touch with God. There is a great need in the world today for prayer which can keep us in touch with God and keep open the channels of communication. None of us should get so busy in our lives that we cannot contemplate with prayer. Prayer is the passport to spiritual power. ("Fortify Your Homes Against Evil," General Conference Address, March 31, 1979.)

Tender Feeling About Prayers. I always have very tender feelings about prayers and the power and blessing of prayer. In my lifetime I have received more blessings than I can ever adequately give thanks for. The Lord has been so good to me. I have had so many experiences in sickness and in health that leave me with no shadow of doubt in my heart and mind that there is a God in heaven, that he is our Father, and that he hears and answers our prayers. ("We Need a Listening Ear," General Conference Address, October 6, 1979.)

I Need Thee. I think the Lord is happy when he hears us say, "I *need* thee." And when he feels that we really do need him. I would like us to sing it—"I *need* thee—Oh, I need thee!" I always tell the missionaries to sing it that way—to give that emphasis on, "I need thee!" How much I need thee. How limited I am, how alone I am if you are not with me. So we sing, "I need thee every hour, most gracious Lord." And then at night, before we retire, we get our families together, and we say, "I need thee *every* hour—*every* hour." Then when we get up in the mornings, before we go to school and seminary and elsewhere, we say to the Lord, one of us of the family, "I need thee, oh, I need thee. Today in my lessons, in my associations, in my friendships—I need thee, *every* hour, most gracious Lord." I hope you sing it with that intent, as you sang it so beautifully here today. (Dedication, Fair Oaks, California, October 9, 1976.)

Ingratitude, Thou Sinful Habit. Did we all fall on our knees to express our gratitude this morning and again tomorrow morning?

In many countries, the homes are barren and the cupboards bare—no books, no radios, no pictures, no furniture, no fire—while we are housed adequately, clothed warmly, fed extravagantly. Did we show our thanks by the proper devotion on our knees last night and this morning and tomorrow morning?

Ingratitude, thou sinful habit! (Thanksgiving Address to Holladay Stakes, November 26, 1975.)

Our People Will Have Very Bounteous Prayers. Some things are best prayed over only in private, where time and confidentiality are not considerations. If in these special moments of prayer we hold back from the Lord, it may mean that some blessings may be withheld from us. After all, we pray as petitioners before an all-wise Heavenly Father, so why should we ever think to hold back feelings or thoughts which bear upon our needs and our blessings? We hope that our people will have very bounteous prayers. ("We Need a Listening Ear," General Conference Address, October 6, 1979.)

We Must Work and Serve

We Were Taming Ourselves. How can one see the slackening of traditional moral standards and not notice the decline in decency? As a boy I saw how all, young and old, *worked* and *worked hard.* We knew that we were taming the Arizona desert. But had I been wiser then, I would have realized that we were taming ourselves, too. Honest toil in subduing sagebrush, taming deserts, channeling rivers, helps to take the wildness out of man's environment but also out of him. The disdain for work among some today may merely signal the return of harshness and wildness—perhaps not to our landscape but to some people. The dignity and self-esteem that honest work produces are essential to happiness. It is so easy for leisure to turn into laziness. ("Listen to the Prophets," General Conference Address, April 2, 1978.)

The More Substance There Is to Our Souls. First, service to others deepens and sweetens this life while we are preparing to live in a better world. It is by serving that we learn how to serve. When we are engaged in the service of our fellowmen, not only do our deeds assist them, but we put our own problems in a fresher perspective. When we concern ourselves more with others, there is less time to be concerned with ourselves! In the midst of the miracle of serving, there is the promise of Jesus that by losing ourselves, we find ourselves!

Not only do we "find ourselves" in terms of acknowledging divine guidance in our lives, but the more we serve our fellowmen in appropriate ways, the more substance there is to our souls. We become more significant individuals as we serve others. We become more substantive as we serve others—indeed, it is easier to "find" ourselves because there is so much more of us to find! ("The Abundant Life," *Ensign*, July 1978.)

A Sense of Peace and Contentment in My Soul. One incident occurred in Santo Domingo that I did not have time to tell you about. I think I should like to relate it to you now.

We held an evening general meeting in Santo Domingo, the capital city of the Dominican Republic. Nearly 1600 souls were present.

About an hour after the close of the general meeting, a busload of one hundred members from the Puerto Plata Branch arrived at the meeting place. They had been delayed because their bus broke down. Under ordinary circumstances, they could have made the trip in about four hours, but they finally arrived after 10:00 P.M. to find the hall dark and empty. Many wept because they were so disappointed. All were converts, some for a few months and others only weeks or days.

Sister Kimball and I had gone to bed after a long and tiring day. Upon learning of the plight of these faithful souls, my secretary knocked on the door of our hotel room and woke us up. He apologized for disturbing us but thought that I would want to know about the late arrivals and perhaps dictate a personal message to them. However, I felt that wouldn't be good enough and not fair to those who had come so far under such trying circumstances—one hundred people jammed into one bus. I got out of bed and dressed and went downstairs to see the members who had made such an effort only to be disappointed because of engine trouble. The Saints were still weeping as we entered the hall, so I spent more than an hour visiting with them.

They then seemed relieved and satisfied and got back on the bus for the long ride home. They had to get back by morning to go to work and to school. Those good people seemed so appreciative of a brief visit together that I felt we just couldn't let them down. As I returned to my bed, I did so with a sense of peace and contentment in my soul.

Brethren, we all have opportunities to render service to others. That is our calling and our privilege. In serving the needs of others, we are mindful of the words of the Savior: "Verily I say unto you, Inasmuch as ye have done it unto one of the least of these my brethren, ye have done it unto me." (Matthew 25:40.) ("Rendering Service to Others," General Conference Address, April 4, 1981.)

We Must Guard Against Selfishness

You Will Need to Guard Against Selfishness. Another word of counsel as you plan the course of your life. To do the special things given to this generation, you will need to guard against selfishness. One of the tendencies most individuals have which simply must be overcome is the tendency to be selfish. All that you can do now while you are young and are more pliant to become less selfish and more selfless will be an important and lasting contribution to the quality of your life in the years, indeed in the eternity, to come. You will be a much better wife or a much better husband, a better mother or a better father, if you can curb the tendency to be selfish. Your children whom you will not know for a few years yet have a stake in your conquest of selfishness. ("Charting Your Course," *New Era*, September 1981.)

From Out of a Selfish World to Speak of Service. Thus, we have gathered together from out of a selfish world to speak of service. Some observers might wonder why we concern ourselves with such simple things in a world surrounded by such dramatic problems. Yet, one of the advantages of the gospel of Jesus Christ is that it gives us perspective about the people on this planet, including ourselves, so that we can see the things that truly matter and avoid getting caught up in the multiplicity of lesser causes that vie for the attention of mankind. (Opening Address, June Conference, June 21, 1974.)

Who Have Served, Led, and Taught Us. If you and I would be good leaders, we should reflect periodically on the qualities of those who have served, led, and taught us. If you were to select just two or three individuals in your life who have been most influential, what specifically did they do that was most helpful to you at critical, or important points in your life? On reflecting for a few moments, you are apt to conclude that such a person really cared for you, that he or she took time for you, that he or she taught you something you needed to know. Reflect now upon your performance, as I do on my own, as to whether or not we now embody in our own ministry those same basic attributes. It is less likely in stirring through one's memories that someone will be remembered because that individual was particularly influential because of a technique. Most often someone has served and helped us by giving us love and understanding, by taking time to assist us, and by showing us the way through the light of their own example. I cannot stress enough, therefore, the importance of our doing these same things for those who now depend upon us, just as we have depended upon others to serve us in the past by special leadership and special teaching. (Opening Address, June Conference, June 21, 1974.)

We Must Do the Will of the Father

There Is No Other Way to Receive These Rewards. Now we made this commitment, ". . . all things whatsoever the Lord our God shall command us." We committed ourselves to our Heavenly Father, that if he would send us to the earth and give us bodies and give to us the priceless opportunities that earth life afforded, we would keep our lives clean and would marry in the holy temple and would rear a family and teach them righteousness. This was *a solemn oath, a solemn promise.* He *promised* us an eventful mortal life with untold privileges and providing we qualified in the way of righteousness, we would receive eternal life and happiness and progress. There is no other way to receive these rewards.

The Faithful from the Careless. Do not take any chances whatever. The Lord will separate his sheep from the goats, the tares from the wheat, the faithful from the careless, when the time comes. ("Marriage and the College Student," Tri-Stake Fireside, Ricks College, February 5, 1978.)

We Must Develop Discipline

You Only Need to Decide Some Things Once! Now may I make a recommendation? Develop discipline of self so that, more and more, you do not have to decide and redecide what you will do when you are confronted with the same temptation time and time again. You only need to decide some things once! ("Charting Your Course," *New Era*, September 1981.)

Christlike Life of Self-Mastery. The lack of chastity, fidelity, and virtue—fast becoming great, worldwide sins which need to be repented of—causes rivers of tears to flow, breaks numerous homes, deprives and frustrates armies of innocent children. Loss of virtue, as you know, has toppled many nations and civilizations. Moral decadence is a villain, and his forehead is branded with the words dishonesty, bribery, irreverence, selfishness, immorality, debauchery, and all forms of sexual deviation.

Each of us is a son or daughter of God and has a responsibility to measure up to a perfect, Christlike life of self-mastery, finally returning to God with our virtue. ("We Need a Listening Ear," General Conference Address, October 6, 1979.)

They Can Have All These Blessings. They can have all these blessings if they are in control of themselves, and if each one takes the experiences in proper order: first some social get-acquainted contacts to develop social skills, then a mission, then courting, then temple marriage and a family, and then schooling and degrees and business. Now the sequence of these things is very serious. If one gets them tipped around topsy-turvy, if sons get married first, many of the other dreams fall flat. But if they will take them one at a time in proper order and sequence, they may have all of them. They don't need to choose among them; they merely time them.

To Be the Master of One's Own Destiny. If we think that through, we will realize that it is very true, that the things we

tolerate in our lives finally become a part of us. It means that all
of the teachings given to us are fundamental and true and need
to be followed. Ugly things, evil thoughts, and evil doings will
take place in our lives if we think about them and tolerate them
in our minds, and then we will suffer. Eventually we will pay for
that which we have done.

And so, brothers and sisters, we govern our lives. Each of us
is the master of his own destiny. We are influenced by our families, by our fathers and mothers, by our brothers and sisters,
and by our friends. We are influenced. But none of us needs to
succumb to or to give way to the feelings of other people. We are
the masters of our own destinies, and we can become great and
strong and powerful, or we can become weak and of little consequence. (Area Conference Address, Manila, Philippines, August
11, 1975.)

What Dignity! What Mastery! What Control! What dignity!
What mastery! What control! Even when he, the perfect, the sin-
less, the good, the Prince of Life, the Just, should be weighed on
one side of the scales against the murderer, the seditionist, the
insurrectionist, Barabbas—and Barabbas won—even when
Barabbas won his liberty at the price of Christ's crucifixion, yet
the Savior said not a word of condemnation to the magistrate
who made the unjust decision.

Yet He Was Calm and Unflustered. Literally did he follow
his own admonition when he turned his other cheek to be also
slapped and smitten. And yet, he showed no cringing, gave no
denials, offered no rebuttals. When false mercenary witnesses
were paid to lie about him, he seemed to condemn them not.
They twisted his words and misinterpreted his meaning, yet he
was calm and unflustered. Had he not taught, "Pray for them
which despitefully use you"? (Matthew 5:44.)

Bless Them That Curse You. Neither did he say anything to
the people who called for Barabbas, crying "Release unto us
Barabbas" (Luke 23:18). Even when they cried for his blood,
saying, "Crucify him. crucify him" (Luke 23:21)—yet he
showed no bitterness nor venom nor condemnation. Only tran-
quility. This is divine dignity, power, control, restraint. Barabbas for Christ! Barabbas released, Christ crucified. The worst

and the best; the just and the unjust; the Holy One crucified, the degenerate malefactor released. Yet no revenge, no name-calling, no condemnation. No lightning struck them, though it could have done. No earthquake, though a severe one could have come. No angels with protective weapons, though legions were ready. No escape, though he could have been translated and moved from their power. He stood and suffered in mind and body. "Bless them that curse you," he had taught (Matthew 5:44).

Yet He Stood Resolute, Unintimidated. In quiet, restrained, divine dignity he stood when they cast their spittle in his face. He remained composed. They pushed him around. Not an angry word escaped his lips. They slapped his face and beat his body. Yet he stood resolute, unintimidated.

He Stood There, the Model of Long-Suffering. Blood from the thorns seemed to be what they wanted. For had they not just said, "His blood be on us, and on our children"? (Matthew 27:25.) Now nothing could stop them. They hungered to satisfy their blood lust, to satiate it. The crucifixion would do that, but first they must satisfy their beastly appetites for sadism; first they must cast their diseased spittle in his holy face, acting out subhuman atrocities.

With a reed in his hand, a scarlet robe over his shoulders, and a crown of thorns on his head, he was made to suffer the worst indignity: they laughed and mocked and jeered and challenged him. Grabbing the reed from his hand, they would strike him on the head. Yet, he stood there, the model of long-suffering.

Such Equanimity. Even when delivered to the soldiers to be crucified, he prayed for them who despitefully used him. How he must have felt when they violated his privacy by stripping off his clothes and then putting on him the scarlet robe!

Then, the crown of thorns. How painful and excruciating! And yet, such equanimity! Such strength! Such control! It is beyond imagination.

Still at His Command. They would have his sore and bruised and bloody body carry the weighty implement of his own death. Their strong backs unburdened, they watched him sweat and heave and strain and pull, a helpless victim. Or was he helpless? Were not the twelve legions of angels still at his command? Did they not still have their swords unsheathed? Were they not still agonizing, yet restrained from taking a hand or coming to the rescue?

How Base Can Man Become? Still they moved about him. In base mockery they feigned worship, praying mockingly to him, doing him false reverence, joking, laughing, giving full vent to their fiendishness. Was all their ugliness, all their pent-up grievances against mankind, all their bitternesses against acquaintances and enemies loosed upon this one so pure, clean, and worthy? Even a bull tires of goring its victim—even a cat tires of playing with its captive mouse—but these tyrants, these bloodthirsty men—would they never tire of blasphemous conduct? Would they never get their fill? How low can the children of God go! How base can man become!—he who may be but a little lower than the angels, he who is created in the image of God. What would they do when their victim could suffer no more and no more please their depravity?

What Excruciating Pain! He goes his way alone. The nails are hammered into his hands and feet, through soft and quivering flesh. The agony increases. The tree is dropped in the hole; the flesh tears. What excruciating pain! Then, new nails are placed in the wrist to make sure that the body will not fall to the ground and recover.

Jesus Shows the Way. He had said, "Love your enemies." Now he showed how much one can love his enemies. He was dying on the cross for those who had nailed him there. As he died, he experienced such agonies that no man had ever before or has since experienced. Yet he cried out, "Father, forgive them; for they know not what they do." (Luke 23:34.) Was this not the last word—the supreme act? How divine to forgive those who were killing him—those who were clamoring for his blood! He had said, "Pray for them which despitefully use you," and here he was praying for them. His life met perfectly his teachings. "Be ye therefore perfect" was his command to us. With his life, his death, and his resurrection, Jesus truly has shown us the way. ("Jesus of Nazareth," *Ensign*, December 1980.)

We Must Maintain Our Personal Journals

Please Follow the Counsel. Please follow the counsel you have been given in the past and maintain your personal journals. Those who keep a book of remembrance are more likely to keep the Lord in remembrance in their daily lives. Journals are a way of counting our blessings and of leaving an inventory of these blessings for our posterity. ("Listen to the Prophets," General Conference Address, April 2, 1978.)

Get a Notebook. Get a notebook, my young folks, a journal that will last through all time, and maybe the angels may quote from it for eternity. Begin today and write in it your goings and comings, your deepest thoughts, your achievements and your failures, your associations and your triumphs, your impressions and your testimonies. ("The Angels May Quote from It," *New Era*, October 1975.)

We Must Obey the Lord

Abraham's Faithfulness. There are many examples of Abraham's obedience to the Lord's will. In Genesis we learn that God commanded Abraham to circumcise every male in his household. Abraham did not say, "Yes, I will obey the Lord, but first I must move my sheep to another pasture, and mend my tents. I should be able to obey by the end of the week, or by the first of next week, at the latest." But instead of so procrastinating his obedience, Abraham went out and complied "in the self-same day." (Genesis 17:26.)

A similar, but even more impressive example is Abraham's obedience to God's command that he sacrifice his only son, Isaac. Abraham could have put this abhorrent task aside or even chosen to ignore the commandment entirely, but instead he arose early the next morning and began the journey to the appointed place.

How often do Church members arise early in the morning to do the will of the Lord? How often do we say, "Yes, I will have home evening with my family, but the children are so young now; I will start when they are older"? How often do we say, "Yes, I will obey the commandment to store food and to help others, but just now I have neither the time nor the money to spare; I will obey later"? Oh, foolish people! While we procrastinate, the harvest will be over and we will not be saved. Now is the time to follow Abraham's example; now is the time to repent; now is the time for prompt obedience to God's will.

Abraham was true with God in all respects. Oft cited is the instance when Abraham gave to God "tithes of all." Do you think it was any easier for Abraham to be righteous than it is for you? Do you inwardly suspect that Abraham was given a little extra help by the Lord so that he could become a great and righteous man, or do you feel that we can all become as Abraham who now, as a result of his valiance, "hath entered into his exaltation and sitteth upon his throne." (D&C 132:29.) Is such exaltation a blessing reserved only for General Authorities, or stake presidents, or quorum presidents, or bishops? It is not. It is a blessing reserved for all who will prepare themselves, by truly receiving the Holy Ghost into their lives, and by following the example Abraham has set. ("The Example of Abraham," *Ensign*, June 1975.)

It Is a Sin to Violate a Vow. I think of young people as sane young folks who are approaching maturity. If they are mature, then they should not need ever to be reminded what is right and what is wrong and what they have covenanted to do. It would certainly show immaturity if a student should need to be reminded. Surely it would be sad if grown young people could not remember their vows. For a young woman to wear shorter skirts or other immodest wear when she has covenanted otherwise would not be a matter of cleverness in escaping detection but a definite flaw in her character. Should any young man promise a certain performance in clothes or grooming or behavior and then evade those restrictions, certainly the error is deep-seated and is not just a difference of opinion. It is nothing to joke about but is a black mark on his character. The scriptures say it is a sin when he so violates his vow. ("Eternal Vigilance—The Price of Victory and Perfection," Salt Lake Institute of Religion Devotional, January 10, 1975.)

Self-Justification Is Easy and Rationalization Seductive. By taking our *covenants* lightly, we will wound our own eternal selves. I use the word *covenant* deliberately; it is a word with sacred connotations, and I mean to use it with all its special spiritual force. Self-justification is easy and rationalization seductive, but the Lord explains in modern revelation that "when we undertake to cover our sins, or to gratify our pride, [or] our vain ambition . . . the heavens withdraw themselves; the Spirit of the Lord is grieved; and . . . [man] is left unto himself, to kick against the pricks." (D&C 121:37-38.) Of course, we can choose; the free agency is ours, but we cannot escape the consequences of our choices. And if there is a chink in our integrity, that is where the devil concentrates his attack. ("Give the Lord Your Loyalty," BYU Address, September 4, 1979.)

With Agency One Can Murder. With agency one can murder, commit all the moral, sexual sins, can steal, lie, use drugs, be unkind. He may hate, envy, swear, or do whatever he would like. One can hate or one can love. One can curse or one can bless. One can help or assist; one can be helpful or hinder. One can blaspheme or one can honor and bless and pray. One can believe in himself or he can believe in an overall, omniscient being. One can do as he pleases. Free agency is his, or he can live his life with the great Redeemer as the center of his life.

One can touch a hot wire, but he cannot stave off the certain death that results. One can step in front of a powerful, oncoming train, but he cannot set aside the mangling that will follow. He can jump from a skyscraper, but he cannot control the results and save his body from the crushing effects of the fall and the abrupt contact with the hard pavement below. ("Eternal Vigilance—The Price of Victory and Perfection," Salt Lake Institute of Religion Devotional, January 10, 1975.)

We Must Be Neat and Clean

What a Powerful Influence You Can Bear. You are nineteen years old when you are called; maybe you will be seventy-nine when you die. In those sixty years, what a powerful influence you can bear. And you must do it! You must do it because it will be wasted life, to a degree, if any one of you go home and let your hair grow and wear sloppy clothes and do ordinary things and break the Sabbath or any other of the laws of God.

You see, the Lord has put you out here in the world, both the foreign and the local missionaries, not only to give the lessons, not only to bear your testimony, but to take this body and this soul of yours and make something of it. And your decision is today, not at the conclusion of your mission. It is today and has already been made. That decision must be right, because when you get back into the swing of things the temptation will be greater. The Lord knew what he was doing when he impressed the Brethren to have you be neat and tidy and clean in the mission field. (Area Conference Address, San Jose, Costa Rica, February 23, 1977.)

We Cleanse Our Lives. Now how can we cleanse our lives if we have been careless? We do it in two ways. We can add more righteousness as you have seen me add pure water until the evils that we might have done will be infinitesimal compared to the total body. That's one way and that's a part of both ways. The other way we can, of course, condense it and the same with our lives. The Lord has made it possible that if in some unguarded moment that we might have done something that was wrong, he has provided repentance and forgiveness. The only thing that cannot be forgiven absolutely is the sin against the Holy Ghost and not any one here in this room could do that because that takes a knowledge that is superior to the knowledge that any of you or us might have. So that we can say that anything we have done is forgivable, can be adjusted, can be cleansed, and we can go on with our lives as the Lord would want us to. The Lord said, "For I the Lord cannot look upon sin with the least degree of allowance; nevertheless, he that repents and does the commandments of the Lord shall be forgiven." (D&C 1:31-32.)

You notice the two elements there again, "He that repents and does the commandments." By doing the commandments we liberate or we dilute the evil that might have been there before by bringing in so much goodness to it. (Layton Region Youth Conference Address, May 5, 1974.)

We Must Perfect Ourselves

Man Has in Himself the Seeds of Godhood. Man can transform himself and he must. Man has in himself the seeds of godhood, which can germinate and grow and develop. As the acorn becomes the oak, the mortal man becomes a god. It is within his power to lift himself by his very bootstraps from the plane on which he finds himself to the plane on which he should be. It may be a long, hard lift with many obstacles, but it is a real possibility.

In other words, environment need not be our limit. Circumstance may not need to be our ruler, nor do granite walls or walls of steel need to be our prison.

To Be Perfect. To be perfect, one can turn to many areas as a starting place. (Converts join often in mid-life and old age.) He or she must become the perfect husband, the perfect wife, the perfect father, the perfect mother, the perfect leader, and the perfect follower. One's marriage must be perfectly performed and perfectly kept on a hallowed plane. One must keep his life circumspect. Each person must keep himself clean and free from lusts, from adultery and homosexuality and from drugs. He must shun ugly, polluted thoughts and acts as he would an enemy. Pornographic and erotic stories and pictures are worse than polluted food. Shun them. The person who entertains filthy stories or pornographic pictures and literature records them in his marvelous human computer, the brain, which can't forget such filth. Once recorded, it will always remain there, subject to recall. ("The Abundant Life," *Ensign*, July 1978.)

We Must Be Good Leaders

The Lord Jesus Christ's Remarkable Leadership. There are far more things to say about the Lord Jesus Christ's remarkable leadership than any single article or book could possibly cover, but I want to point out a few of the attributes and skills he demonstrated so perfectly. These same skills and qualities are important for us all if we wish to succeed as leaders in any lasting way.

Do What I Do. Jesus knew who he was and why he was here on this planet. That meant he could lead from strength rather than from uncertainty or weakness.

Jesus operated from a base of fixed principles or truths rather than making up the rules as he went along. Thus, his leadership style was not only correct, but also constant. So many secular leaders today are like chameleons; they change their hues and views to fit the situation—which only tends to confuse associates and followers who cannot be certain what course is being pursued. Those who cling to power at the expense of principle often end up doing almost anything to perpetuate their power.

Jesus said several times, "Come, follow me." His was a program of "do what I do," rather than "do what I say." His innate brilliance would have permitted him to put on a dazzling display, but that would have left his followers far behind. He walked and worked with those he was to serve. His was not a long-distance leadership. He was not afraid of close friendships; he was not afraid that proximity to him would disappoint his followers. The leaven of true leadership cannot lift others unless we are with and serve those to be led.

Jesus kept himself virtuous, and thus, when his closeness to the people permitted them to touch the hem of his garment, virtue could flow from him. (See Mark 5:24-34.)

The Perfect Leader. I make no apology for giving something of the accomplishments of Jesus Christ to those who seek success as leaders.

If we would be eminently successful, here is our pattern. All the ennobling, perfect, and beautiful qualities of maturity, of strength, and of courage are found in this one person. As a large, surly mob, armed to the teeth, came to take him prisoner, he faced them resolutely and said, "Whom seek ye?"

The mob, startled, mumbled his name. "Jesus of Nazareth."

"I am he," answered Jesus of Nazareth with pride and courage—and with power: the soldiers "went backward, and fell to the ground."

A second time he said, "Whom seek ye?" and when they named him, he said, "I have told you that I am he; if therefore ye seek me, let these [his disciples] go their way." (John 18:4-8.) ("Jesus: The Perfect Leader," Young Presidents Organization Address, Sun Valley, Idaho, 15 January 1977, *Ensign,* August 1979.)

We Must Be Loyal and True

Recipients of Divine Inspiration. Loyalty to the Lord also includes loyalty to those leaders he has chosen. I know that those whom the Lord has called to give leadership to his children in this dispensation of time are recipients of divine inspiration. My grandfather sat in the first Quorum of the Twelve; my father served as mission president and stake president in a much smaller church than we have today, under five presidents of the Church; I have served as stake officer and General Authority for sixty-one years. Our three lives have encompassed essentially the whole period of the restored Church; taken together, we have known with some intimacy almost all of the General Authorities since the Restoration. On that basis I tell you that those Church leaders were men whose great accomplishments have transcended even their substantial innate abilities, for the Lord has given them power to do his work. ("Give the Lord Your Loyalty," BYU Address, September 4, 1979.)

A Total Loyalty Is Still Expected. Now, this institution, the kingdom of God, is different from the Brigham Young University but only in specifics. A total loyalty is still expected from every soul who is a worker in the Lord's kingdom. Cleanliness of life is expected, and if anyone is breaking the Word of Wisdom or failing to pay his tithing or is dishonest in any way or is immoral in any of the ugly ways, he or she should change those errors and repent of those sins immediately or he should go to the one under whom he or she is serving and explain, "The laws and commandments of the Lord are too heavy for me; I cannot live them. Therefore, I will seek service with some firm that does not care about these eternal values." That would be the position of honesty. ("What Think Ye of Christ?" Church Employees Christmas Devotional, December 12, 1974.)

Deal Honestly and Uprightly. We have talked about cheating in school and in examinations. I never could quite understand that, how anyone could figure that he could cheat and get by? What good would he be doing going to school? It disturbs me a great deal. Thomas Dekker said, "Honest labor bears a lovely face." (*Patient Grissil* [1603], act 1, scene 1.) Brigham Young said, "Cease speaking evil. . . . masters, deal honestly and justly with those whom you hire, who are called servants. [Servants] deal honestly and uprightly with those who employ you, that confidence and the spirit of brotherhood may be kindled." (*Discourses of Brigham Young*, comp. John A. Widtsoe [Salt Lake City: Deseret Book Co., ed. 1971], p. 280.) It isn't a matter of whether the employer or the employee, or both are very careless and indecent in this particular matter. (Area Conference Address, Monterrey, Mexico, February 19-20, 1977.)

Keep Your Promises. Keep your promises. Maintain your integrity. Abide by your covenants. Give the Lord this year and every year your high fidelity and fullest expression of faith. Do it "on your honor" and you will be blessed now and forever. ("On My Honor," BYU Devotional Address, September 12, 1978.)

We Must Be Good Companions

I Love Both of My Counselors. I also love both of my counselors for being men of good humor as well as good will. In the heavy burdens we bear in the First Presidency there is a sweet quality in my counselors which permits us some smiles and moments of respite in the midst of the heavy and serious problems that we must encounter.

Further, we are not only the First Presidency, we are friends!

My counselors always think in terms of what is best for the kingdom, not their own needs. They also seem unhurried even though they get so much done!

I wanted to mention these matters to you as a few examples of how all of us must strive to be leader-servants.

A Humble Leader-Servant. President Tanner never uses unnecessary words. He is a doer and decider more than a talker. He is very quick to focus on the central issue under discussion, and then when he says something, it is very much worth listening to. I am sure this takes a certain amount of discipline for him at times when some of the rest of us are not quite so focused, but he is very kindly in the way he does this and it moves the work forward more expeditiously. His economy in words means, of course, that he is really listened to when he speaks. He is so humble and is a good example of the leader-servant, and I wanted to make mention of this quality among many that he has.

He Understands the Thoughts of Those Whom He Is to Serve. President Romney is able to reflect on an issue before us in the context of the scriptures which he knows so well, and he relates problems to the scriptures in an especially keen way. He is persistent in his effort to make certain that he understands the views of those who are presenting matters to us and will ask some clarifying questions if needed. He makes certain, in other words, that he understands the thoughts of those whom he is to serve even if he may not agree with them. (Regional Representatives Seminar, October 5, 1979.)

We Must Develop Spiritual Strength in Ourselves

If We Are Converted. Develop spiritual strength in yourself, and there will be felicity in the family. Righteousness proceeds outward from the individual to the group. We will find that if we are converted (through studying, searching, and praying), our immediate desire is to want to help others. True conversion causes us to want to reach out to the living and to the deceased to do what we can to help in each case. If we are truly converted, we will also want to provide for our own in the fullness of what welfare service means. ("Boys Need Heroes Close By," General Conference Address, April 3, 1976.)

Models of Reverent Behavior. True reverence is a vital quality, but one that is fast disappearing in the world as the forces of evil broaden their influences. We cannot fully comprehend the power for good we can wield if the millions of members of Christ's true church will serve as models of reverent behavior. We cannot imagine the additional numbers of lives we could touch.

The Greatest Spiritual Impact. Perhaps even more important, we cannot foresee the great spiritual impact on our own families if we become the reverent people we know we should be. That we might work to develop greater reverence in our lives is my prayer.

Reverence Leads to Increased Joy. As with the other principles of the gospel, reverence leads to increased joy.

We must remember that reverence is not a somber, temporary behavior that we adopt on Sunday. True reverence involves happiness, as well as love, respect, gratitude, and godly fear. It is a virtue that should be part of our way of life. In fact, Latter-day Saints should be the most reverent people in all the earth. ("We Should Be a Reverent People," *Church News*, September 18, 1976.)

How They Take My Name in Their Lips

That Is My Lord. In the hospital one day I was wheeled out of the operating room by an attendant who stumbled, and there issued from his angry lips vicious cursing with a combination of the names of the Savior. Even half-conscious, I recoiled and implored: "Please! Please! That is my Lord whose names you revile."

There was a deathly silence; then a subdued voice whispered, "I am sorry." He had forgotten for the moment that the Lord had forcefully commanded all this people, "Thou shalt not take the name of the Lord thy God in vain; for the Lord will not hold him guiltless that taketh his name in vain." (Exodus 20:7.)

Speaking the Lord's Name with Reverence. Speaking the Lord's name with reverence must simply be part of our lives as members of the Church. For example, we, as good Latter-day Saints, do not smoke. We do not drink. We do not use tea and coffee. We do not use dope. By the same token, we do not use foul language. We do not curse or defame. We do not use the Lord's name in vain. It is not difficult to become perfect in avoiding a swearing habit, for if one locks his mouth against all words of cursing, he is en route to perfection in that matter.

But our responsibility does not end there. That would merely be to refrain from committing sin. To perform righteousness, we must speak our Lord's name with reverence and holiness in our prayers, our discourses, and our discussions. Isaiah sang: "For unto us a child is born, unto us a son is given: and the government shall be upon his shoulder: and his name shall be called Wonderful, Counsellor, The mighty God, The everlasting Father, The Prince of Peace." (Isaiah 9:6.)

Jesus perfected his life and became our Christ. Priceless blood of a god was shed, and he became our Savior; his perfected life was given, and he became our Redeemer; his atonement for us made possible our return to our Heavenly Father, and yet how thoughtless, how unappreciative are most beneficiaries! Ingratitude is a sin of the ages.

Great numbers profess belief in him and his works, and yet relatively few honor him. Millions of us call ourselves Christians, yet seldom kneel in gratitude for his supreme gift, his life.

Let us rededicate ourselves to reverential attitudes, toward an expression of gratitude to our Lord for his incomparable sacrifice. Let us remember the modern command, "Wherefore, let all men beware how they take my name in their lips." (D&C 63:61.) ("President Kimball Speaks Out on Profanity," *New Era*, January-February 1981; *Ensign*, February 1981.)

God Bless Our Missionaries

They Look Like Young Men Ought to Look. I meet with prime ministers and presidents, with sovereigns and rulers, political and public figures all over the world, and one of the things they inevitably say about us (and always with warmth and appreciation) is, "We have seen your missionaries. We've seen them all over the globe, in every state of the union and in most countries of the world. Without exception, they look like young men ought to look. They are clean cut, neatly dressed, well-groomed, and dignified." My, that makes me proud! I'm trying to do my own little part in missionary work and that kind of comment makes me so proud of you. Then sometimes these great leaders say, "Your missionaries look like just the kind of young men I would want in my business, or in my government, or in my embassy, or in my law firm." Sometimes they even say, "They look just like the young man I would like for a son-in-law." That makes me proudest of all. ("On My Honor," BYU Devotional Address, September 12, 1978.)

The World Will Be Revolutionized. You live in a time of wars and revolutions. And yet, as President Brigham Young said, *the world will be revolutionized by the preaching of the gospel* and the power of the priesthood. And this work we are called to do. Women and men, our keeping the commandments is the most revolutionary development in the world, though it is often less noticed and less glamorous. Do not be discouraged, in the midst of the sweep of events of our time, if your life sometimes seems so small. Phillips Brooks observed, "Greatness, after all, in spite of its name, appears to be not so much a certain size as a certain quality in human lives." It may be present in lives whose range is very small. May I assure you of the everlasting significance of your personal life. And even though at times the range of your life may seem to be very small, there can be greatness in the quality of your life. I promise you further that where that quality exists, your opportunities for service and goodness will outnumber your fondest dreams. There is always more work to be done around us than we manage to get done. It is important in this time of preparation that you do all you can to gather in the truths, the information, and the skills which go with Christian living. Apply what you have come to know as you come to know it. The same Phillips Brooks said, "The hills are full of marble before the world blooms with statues." (*Literature and Life*.) There must be an assembling in you of those basic qualities of goodness which will permit the Lord to do his own sculpturing on your soul. Use, therefore, the talents that you have. Use the opportunities for service around you. Use the chances for learning that are yours, sifting as always the wheat from the chaff. Learn to be effective first in the small human universe that is your own family if you would prepare yourselves to be effective in contributing to the larger human family. Do not be surprised if Church leaders continue to emphasize the importance of the family institution when so many think otherwise. ("The Savior: The Center of Our Lives," *New Era*, April 1980.)

CHAPTER TWENTY

Blessings:
The Fruit of the Missionary Work

Think what a power these trained and testifying elders would be in the wards, branches, stakes, and missions when they returned.

Good Reason for Calling Missionaries

When You Begin Sending All of Your Sons. One of the stakes in Utah made a survey. The stake sent out 318 missionaries in a given time. Of the 318, ninety-four percent of them continued faithful in the Church upon their return; and only six percent of them were inactive, which is a marvelous record. Of the 204 who had been married by the time of the survey, all had been to the temple for marriage except ten. There were only two divorces. What a record of achievement! Even if fewer had remained active, what a strength they would be to the growing Church. How great the dividends. Ninety-four percent is phenomenal.

Think what a power these trained and testifying elders would be in the wards, branches, stakes, and missions when they returned. When you begin sending all of your normal sons into the mission field, there will be a new growth and power and devotion and righteousness that you can little imagine. (Area General Conference Address, Stockholm, Sweden, August 17, 1974.)

We Will No Longer Import Testimony. These statistics are most heartening. No longer will we import testimony from these countries. No longer will we import experience, training, dedication, and leadership. After their missions these young men will stay in their own countries and serve in leadership capacities among their own people in their own tongue. Think, too, what this will mean when these numbers are in hundreds and thousands, instead of dozens in leading positions. I repeat, brethren, we look to you to continue to give this work a continued thrust. (Regional Representatives Seminar, April 3, 1975.)

A Great Chain Reaction. Young men having planned for nineteen years to fill a mission will be more fruitful, more effective, and more successful when they serve and more people will come into the Church and will create more enthusiasm and there will be a chain reaction. Is there any other thing that would have a greater chain reaction and affect more interests and people? ("President Kimball Speaks Out on Being a Missionary," *New Era*, May 1981.)

Returning Missionaries to Serve. I am anxious, however, that we give to these returning missionaries opportunities to serve. I remember as we recently received a statement from the missionary committee that some missionaries, a very few, become inactive and the reason that they gave as they made their survey was, that some few missionaries are not given anything to do. Now, that goes back to the bishop, doesn't it; to the bishop and the stake president and leaders of the stakes and wards. We want them to have an opportunity, but we want them not to think that they have to have one in order to prove true to their great work. (Area Conference Address, Houston, Texas, June 24, 1979.)

Much Enlarged and Blessed. We expect that you will come back from your missions much enlarged and blessed and more serviceable than ever before. (New Mission Presidents Seminar, June 1977.)

Another Great Reason for Having All Boys Become Missionaries. Also, another great reason for having all boys become missionaries is the fact that two years of training and preaching and indoctrinating themselves is a great education for them as they return home and enter the ecclesiastical field. We will need large numbers of bishops and stake presidents and mission presidents and other ecclesiastical authorities for the fast, constantly growing Church, and especially abroad.

We can never be totally happy with a few missionaries from a country when they should send hundreds, eventually thousands, of young people into the mission field. Yes, of course, it is a sacrifice, but not too great a sacrifice when we consider the advantages and the blessing which come therefrom. (New Mission Presidents Seminar, June 25, 1976.)

Making Final Preparation for Their Life's Work

They Are Building Their Life. What a marvelous opportunity our missionaries have. They are making the final preparation for their life's work. They are not going to be common men and women. Every one of them must be special so that the Lord will approve of them and appreciate them. I am speaking of all those who should be on missions as well as those who are on missions.

Today they are building their life just as much as if they had loads of gravel and stacks of timber to build it with. If we could see our lives today and then see them 20 years from now, we could each go back and decide: It was back there during those years when I was a missionary where I made my life's decision. ("President Kimball Speaks Out on Being a Missionary," *New Era*, May 1981.)

To Make Men Sons of God. Do you think that the only reason the Lord has called you to the mission field is to preach the gospel? Absolutely not. That is important. But you are called into the mission field to make men, sons of God, strong, powerful leaders.

I had a companion once in the mission field in Missouri. He was a married man. He was a little flighty. As he neared the end of his mission, he kept saying to the rest of us missionaries, "Well, I've done my job for the Lord. Now I'm going home and work for me." It sounded rather strange to me, so I watched him through the next forty years. That's exactly what he did. He went to his home. He didn't have time to follow the gospel program; he had to take care of the motion picture shows that he owned and his other investments. He died a few years ago. Not very much was said in his funeral about the life he had lived. I think they did say that he filled a mission. That isn't very much, is it? (Area Conference Address, San Jose, Costa Rica, February 23, 1977.)

Today Is the Day. When I returned from my mission, I started to do some dating. I was only twenty years old, and I liked the girls. I had many friends. One Saturday night, when I went to college, I invited a young lady to go to a motion picture show, I think it was. When we went to her home, she got some peaches and cream to serve me. I thought she was a wonderful girl because I liked peaches and cream. But I didn't get up very early the next morning. It was Sunday morning. And when my brother called me I said, "All right, I will after a while." Then I decided to skip the priesthood meeting that morning. I said, "I'll go to the sacrament meeting tonight." That was the great temptation. And so the next week I thought about it very often. "Spencer Kimball, you missed another priesthood meeting. When you were baptized, you promised the Lord you would always attend, and here you are missing your priesthood meeting. That is the big temptation. Next Sunday it will be harder and the following Sunday even harder. Now you better get on your toes, Spencer Kimball." I made up my mind that week I wouldn't miss any more priesthood meetings. I promised to attend them. I needed them.

So today is the day. What are you going to do with your life? Will it be superior? Or common? Or disgraceful?

The two years that a missionary spends in the mission field can be the most prosperous two years of his life. Again, I ask, not because of the hundred people that you can baptize, though that is extremely important, but what are you going to do for yourself? What kind of man are you going to be? Are you going to be common? Ordinary? Or are you going to be sparkling? That is up to you today.

Too often we put off these days. This applies to every man and boy in the congregation. Today is the day. If you haven't already made your mind up unchangeably, today, the twenty-fourth of February, 1977, is the day. You all have great potential. You can become leaders, you can become wonderful citizens, or you can become very ordinary. (Area Conference Address, San Jose, Costa Rica, February 24, 1977.)

Honorable Missionaries Become Honorable Men

We May Stand Blameless Before God. The Lord has promised great blessings to us in proportion to how well we share the gospel. We will receive help from the other side of the veil as the spiritual miracles occur. The Lord has told us that our sins will be forgiven more readily as we bring souls unto Christ and remain steadfast in bearing testimony to the world, and surely every one of us is looking for additional help in being forgiven of our sins. (See D&C 84:61.) In one of the greatest of missionary scriptures, section 4 of the Doctrine and Covenants, we are told that if we serve the Lord in missionary service "with all [our] heart, might, mind and strength," then we may "stand blameless before God at the last day." (v. 2.)

And, further, the Lord said:

> And if it so be that you should labor all your days in crying repentance unto this people, and bring, save it be one soul unto me, how great shall be your joy with him in the kingdom of my Father!
>
> And now, if your joy will be great with one soul that you have brought unto me into the kingdom of my Father, how great will be your joy if you should bring many souls unto me! (D&C 18:15-16.)

If one labors all his days and brings in save it be one soul! What joy! One soul! How precious! Oh, that God would give us that kind of love for souls! ("President Kimball Speaks Out on Being a Missionary," *New Era*, May 1981.)

He Should Become a Man. Now, there are probably some returned missionaries here today, who have fulfilled a mission, and have come home with a feeling of achievement, a feeling that they have done much good and that they have completed and fulfilled an obligation that their Heavenly Father gave to them. Now let me say a word to those missionaries. When a boy goes on a mission, he becomes a man. He should become a man. He is no longer a kid. He is a man. He is an adult; he is mature. And when he comes home from his mission, he should be a man of strength and power and have ideals and the controls, so that any girl who would date a returned missionary should be able to say, "He has been a missionary; therefore, I have full confidence in him. He would never propose anything that would compromise us in the slightest. I have confidence in him." That is what a returned missionary should be. Two years make a tremendous difference in the life of a young man. He goes out a boy and comes back a man. He goes out immature, he comes back mature and strong, gracious, and a worker and willing to serve.

He goes back to college in most cases and there he will make higher grades than he ever made before, because he has purpose in his life. He is already enjoying purpose, and now he has a new purpose. (Devotional—Expo '74, Spokane, Washington, July 24, 1974.)

She Was in Tears. It was our privilege also to attend the dedication of the Swiss Temple. We had just completed a six-month tour of the European missions. In the northern part of Germany we had met a mother whose husband had been lost in World War II and never again been heard from, but in her sorrow and loneliness she parted with her one son and sent him on a mission. When I visited her in her home town and met her, I asked her, "Will you be able to go to the temple dedication next month?" Her face dropped and she said, "No, I will not be able to do so." She told me about her son who was on a mission and how deeply she loved him and how much she counted on him.

I had been given $50 by a good faithful member of the Church in Utah and had been asked to give it to someone who needed it much. She had given this $50 as a gift to the Savior on his birthday on April 6. I had carried the $50 with me for the six months. It came to my mind quickly. Here is a chance to give the birthday gift of the Savior.

I left $25 with the branch president to give to her to help her with her transportation to Switzerland.

As we continued on our tour, we came to France and because we needed to cross a high mountain range with slow, winding and rough roads, we were two hours late to the meeting which we had set up.

As we came to the meeting place there were still many people waiting for us, and a small widow lady pianist was playing the piano to keep them interested and to dissuade their going home. She was an older woman. She had lost her husband but she wished to do all in her power to hold the people till we came for the meeting.

After the meeting was over, I learned from her branch president that she was wholly worthy, that she had been a widow for some time and that she was in impecunious circumstances. I handed the other $25 to him to obtain transportation for her to Switzerland.

It was a matter of only days until the dedication service for the temple. President David O. McKay and several of the Brethren were in attendance. We sat for thirty minutes prior to the conference in total silence. The Tabernacle Choir was there. Finally when the time came, President McKay in his white suit and his beautiful white mane of hair stood up and conducted the dedication services.

After the services were over and the temple was dedicated, it was opened to service of the people from Europe who had come for that purpose. Seldom have I ever been so enthralled as I was to see this little mother from northern Germany meet her missionary son and embrace him and my eyes and interest followed them as they went through this temple for their endowments, and to be sealed to their husband [and father] and to each other. And here, also, was the little pianist woman and she was in tears as she was sealed to her late husband. (Address at Arizona Temple Dedication, April 15-16, 1975.)

We Are Proud of Their Service. The missionaries are now baptizing nearly 160-170,000 members per year. They brought 100,000 Scandinavians, Britons, Germans, and others to Zion in 286 sailing vessels. They crossed the ocean to the Mississippi River, up the river to St. Joseph, then continued west by wagon and later by train. The Church has measured phenomenal growth from six members to four million. There are now 156 missions. Since the actual cost of supporting a missionary is approximately $1,872 each, per year, they are now, with their services, contributing perhaps $50,000,000 per year, plus other incidental costs of doing missionary work. We are proud of their service. (Regional Representatives Seminar, March 31, 1978.)

A Utopia, Heaven on Earth. Other stakes have made surveys and have approached that figure. Can you see what would happen in tomorrow's world if 90% or 80% or even less of all the young men are returning from their missions full of zeal and faith and with temple marriages rear the families really in Israel? It will be a different day, a utopia, heaven on earth. (Regional Representatives Seminar, October 3, 1974.)

People Will Cease to Pray for Me. Every little boy is under the protection of the Lord when he is in the mission field. In one of the missionary meetings in South America I heard a missionary report on his mission. He said this: "Today is my last day in the mission. I go home tomorrow." He said, "I'm almost afraid to go home, because tomorrow two million people will cease to pray for me." Nearly every family prays for the missionaries, and the Lord is constantly conscious of their faith and their prayers.

Now if your little boys pray in their turn in the home and pray for the missionaries, they are almost certain to plan their lives in that direction. If all of your little boys are trained to earn money and to save money for their missions, the finances are in their favor because in nineteen years they can save a good deal of money. But the more powerful instrument is the fact that they are converting themselves all through those years.

Now, there is no compulsion to go into the mission field, but it is an obligation. It is not enough just merely to go to church; there are other obligations likewise. And this is the way to get your boys and girls into the temple for their marriages. A very high percentage of the returned missionaries are married in the holy temple, and so that in itself is a good way to convert them. (Area General Conference Address, Tokyo, Japan, August 9, 1975.)

We Want You to Stay Clean

Don't Slip Back to Some Other Method of Living. Don't forget that there will be invitations for you to slip back to some other method of living, but we want you to stay clean and sweet and above reproach; and we hope that will be the case in every situation. Another thing, but being more specific, I would like to have you remember that you are going to continue your education when you get home, and go forward with your training to make yourself more proficient in the world so that you can have a better livelihood for your wife and for the children that will come. That is all proper. That can be done simultaneously with your courtship, if you want to do that. The courtship can go forward without any great delay, and there shouldn't be any great delay, for the Lord placed man and woman to be together, a father and mother, a husband and a wife. They twain shall be one flesh, and they shall forsake their parents, even to find their wife or their husband and go forward with their family life. . . .

If We Don't Have Families We Have Missed the Boat. The Church is oriented by the family and that is the center of all things. If we don't have families and children who we love and train, then we have missed the boat, haven't we? We have many people today who are proclaiming a new program whereby young men don't marry and young women don't marry. They go forward and participate in the things of life without marriage, which is one of the most despicable things that you can ever think about. We hope that no thought would ever be given to it. Marriage is proper. Marriage is honorable, and it is the only honorable state; and every person who lives would expect to marry, unless there be some very unusual situation which made it impossible; but every boy will think about a marriage. When he thinks about marriage, he realizes, as I mentioned yesterday, that the mother is the principal one who trains the children. She teaches them their ABC's. She teaches them the right and wrong. She is with them night and day. The father will do as much as he can also so that he and his wife together will train the children in all the things that they should know.

Of course, the marriage that you plan will be a temple marriage, even if you have to travel around the world. It is a long way in some cases, but it isn't too much to ask anybody who wants joy and peace and happiness all his life to find the proper person and then to be sealed to her or to him for all eternity. Nothing else will do for any missionary, unless it is absolutely impossible to have, which might be considered but isn't likely. When your children begin to grow up, we hope fathers will plan their lives and their time so the father can hold his boy's hand and can lead him and direct him and kiss him when he wants.

Now there is much else to think about. There are many expenses, of course, as one carries forward his life and there are many demands—the children, their missions, their weddings, and all of their experiences. It is a part of life. That is why you want to be prepared with a good education to go forward and make a good living for your family so that you can provide for them all of the important things of life.

As you think about these things, you realize that they are wholesome. They are total. The Lord has given them to us. It wasn't an accident that a man and woman came together to live together, to be husband and wife, and to be the parents of the children. No accident was there. The Lord recognized that before he even created this world, when he placed Adam and Eve on the earth and said, "Multiply and replenish the earth and subdue it." That was the command that comes to you through Adam as it does to all of the descendants of Adam and Eve, who were the first man and first woman and the mother and father of all the mortals that are living. (Area Conference Address, Johannesburg, South Africa, October 23, 1978.)

One of the Great Disappointments. Let me confess one of the sad disappointments I sometimes feel: The returned missionary who, after two years of taking great pride in how he looks and what he represents, returns to this campus or some other similar place to see how quickly he can let his hair grow, how fully he can develop a moustache and long sideburns and push to the very margins of appropriate grooming, how clumpy his shoes get, how tattered his clothes are, how close to being grubby he can get without being refused admittance to the school. That, my young returned missionary brethren, is one of the great disappointments in my life.

Like Alma and the Sons of Mosiah. Please, you returned missionaries and all young men who can understand my concern in this matter, please do not abandon in appearance or principle or habit the great experience of the mission field when you were like Alma and the sons of Mosiah, and where you were as the very angels of God to the people you met and taught and baptized. ("On My Honor," BYU Devotional Address, September 12, 1978.)

You Cannot Afford to Take a Chance

The Hazards of Interfaith Marriages. I have warned youth about the hazards of interfaith marriages—the sorrows and disillusionments which come from marrying out of the Church. But there seems to be a tendency on the part of many young people today to form their own opinions and their own conclusions to determine the right and the wrong of everything.

We are concerned and disturbed that many of the people are married by justices of the peace or bishops or ministers, when there are temples of God which guarantee that if there is righteousness there will be happiness forever and eternally.

It is very shortsighted for any girl to choose someone who cannot take her to the temple, or for any boy to go with a girl who cannot go to the temple with him. You cannot afford to take a chance on falling in love with someone who may never accept the gospel.

Yes, a small minority are finally baptized. Some good men and women have joined the Church after the interfaith marriage and have remained most devout and active. God bless them! We are proud of them and grateful for them. These are our blessed minority.

Others who do not join the Church are still kind, considerate, and cooperative, and permit the member spouse to worship and serve according to the Church pattern. God bless them also!

Many others join the Church ostensibly for the marriage, then fail to live the commandments. Many of them are later divorced. Others, though not divorced, continue to have friction, particularly in religious matters in the home.

The majority however, do not join the Church. Surveys have indicated that only one of seven finally join the Church—the odds are against the others. And nearly half of those who marry out of the Church become inactive. As parents give up their religion, an increasing number of their children are brought up without any religion.

So you are taking a desperate chance if you say, "Well, maybe he will join after we are married. We will go ahead and try it and see." It is a pretty serious thing to take a chance on.

Frequently young people think, "Oh, that doesn't matter. We'll get along all right. We'll adjust ourselves. My spouse will permit me to do as I please or I will make adjustments. We'll both live and worship according to our own pattern." This is not broad-mindedness, but even if it were, to be broad-minded with the Lord's eternal program is somewhat like being generous with other people's money.

Over the years many times women have come to me in tears. How they would love to train their children in the Church, in the gospel of Jesus Christ! But they were unable to do so. How they would like to accept positions of responsibility in the Church! How they would like to pay their tithing! How they would love to go to the temple and do the work for the dead, to do work for themselves, to be sealed for eternity, and to have their own flesh and blood, their children, sealed to them for eternity!

But the doors are locked! They themselves have locked them, and the doors have often rusted on their hinges. Someone did not teach these individuals sufficiently, or they did not study the scriptures and they did not understand, or they ignored the warnings which came to them. They married out of the Church. Perhaps he was a good man. Maybe he was handsome. He may have been cultured and well trained; but he did not have the qualification that he needed most and which they overlooked. He did not have membership in the kingdom; he did not have the priesthood, the ordinances, and the righteousness that would carry them to exaltation.

It Is a Most Important Event. Now, since life is eternal—and that is absolutely certain—true marriage must also be eternal. It is a most important event and a most necessary one. Marriage by civil officers or local leaders is "till death do you part," and terminates with death. Only celestial marriage extends beyond the grave. Celestial marriage is performed in holy temples erected and dedicated for that special purpose. Only such marriage transcends the grave and perpetuates the husband/wife and parent/child relationships. ("The Importance of Celestial Marriage," *Ensign*, October 1979.)

She Married a Returned Missionary. This is a signal honor to come to this place and say a few words to you. I have noticed what was just repeated—that Sister Kimball did not marry a prophet. She married a returned missionary, and that is my theme today, only I did not suggest it. ("The Matter of Marriage," Salt Lake Institute of Religion Devotional, University of Utah, October 22, 1976.)

CHAPTER TWENTY-ONE

Stake Missionary Work

*Is the Lord trying to tell us that stake missionary
work is vital and important? I personally feel that
we have greatly slipped on stake missionary work.*

Stake Missionary Work Is Vital and Important

Is the Work Being Carried Forward? Are you satisfied,
brethren? As you go into the stakes, is the work being carried
forward as well as you feel it should be? Are there as many of
the people who are basking in the glory of the gospel who are
helping their neighbors to get the gospel as you think there
should be? Think of the work that we could do, just even here in
Salt Lake City, the center. Think of the thousands there are here
and how eagerly they accept the gospel when it is properly prepared to give to them. (Regional Representatives Seminar, October 2, 1975.)

*Complete Cooperation Between the Stake and the Full-
Time Missionaries.* We expect to have complete cooperation
between the stake missionaries and the full-time missionaries
and to involve the members of the Church generally in opening
the gospel door to our Father's other children. One of the main
ways in which this can be done is to use the organizations and
programs of the Church for proselyting. Thus all officers,
teachers, and members of the priesthood and the auxiliaries
should keep their organizations in proper order, making them
truly lights set upon a hill that can give light to the whole world.
We cannot stress too strongly the need to do missionary work in

the framework of priesthood correlation so that investigators are fellowshipped and tied into the programs of the Church in such a way that they promptly become active and faithful members. This, then, is another way in which all members of the Church can be actively and constantly engaged in missionary service—by fellowshipping, befriending, and encouraging the new members of the Church. ("It Becometh Every Man," *Ensign*, October 1977.)

A Family a Year. In stake missionary work, I know a good man who with his family set their goal to bring into the Church a family a year. I believe it was about fourteen years they have been doing this and they have brought about fourteen families into the Church to their credit. (Regional Representatives Seminar, October 3, 1974.)

Every One of You Should Be a Missionary

Every Man Should Give to the People His Testimony. Now there are two phases of missionary work. Let me touch very briefly on them again. *One* is the full-time missionary work, and every boy in the Church in Peru, or in Chile, or in Brazil, or wherever he lives should be preparing all his life for a mission and then fill an honorable mission. And then, having that good training, he goes into the organizations of the Church, the stake, the branch, the mission. He goes into the organizations with much ability and power and training. We have talked about that phase.

Now, *the other phase* is the local stake missionary work. In every district, in every mission, in every stake, there should be stake or local mission groups. Every man should give to the people his testimony. Every one of you, every one of you should be a missionary in addition to whatever else you are doing. You have neighbors, you have friends, you have fellow workers; it's your responsibility. You cannot go into eternity and look the Lord in the face if you've done nothing toward teaching the gospel to others. Have your wives do the same. Have your children do the same. Little children have brought thousands of people into the Church—little girls and little boys who have invited their friends to go to Primary. And that is the seed from which a great orchard has grown, and many converts. (Area Conference Address, São Paulo, Brazil, March 1, 1975.)

Call Many Stake Missionaries. There are so many of our people who excuse themselves from proselyting, perhaps for age, perhaps for infirmity, perhaps for business. Would you feel that if you stimulated the bishops to call many stake missionaries, including older and younger ones, that it would get them busy and all others would get some inspiration therefrom? (Regional Representatives Seminar, September 30, 1976.)

Finding

Members must be finders. The valuable time of our teaching missionaries is too often spent in "finding."

CHAPTER TWENTY-TWO

Every Member a Missionary

Several decades ago when President David O. McKay presided over the Church, he gave impetus to the missionary work in the stakes of Zion. He coined the term, "Every member a missionary," and it is obvious that would be a giant step toward the accomplishment of our directives.

Every Member a Missionary

A Total Dependence upon the Lord. A monk is said to have built a tower sixty feet high and three feet wide. On a certain day he would climb up to the top of the tower and pray, and the words of his prayers were generally about like this, "Oh, God, where art thou?" No answer. "Oh, God, where art thou?" No answer. Finally when he had exhausted someone's patience, there came a voice and it said, "I am down among the people." You have to be humble. Our wealth, our affluence, our liberties, all that we possess must never make us feel above anyone. We must always keep in mind a deep sincerity, a great humility, and a total dependence upon the Lord. ("The Vision of Visiting Teaching," *Ensign*, June 1978.)

Many Unconsciously Waiting for the Gospel

This Gospel Must Be Presented to All the World. Many of us sit in luxury and wealth while neighbors and friends and relatives are anxiously or unconsciously waiting for the gospel message.

Many of our good people have reared their families and settled down in advancing years and have relaxed to enjoy life without selflessly sharing it.

We are the disciples of Christ. The common dictionary gives to us the definition of the word disciple as "one who is receiving instructions from others; one who accepts the doctrines of another and assists in spreading or implementing them; who is a follower; one of the Twelve Apostles; one who is a convinced adherent of a school of philosophy or art or politics."

In a word, then, we are all disciples of Christ and by our efforts this gospel must be presented to all the world.

And then he gives the authority and power to all of us when he says, "Behold, this is mine authority, and the authority of my servants, and my preface unto the book of my commandments, which I have given them to publish unto you, O inhabitants of the earth." (D&C 1:6.)

He is speaking to all the nations of the earth. (Regional Representatives Seminar, September 30, 1977.)

Abraham to Serve as a Missionary. Just as the Lord called his servant Abraham to serve as a missionary 4,000 years ago, so is he calling the Saints today. We must all be missionaries and prepare our sons to be full-time missionaries. Those who have made even a slight effort to share the gospel can testify of the joy they find through sharing it with their earthly brothers and sisters. Our efforts to spread the gospel have been feeble; we must do more. Like Abraham, we must declare the gospel to the world, not stopping with a vocal declaration, but living the gospel so others can see the truth. ("The Example of Abraham," *Ensign*, June 1975.)

Work for the Dead. Now, there is another kind of missionary work that must be done, and it is the responsibility of the older people, the middle-aged people, the young people—all of us. That is the work for the dead and for our own families. We expect that every family will talk about this constantly in their home evenings and in their family firesides, and they will get busy doing it. (Area Conference Address, St. Louis, Missouri, June 8, 1980.)

Far More Than All the Money or the Jewels

Warn Thy Neighbor. You remember that it was the Lord who said, "They who have been warned must warn their neighbor." (See D&C 88:81.)

If you found the pearl of great price, would you just hold it in your pocket and not divide it with anyone? Far more than all the money or the jewels of the earth is the gospel of Jesus Christ, so we divide it with our neighbors and our friends and our relatives. Now, we all have relatives who are precious, wonderful people. Maybe sometimes they think we are eccentric, but if we live so righteously that they cannot help but respect us, that will make a lot of difference.

As to our relatives, we will not push and force them. We try to live our lives so that we will show to them that we are extremely happy.

Now, we had about eight thousand people at the conference yesterday. Think of what six or eight thousand people could do if they exerted themselves to bring the gospel into other homes.

Now, these young missionaries are equipped to teach the gospel, and if you do not understand all the doctrines, you can call on the missionaries. So we have a program that is for everybody.

We hope you fathers are training your boys to save their money so that just as soon as the day comes they will have funds to take them on their missions. The Church does have some funds that are contributed by interested people, but not enough to send all the missionaries. It is necessary that every missionary do as much as he can, and then some of them can be helped by the Church. (Area Conference Address, Santiago, Chile, March 1, 1977.)

All Five Were Baptized. In an eastern city a woman member of the Church worked in a bakery. She explained the gospel to five women who worked with her, and all five were baptized into the Church. A Relief Society of twenty-three members got busy. They converted, with the help of the missionaries, twenty-four other women, one for each. A prominent high priest and his wife entertained seventy-eight people in their home and preached the gospel to them. The missionaries baptized twenty-five of the seventy-eight, and the others were friendly. A brother in the hospital spoke to his nurses, and they listened and joined the Church. One ward in California stimulated the members to this work, and they held seventy-six meetings and baptized thirty-four of the people who attended. (Area General Conference Address, Stockholm, Sweden, August 17, 1974.)

We Must Not Slacken Our Hands. Brothers and sisters—all fellow members in this most important work—we must not slacken our hands in this work. Not only is our eternal welfare at stake, but also the eternal welfare of many of our brothers and sisters who are not now members of this Church. Let us be faithful in discharging our responsibilities and obligations to ourselves and to them. By so doing, we shall all be blessed as President George Albert Smith indicated when he was an Apostle:

> Do we realize that every man is in the image of God and is a son of God, and every woman his daughter? No matter where they may be they are his children, and he loves them and desires their salvation. Surely as members of this Church we cannot sit idly by. We cannot receive the beneficent favor of our Heavenly Father that is bestowed upon us, the knowledge of eternal life, and selfishly retain it, thinking that we may be blessed thereby. It is not what we receive that enriches our lives, it is what we give. (Conference Report, April 1935, p. 46.) ("It Becometh Every Man," *Ensign*, October 1977.)

Love Your Neighbors

Lovest Thou Me? Now the Lord has said that to every man, woman, and child in this congregation and in this world who has joined his church: "Lovest thou me?" Then show me! Show me: feed my sheep. We have in many of the lands of this world large, fast-growing, delightful, wonderful congregations; and we say to you again that the Lord is saying, "Feed my sheep." And he knows whether we are or not. He knows all the time. We don't need to put it into words; we don't need to express that for ourselves. All we need to do is to feed his sheep. ("Let Us Move Forward and Upward," General Conference Address, April 1, 1979.)

We Must Warm Our Neighbors Before We Can Warn. It should be clear to us that usually *we must warm our neighbors before we can warn them properly.* Our neighbors must experience our genuine friendship and fellowship. We want members to entreat neighbors, not to scold them or scare them.

What we need are not more quotas but *fewer qualms about sharing the gospel. We hope our members will not simply go through the motions but will keep this requirement of sharing the gospel.*

Someone has said that the only true form of slavery is "service without joy."

We know that some of those who will claim at the judgment time to have known the Lord will be told that they refused a neighbor in need when hungry and thirsting. (Regional Representatives Seminar, September 30, 1976.)

Members Should Shoulder This Responsibility

Every Member Knows of Nonmembers. Members should shoulder this responsibility. Every member knows of nonmembers he or she can refer to the missionaries. Every father, mother, and youth in this Church should share the gospel by giving a Book of Mormon, telling the account of the Prophet Joseph Smith, or inviting our acquaintances to a special meeting. If we are in tune, the Spirit of the Lord will speak to us and guide us to those with whom we should share the gospel. The Lord will help us if we will but listen.

It is the responsibility of the members to provide the stake and full-time missionaries with the names of individuals and families to teach. Sometimes we forget that *it is better to risk a little ruffling in the relationship of a friend than it is to deprive him of eternal life by keeping silent.* (Regional Representatives Seminar, April 3, 1975.)

Service Through Missionary Work. One of the most rewarding ways in which we can serve our fellowmen is by *living* and *sharing the principles of the gospel.* We need to help those whom we seek to serve to know for themselves that God not only loves them but he is ever mindful of them and their needs. To teach our neighbors of the divinity of the gospel is a command reiterated by the Lord: "It becometh every man who hath been warned to warn his neighbor." (D&C 88:81.)

Not all of us can engage in full-time missionary work, where one might have opportunity to explain the gospel and bear testimony of its divinity many times a day. *But what every member most definitely can do is follow President David O. McKay's inspired slogan, "Every member a missionary." He can be-*

friend and fellowship nonmember neighbors, fellow em-
ployees, friends and acquaintances, and those with whom he
is engaged in community service. By his interest and association, he should strive to bring those nonmembers to the point
where they will willingly receive the stake or full-time missionaries. *What every member ought to do, by good example and*
by bearing testimony, is to portray to nonmembers the joys of
gospel living and understanding and thus help to bring them
to the stage where they will accept more formal teaching.

The proper motivation for missionary work of any kind, as
for all Church service, is of course *love for fellowmen;* but
always such work has its by-product effect on one's own life.
Thus, as *we become instruments in God's hands in changing*
the lives of others, our own lives cannot help being lifted. One
can hardly help another to the top of the hill without climbing
there himself. ("President Kimball Speaks Out on Service to
Others," *New Era*, March 1981.)

The Local People as Member Missionaries. Brothers and
sisters, we need not only more missionaries, we need the local
people as member missionaries. We need fathers and mothers
and sons and daughters who will extend themselves and try to
bring the gospel to many people. We have evidence and we have
record of numerous little girls and little boys that are only six
and eight and ten and twelve who have told their teachers about
the gospel, who have told their school friends about the gospel,
who have taken their best friends to Primary and to Sunday
School and to other meetings, and who thus have started whole
families toward the Church. We have numerous situations
where the members of the Church have done unusual work.

Brother Robert D. Hales told me recently of a young man who
was asked about his missionary work in Mexico. Brother Hales
said that when he was asked, "How many have you baptized?"
he was happy to answer he had baptized 840 people. He was just
nineteen years old and hadn't had a college education yet and
hadn't had all the blessings that many of you have had.

One mission in Mexico had 3,000 convert baptisms in a
month, if you can believe that. It is almost unbelievable because
of its greatness. Well, that means that we must go to work with
all our souls. (Area General Conference Address, Glasgow, Scotland, June 21, 1976.)

O Lord, How Long Shall I Cry? Now, we are a busy people; but the Lord did not say, "If it is convenient for you, would you consider preaching the gospel." He has said, "Let every man learn his duty" (D&C 107:99), and "Behold . . . it becometh every man who hath been warned to warn his neighbor." (D&C 88:81.)

We must remember that God is our ally in this. He is our help. He will open the way, for he gave the commandment. ("Are We Doing All We Can?" *Ensign*, February 1983.)

Personal Purity

Personal Purity and Veracity. It was the Master who observed of his relationship to others, "For their sakes I sanctify myself." (John 17:19.) Personal purity and veracity are essential if we are to give sanctified service to others. We must expend our energies and use our skills for purposes larger than our own self-interest, if we desire true happiness. (Commencement Address, Church College of Hawaii, April 13, 1974.)

Purify Your Hearts. We talk about duty—"I must go and do my [home] teaching": "I must go and do my visiting teacher's work"—but we have already lost the enthusiasm, the vision, and the objective when we say, "I must go this morning and do my visiting teaching." Rather it could be: *"Today is the day I have been waiting for. I am happy to go into the homes of my sisters and help lift them to new heights."*

You have a responsibility. You have been called of God, through the properly constituted authorities. You just can't go to the homes if you have "blood" on your skirts. It says in the eighty-eighth section: "Purify your hearts, and cleanse your hands and your feet before me, that I may make you clean: That I may testify unto your Father, and your God, and my God, that you are clean from the blood [and sins] of this wicked generation." (D&C 88:74-75.) ("The Vision of Visiting Teaching," *Ensign*, June 1978.)

We Pray for Our Neighbors

We May Be Good Neighbors. Father, we pray for our neighbors—the good people who live among us, many of whom are good men and good women and good youth, and want to do only right. They have only lacked to this time the knowledge of what is right and truth and should be done. Help us to send the message to them so that they may receive the truth in the gospel. Bless us, our Father, that we may be good neighbors and that we may teach truth by our actions, as well as by the things that we shall say. (Dedicatory Prayer, Fair Oaks, California, October 9, 1976.)

Prayer Can Touch Hearts. You know the Lord has intangible methods and ways and means and forces that can touch hearts. Remember Alma? Alma, persecuting the Church one day, and the next day he was a great advocate of it. (See Mosiah 27.) Remember Paul? One day he was persecuting the Saints or imprisoning them and in a few days here he was preaching the gospel in the synagogue with great power. (See Acts 9.) What was the difference? It was some intangible force that had been brought to bear by the Lord in his wisdom. He touched their hearts. He did something else, too; we know what it was, of course.

Now you say, "Well, that woman can never be touched." Of course she can be touched. She can be brought in. President John Taylor said there is none who cannot be converted if the right person makes the right approach at the right time in the right way with the right spirit. He didn't pull all those rights in. I have added them, but don't you think that it is impossible. ("The Vision of Visiting Teaching," *Ensign*, June 1978.)

Pray for the Critics. Brothers and sisters, pray for the critics of the Church; love your enemies. (See Matthew 5:44.) Use wisdom and judgment in what you do and say, so that we do not give cause to others to hold the Church or its people in disrepute. This work, which Satan seeks in vain to tear down, is that which God has placed on earth to lift mankind up! ("Remember the Mission of the Church," General Conference Address, April 3, 1982.)

CHAPTER TWENTY-THREE

Becoming Effective Member Missionaries

If we are in tune, the Spirit of the Lord will speak to us and guide us to those with whom we should share the gospel. The Lord will help us if we will but listen.

Prayerfully Identify Those Persons

Why Should We Fear? I feel the Lord has placed, in a very natural way within our circles of friends and acquaintances, many persons who are ready to enter into his Church. *We ask that you prayerfully identify those persons and then ask the Lord's assistance in helping you introduce them to the gospel.* And in your conversations, if you can't think of anything you feel is important, you can say, "I know that God lives." That is the greatest testimony in the world. A conversation telling how you acquired such knowledge and what it means to you and what it might mean to someone else is a powerful witness for the Lord.

Some of your acquaintances will be chance ones and others will be persons warmed and cultivated by you because of your sincere friendship and interest in them.

With the opportunities all around us, why should we fear? *The gospel is indeed the power of God unto salvation. All people need it in their lives. The gospel will make new people out of them. It changes and transforms their lives as they live it. People who receive the gospel deeply into their hearts are not the same. They change.* And to every person, family, nation, and people which opens its heart or borders to the gospel will come unbelievable blessings. There will come joy and peace to all recipients, and eternal life to those who accept and magnify gospel teachings.

Again, why should we fear? Sharing the gospel brings peace and joy into our own lives, enlarges our own hearts and souls in behalf of others, increases our own faith, strengthens our own relationship with the Lord, and increases our own understanding of gospel truths. Perhaps almost more comes to us than to those to whom we introduce the gospel.

I know of no home that is not revitalized when the spirit of missionary work becomes part of that family's way of life. There is a concern to be healthy so we can be of constant service, a concern to manage our resources so we can be of assistance, a hunger to learn the gospel so we can be a more effective witness, *a desire to be in tune with the Spirit so we can receive its continual whisperings and guidance. We need to prepare to receive these blessings. Let us prepare ourselves and take the necessary steps to be missionaries in our daily lives.* Let us also prepare for the day when we may either go on missions ourselves or help someone else to go. ("Are We Doing All We Can?" *Ensign*, February 1983.)

Good Neighbors. Good neighbors are best suited to bringing to others the good news of the gospel, just as righteous members, living the gospel by example, as well as by precept, are the Church's best advertisement. (Regional Representatives Seminar, October 3, 1980.)

Members Should Strive to Refer Entire Families. Members should strive to refer entire families. The missionaries will teach single people, but they are sent out especially to bring entire families into the Church. A family will tend to remain stronger in the Church than individuals. Even one strong person in a family will help to keep them all active and will help solve the occasional laxity of one or more members of the family. ("It Becometh Every Man," *Ensign*, October 1977.)

Every Year One Family. Now, I would like, before leaving this matter, to make that as an appeal to you wonderful people here today. Go out tomorrow and start your program. Now that is not just the missionaries who are here, just the foreign missionaries; it is not just your local missionaries, it is not just the youth—it is the older people. Imagine what an older man or an older woman with a lifetime of rich living could do with other people.

When I visited Uruguay the first time many years ago, there was a woman there who talked Spanish. The mission president said, "Sister Gonzales," (or whatever her name was) "Tell Brother Kimball how many people you have brought into the church." She said, "Oh, I haven't done much." He said, "Well, tell Brother Kimball. He would like to know." She said, "Well, I think it was just eighty."

Now, what would happen here if a dozen of you women would bring in eighty people, or *eight* people, or *one* person; or if every one of you every year brought in one person? I know a very fine young man who now is a regional representative. Long years ago when they were first married, they made up their minds, he and his wife, that every year they would baptize *at least* one new family. So at the beginning of the year, they would always pick out this family, or that one, somewhere in their neighborhood that they liked very well, and thought they would be good members. Before the year was up, they had baptized them, by fellowshipping them and taking them to church with them. Every year—one family! Suppose you did that here. That would be wonderful! Soon we would have the land dotted with stakes as it is now with wards. We have scores of stakes in California. We could have hundreds of stakes, thousands of stakes, perhaps, because the people are here and there are a lot of wonderful people. (Dedication, Fair Oaks, California, October 9, 1976.)

Bring a Family to Church. As our April Conference came to a close, my mind and heart were filled and I then said these things pertaining to the missionary work. This impression weighed upon me, that the Church is at a point in its growth and maturing when we are at last ready to move forward in a major way. We have paused on some plateaus long enough. Think, brothers and sisters, of having a "Bring a Family to Church" week, open houses, special missionary firesides. Certain numbers of the Church were even taught how to teach their nonmember friends to pray and after they were taught, those nonmember friends began to get answers confirming that that which they were taught was true. Full-time missionaries worked closely with stake missionaries and the latter, therefore, [got] solid missionary experiences. Members in eight stakes are involved and increasingly used in many of the visiting centers. A mission that not too long ago was baptizing around fifty a month is now over

100 per month and the retention rate is excellent. *It can be done where we are, brothers and sisters, if we will follow a few simple steps which emphasize that members should do the finding and fellowshipping and the missionaries the teaching.* (New Mission Presidents Seminar, June 22, 1979.)

There Is a Spiritual Adventure in Doing Missionary Work

Imagine How Wonderful You Would Feel. There is a spiritual adventure in doing missionary work, in giving referrals, in accompanying the missionaries as they give the discussions. It is exciting and rewarding. The hours, the effort, the wondering, all are worth it when even one soul expresses repentance and faith and a desire to be baptized. Imagine how wonderful you would feel when they say, "When you are here, and we're talking about these things, it seems like I'm remembering things I knew before," or "You can't leave here until you've told us all you know about the restored Church."

Don't Be Discouraged. Sometimes it takes more time for some to come into the Church than for others. Don't be discouraged just because of a temporary lack of progress. There are hundreds of stories about the value of perseverance in missionary service. ("It Becometh Every Man," *Ensign*, October 1977.)

Examples of Effective Proselyting

The Members Do the Finding. The real goal for effective proselyting is that the members do the finding and the full-time missionaries do the teaching. This tends to solve many of the old missionary problems. When members do the finding they have a personal interest in fellowshipping, there are fewer investigators lost before baptism, and those who are baptized tend to remain active. Another by-product is that when a member is involved, even if only from a casual relationship, the investigator seems to sense much more quickly that Mormons have a special health code (the Word of Wisdom comes as no surprise), that Mormons spend Sunday in church and not fishing or playing golf (keeping the Sabbath Day holy comes as no surprise), and that Mormons contribute readily to the Church programs (tithing, fast offerings, budget, building fund, missionary funds, etc., are more readily understood.) When there is little or no surprise, the reluctance to be baptized is more easily overcome.

A Beauty Operator. A beauty operator, a member, asked her new client if she would like to read a Church tract while waiting and placed it in her client's hand. The answer was "No." Not giving up, the member picked up a Church magazine from another table as though it were a commercial magazine and gave that to her client to read. Quickly thumbing through the pages the client readily realized it was also Church material, but as she moved to lay it down, she noticed an article entitled, "Love at Home." Having some serious troubles with her husband, she decided to read the article. Then during the rest of the visit a lengthy conversation developed around Mormon home life. The result was a visit arranged immediately with the missionaries. The husband wasn't present at the first visit, but the wife gave him an ultimatum: "Listen to these missionaries or the children and I may leave." He listened. They were baptized as a family. He is a high councilor today.

A Young Mother Turned to Her Own Mother. We have profound influences upon our relatives. A young mother turned to her own mother who was a guest in the home and who had just enjoyed a visit with the missionaries and said, "Mother, what has gotten into you? You don't even treat relatives that nice!" The lady, wise and perceptive and spiritual, looked at her daughter and replied, "My dear, can't you see: they are angels!" They joined the Church. That phrase is a tradition in that family. They will always look upon all missionaries as ministering angels.

Everybody's Job Has Become Nobody's Job. Another old missionary dilemma is when the investigator says, "Yes, it's easy for you to be a Mormon because you haven't had to raise a family or change your life." The adult member or peer is the one who can effectively step in with his testimony to say, "I am no different than you are. I live the Mormon way of life. I'm happier and healthier and have more left over at the end of the month than if I didn't live the commandments. Besides, I know it is true."

As mentioned, in many areas the members have truly caught the vision, and they are keeping the missionaries fully occupied teaching all day long and bringing hundreds and thousands into the kingdom. But in other areas it seems that "everybody's job has become nobody's job." Let me point out a common error in the mind of man. When someone speaks of what has been accomplished, we tend to think "me," but when someone mentions what should be done, we tend to think "them." But I ask all of us to honestly evaluate our responsibilities and our performances in giving missionary service. When we say every member should give referrals, it is too easy to let someone else do it. There doesn't seem to be enough sense of responsibility on the part of some individual members to do what could and should be done in missionary service. ("It Becometh Every Man," *Ensign*, October 1977.)

Every Day She Would Go to the Market. Down in South America there was one woman who had joined the Church, and she loved it so much that every day she would go to the market place where lots of women came and there she'd say, "Have you ever heard of the Mormon boys?" The women would say, "No." "Well, you know, we have two that come and preach the gospel in our home, in our ward, in our building. Why don't you come over and listen to them?" And do you know that that one middle-aged woman brought in ninety-one members of the Church? She would introduce them to the missionaries, and the missionaries converted them. Ninety-one!

This Is a Missionary Church. Now, *this is a missionary church.* We're not going to be wholly happy with what the missionaries do, either. From now on we want to go to work and let every man, woman and child assume this responsibility. It's very important. Every mother should watch the children that come to play with her own children. She can work out some way to use her little ones to teach the gospel. We want every father and every mother and every youth and every child to assume the responsibility and move forward with this kind of a program. Thousands of fine young people have been brought into the Church by their neighbors, by their young boys and young girls.

For instance, here's a little girl who is five or six years old, and she invited her neighbor child to go to Sunday School with her. The neighbor child liked it, so they went quite often, and after a while—as soon as she got eight years old—she said, "I'd like to be baptized, too." Fortunately, her parents were willing. There was another member of the Church.

The seminaries and institutes of the Church all over the world, where we have hundreds of thousands now, are one of the most fruitful fields we have. The youth go and they invite some of their closest friends to come to seminary with them. They get enthralled in the seminary work, they get their testimonies built up, and then they ask for baptism. *That's the way we want all the people of the Church to get busy.* (Area Conference Address, Suva, Fiji, February 23, 1976.)

Nothing Is Ever Lost. Every gospel teaching experience is a spiritual experience for all parties, regardless of whether it leads to baptism or not. *Our goal should be to identify as soon as possible which of our Father's children are spiritually prepared to proceed all the way to baptism into the kingdom.* One of the best ways to find out is to expose your friends, relatives, neighbors, and acquaintances to the full-time missionaries *as soon as possible. Don't wait for long* fellowshipping nor for the precise, perfect moment. What you need to do is find out if they are the elect. "[My] elect hear my voice and harden not their hearts." (D&C 29:7.) If they hear and have hearts open to the gospel, it will be evident immediately. If they won't listen and their hearts are hardened with skepticism or negative comments, they are not ready. In this case, *keep loving them and fellowshipping them and wait for the next opportunity to find out if they are ready.* You will not lose their friendship. They will still respect you.

Of course, there are discouragements, but nothing is ever lost. No one ever loses a friend just because he doesn't want to continue with the visits from the missionaries. The member can continue the association with no threat to his friendship or special relationship with that family. Sometimes it takes more time for some to come into the Church than for others. ("It Becometh Every Man," *Ensign*, October 1977.)

Many, Many Children Have Come into the Church. I remember a stake president in this general area who told me one day—in fact, he admitted and he confessed to his people. He said, "You know, I had a young woman, a little girl, that grew up right next door to me. The houses were right against each other, almost. She grew up, she went to grade school, she went to high school, she went to college, and she went off to the university. One day she came back, all excited, and she came rushing over and said, "President, why didn't you ever tell me about the gospel? I had to go off to another city to find the gospel and here I have been deprived of the blessings of the gospel for all these years." She had become a schoolteacher and was in her late twenties or early thirties, probably.

This stake president admitted he had failed to ever mention to her what church he belonged to even, or what he believed. And here she had gone year after year knowing he was a good man, but didn't know what he believed. When she got among strangers that were fellow citizens, not strangers, who told her about the gospel, she accepted it readily. Maybe he had made a contribution toward her conversion, I don't know, but he didn't think that he had.

Many, many children have come into the Church, as I mentioned before. Many, many youth are baptizing thousands of young people in their teen ages, in their early twenties—thousands of them. Why? Because they are honorable, sweet, wonderful young people just searching for right and truth, and when they hear it, they want it. They go against their parents even in some cases, and defy them, to take the gospel. We don't encourage that. We ask them always to get their parents' consent, but even with that restriction there are many who are joining the Church. (Dedication, Fair Oaks, California, October 9, 1976).

Break Down Prejudice, Overcome Resistance. The cooperating member families, having been fully instructed, will proceed to meet the people who might be invited into their homes. They will screen them carefully with the two questions: (1) How much do you know about the Mormon church? (2) Would you like to know more?

They will be sure there is no obligation nor pressures exerted and only those who express a genuine interest will be invited. They will report to the ward mission leader their readiness to hold the meetings.

The bishopric and the ward mission leader will classify the nonmember families in two categories: First will be those interested families who answer "yes" to the questions. Those who say "no" might be placed in the "unready" or the "resistant" group.

The cooperating member families will now simultaneously work with "resistant" or "unready" families doing what might be called "preproselyting" fellowshipping. Without pressing further about the Church or the gospel, there will be a consistent effort to break down prejudice, overcome resistance, and cultivate toward later proselyting. The host wife could take a homemade loaf of bread, a pie, a cake, some homemade jelly to the resisting families. The host husband could share rides, take the nonmember husband to a ball game, fishing, hunting. The host family children could walk to school with the other children and take them to Primary, MIA, and seminary. Gradually the walls of prejudice are leveled, the resistance is crumbled and the question may be asked again about a month or a year or two later, and the resistant family becomes a "ready" family and proselyting brings the family into the Church.

The ward mission leader, in cooperation with the full-time missionary district leader, will keep all advised as certain families are ready and will coordinate the assignment of missionaries—full-time and stake to work with the families.

How else could the Lord expect to perform his work except through the Saints who have covenanted to serve him? You and I have made such a covenant. Will we honor our sacred covenant? (Regional Representatives Seminar, September 30, 1977.)

I Am a Mormon. In missionary service, members of the Church are having experiences similar to this:

A member asked a salesman on impulse, "Would you like to know more about the Mormon church? I am a Mormon." The answer brought knowing tears of the Spirit. "Yes, I really would. You know, when I was young I seemed to know the difference between right and wrong, but now I have a problem with my son. He doesn't seem to sense the difference. Do you have something that will help me teach my son?" The affirmative answer by the member led to a date with the missionaries the next day. The testimony of the member during the discussions and the frequent fellowshipping led to a family baptism. ("It Becometh Every Man," *Ensign*, October 1977.)

She Was Not a Set-Apart Missionary. I mentioned in one of the meetings that we had a woman over in Cordoba or Mendoza who had brought thirty-two people into the Church. She was not a set-apart missionary, just a housewife, but if a housewife can do that, certainly her husband can do it and all the other members of the Church can do it.

I met a woman up in Uruguay who had brought in eighty-two members of the Church. Now why couldn't a stake president do that? The other day we met a taxi driver who had joined the Church. *He had given copies of the Book of Mormon to many people*, and he watched the people who would come to ride in his taxi. He asked them, "Do you know about the Mormon Church? Would you like to know more about it?" He said, "Would you like to talk to one who has talked to the Lord? In other words, would you like to meet a prophet of God?" Why couldn't all the taxi drivers do that well? Why couldn't the elders quorum presidency do that well?

Now we would hope you would use your homes for this purpose. Invite your neighbors and your friends to come to your home and participate with you in a home evening.

In the Northwest, a little girl was riding with her daddy on the streetcar. There were no double seats available, so she couldn't sit by her father. She sat by a man she had never seen before. She said to him, "Do you know anything about the Mormon church?"

He replied, "Not very much."

"Would you like to know more?"

He said, "Yes, I think I would."

So she ran up to the front of the bus and said, "Daddy, what should I do now?" And, of course, he got in touch with the man and told him about the gospel.

Do You Have Any Children? We have had Primaries where nearly all the children were nonmembers. Up in Canada, a woman who had a Primary group invited all the neighbor children in. Two lady missionaries went out from the mission home and went within walking distance and found all the children in that area and said to the mothers, "Do you have any little children? We're holding a Primary. Would you like to send your children there?"

The women said, "What do you do there?" That gave the lady missionaries an opportunity to explain the gospel to the mothers.

When they called the roll, there were fifty-seven nonmember children hearing the gospel at Primary.

Now this is a program for all of us. Will you keep this in mind and go forward with it? Organize carefully and well, and let your people understand their responsibility. (Area Conference Address, Luna Park, Buenos Aires, Argentina, March 8, 1975.)

Church Leaders Must Be Missionaries

You Are Missionaries. Brother Bernard P. Brockbank has called to your attention very pointedly that you have a responsibility. Perhaps ten percent of this audience are missionaries who have come from afar. *You are missionaries. Every member is a missionary. We expect you stake presidents, you bishops, you regional representatives, you leaders in the organizations of the Church, we expect you will open your homes and invite people into them, and invite the missionaries to present the gospel to them if you need assistance. This is your responsibility.* We hope you will follow it carefully. (Area Conference Address, London, England, June 20, 1976.)

Devote a Sacrament Meeting to Missionary Work. In sacrament meeting, every bishop should periodically devote a sacrament meeting to missionary work with perfectly trained stake or full-time missionaries presenting the discussion, being certain that full preparation has been made and that the whole program has been rehearsed sufficiently that it moves forward with dispatch and effectiveness and impressiveness. Proper preliminary explanations will have been made; the family portraying the role of host will have been carefully selected and trained; the previous rehearsals of the cast will insure a perfect, impressive performance. There will be no facetiousness. This is a serious conversion program, not to convert the members to the gospel but to convert them all to a willingness to secure investigator families and hold meetings in the homes. The ward mission leader will coordinate for the bishop the securing of pledges from members to hold meetings in their homes. (Regional Representatives Seminar, September 30, 1977.)

Stress the Sharing. We hope in your work with your stake presidents that you will stress this reality in a fresh, improved way. We do not want goals imposed from the top down on individual members or families. We do want them to set their own goals which they will do if encouraged. I am confident of that, if we stress again the importance of their sharing the gospel as well as living it so that they can be a light unto the world. (Regional Representatives Seminar, September 30, 1976.)

PART FOUR

A Great Increase
in the Conversions

We expect that every year there will be a great increase in the conversions and baptisms.

CHAPTER TWENTY-FOUR

Teaching and Fellowshipping for Integration

Truly converted persons change their old sinful ways and turn to a new life in Christ: There is truly a "converting" or a changing in their lives.

Better Teaching and Better Integration

Let Them See the Principles at Work. The gospel of Jesus Christ is true. An earnest seeker can know for himself that it is true by studying and living its principles and seeking the companionship and help of the Holy Ghost. But how much easier it is to understand and accept if the seeker after the truth can also see the principles of the gospel at work in the lives of others. No greater service can be given to the missionary calling of the Church than to exemplify positive Christian virtues in our lives. ("Hold Fast to the Iron Rod," General Conference Address, September 30, 1978.)

We Cannot Stress Too Strongly. We cannot stress too strongly the need for investigators to be fellowshipped and tied into the programs of the Church. This, then, is another way in which all members of the Church can be actively and constantly engaged in missionary service—by fellowshipping, befriending, and encouraging the new members of the Church. ("It Becometh Every Man," *Ensign*, October 1977.)

Fellowshipping, Befriending, and Encouraging

It Is a Crime. I would like to talk about missionary work all the time, but I have some other things to do and some other things to talk about. One thing, brethren, and we leave this with you stake presidents, and bishoprics, mission presidents, and branch presidents: We expect you to carry forward this work in detail. We hope you will know that it isn't just busy work. We are really serious about this program.

When we baptize somebody it is a crime to let them just slide slowly back out of the Church and out of the gospel because of a lack of fellowship. Fellowshipping is an important responsibility. We should be able to fellowship everybody that comes in. That is the reason we want the members to do the missionary work as well as to get help from the missionaries. We want the people, the high priests, the seventies, and the elders to go out and do this work because they are still the neighbors after the person is baptized. They can still fellowship them; they can still call for them and take them to priesthood meeting; they can still encourage them and help them in their home evenings and so on. This is what we would like to emphasize with you. (Area General Conference Address, Glasgow, Scotland, June 21, 1976.)

Nurturing These Members. As the rapid growth in Church membership continues throughout the world, we must direct increased attention to the task of nurturing these members in rewarding and productive activity. We have an alarming number of our members we are not able to contact, because we do not know their current addresses. Not only are they inactive, but we no longer know where they are and what kind of lives they are living; and even a greater number of men, women, youth, and children are living in our wards and stakes where they are identified but are no longer participating in any Church activities. Among this group are many heads of families whose homes are not blessed by the full advantages of the priesthood, the gospel and Church membership.

Our records indicate that in many areas of the Church, this number of inactive members is increasing. As you continue to study the records available to you for your own areas of responsibility, you will realize the magnitude of this problem. We cannot be content with our performance in regard to this.

As we have said to you before, we must now make a magnified effort to change the trends. The cycles of inactivity and indifference are recurring cycles from fathers and mothers to sons and daughters. We must break that cycle at two points simultaneously. We must reach out and hold many more of our young men and women to keep them faithful, to help them to be worthy to go on missions, and to be married in the holy temples. At the same time, we must reach and hold many more of the fathers and mothers.

The sad truth is that if we do not act preventively in the early years, we must later act redemptively, but with much less efficiency and fewer and more labored results.

We must find improved ways of vitalizing our Aaronic Priesthood and Melchizedek Priesthood quorums. Particular attention should be given to the vast number of prospective elders.

The Young Men's organization exists to strengthen the work of the Aaronic Priesthood in the ward.

Under the revelations of the Lord, the bishop is given responsibility for the Aaronic Priesthood. There are now more than 213,000 of these young men. This group is the reservoir for the future missionaries of the Church. The degree to which they are kept active and growing will develop them in their work and they will go into the world to preach the gospel.

The Young Women and Relief Society organizations must do a better job of training and building faith in our girls and mothers. Continued attention must be given to our young women during their years of discovery from twelve to eighteen as they prepare for the time when they will establish their own homes. They must have an equal responsibility with our young men to develop a thorough and solid foundation in the scriptures.

President J. Reuben Clark, Jr., said: "The youth of the Church are hungry for things of the Spirit; they are eager to learn the gospel, and they want to go straight, and have an undiluted life in the gospel and the Church. . . . Our youth are not children spiritually; they are well on towards the normal spiritual maturity of the world." ("The Chartered Course of the Church in Education.")

We Must Build Bridges. Families must give increased attention to a study of the scriptures and practice obedience in the homes. The Primary, the Sunday School, the seminary, and the institutes of religion—they must give more effective support to the building of faith and testimonies which should find root in the family. An effective activity program for members of all ages must provide attractions in the areas of the cultural arts and recreation.

The Young Women's organization focuses on developing in each young woman her great potentialities. There is an emphasis on helping each girl to establish a pattern for living, a way of life which points to her destination as a wife and homemaker. In addition, there is guidance and direction given to helping her live her life to the fullest measure at all times.

Brethren, we already have all the tools. We must build bridges to those who, for one reason or another, have become indifferent and inactive, and we must see that those who are now participating do not become disillusioned or disaffected. They must not go unfulfilled in their desire to find fellowship and to serve.

We stressed in earlier seminars that our efforts directed towards those who have become inactive must be sustained. These efforts require a continued emphasis. Temporary flashes of interest and enthusiasm for the welfare of these, our brothers and sisters, will not produce the desired results. We must marshal all of our resources to stem the tide of inactivity.

Much of the responsibility for this rests with our home teachers. They must be encouraged to go with prayer in their hearts to the homes of these inactive men and women and there strive to rekindle in the lives of these people that which they have felt themselves—a more intense and active interest and a more sustained effort. (Regional Representatives Seminar, September 30, 1977.)

To Bring the People to Belief. I was going to mention this matter down in Brazil. The mission president, he was the highest official in South America at that time, he invited all his people to come to a meeting, all his menfolk to come into a meeting, about this size, and they sang and bore testimony all day long while they were waiting for me to help to work out this stake. So we went to work and we found the leaders to be the stake presidency, called the high council and other leaders, as you know they are needed, bishoprics, and so on.

We found all of them and before I came back to the other room, I said to these men as I interviewed them: "What about your life, up to this moment?" They said, "It is different than it used to be." I said, "What about your drinking habits? Did you ever do any drinking?" They said, "Yes, plenty of it before I joined the Church." "What about your smoking habits?" "I used to smoke all the time but not any since my baptism." "What about your gambling? Do you ever do any of that?" "Oh, yes, in the old days I used to get my paycheck and go down on the street with the other boys and we did a lot of gambling and had a lot of fun." He said, "Not since my baptism—never have I done any more. My wife takes the paycheck and together we organized our family life." "What about—did you ever pay any tithing?" "Oh, no, never dreamed of that, of course." "But you're doing that now?" "Oh, yes, since our baptism, we pay our tithing." And we went on from A to Z.

In those matters I wanted to know what kind of lives they were now living, not so much what had happened long before. "Not since my baptism"—that has rung in my ears ever since. To know that lives can be changed, there is nothing in the world like the spirit of truth and the gospel of Christ to bring people to believing, to change in their lives. Absolutely changing. It isn't just a suggestion, it is an absolute certainty. (Missionary Farewell, Scottsdale, Arizona, May 14, 1978.)

CHAPTER TWENTY-FIVE

A New World

Baptism into Christ's true Church by proper authority opens the doors for exaltation in the eternal kingdoms of glory, exaltation to be earned by repentance, by living righteously, keeping the commandments of the Lord, and service to one's fellowmen.

Great Changes Have Come

We Have Been Taking the Gospel to the People. So long as the body of the Church was in Utah or even in the Intermountain West, it was not an impossible thing to call to headquarters the women of the Church for their delightful period of fellowship, learning, and training. But now conditions are different. Great changes have come. In the old days perhaps a few representatives could come for the messages and relay them to the scattered membership, but now the church of the Lord is in a different age and we have different conditions. We now have some 707 stakes, 133 missions, and 3½ million people and we have to approach our problems a little differently than when we had one-tenth of that number. This we have found in the total Church; so as you know, for the past four years, we have been taking to the people in their own homelands area conferences where the General Authorities give the gospel directly to them. For four years we have held these conferences—in Manchester, England; Mexico City; Munich, Germany; and Stockholm, Sweden: and last year down in South America, and just recently over in the Orient. We were well received. We estimate that we talked to 114,000 people in those conferences; the most we would get here would be a small fraction of that number. ("The Blessings and Responsibilities of Womanhood," *Ensign*, March 1976.)

The Church Will Spread. Now, my brothers and sisters, do not be dismayed as evil in the world increases. Remember the prophecy of President Brigham Young when he said, "It was revealed to me in the commencement of this Church that the Church would spread, prosper, grow, and extend that in proportion to the spread of the gospel among the nations of the earth, so would the power of Satan rise."

The prophecy indicates that the progress of the Church will be paralleled by a growing wickedness among mankind. We rejoice in one and deplore the other. But so far as our part in human affairs is concerned, we must be of good cheer. (New Mission Presidents Seminar, June 22, 1979.)

Approximately 100 New Stakes—Every Year. Every year now we are adding approximately 100 new stakes—the locally governed ecclesiastical units of Mormonism composed of several wards and branches each. Only a few weeks ago we created the thousandth such stake of Zion at Nauvoo, Illinois, a place of deep historical significance to the Church.

I rejoice with you, my brothers and sisters, in these statistical evidences of the progress and growth throughout Zion. It is indeed progress to add new thousands of people to a membership now in excess of four million. It is pleasing to build the temples and places of worship in so many lands and to add thousands of students to our expanding educational and training programs for both youth and adults. ("Fortify Your Homes Against Evil," General Conference Address, March 31, 1979.)

It's a New World. When I went to Mexico a year or so ago, we invited the stake presidents. Now we have twenty or thirty stake presidents right there within the area around São Paulo, and we invited them to come to this banquet. They came. The women were all in long evening gowns and corsages; the men were all beautifully dressed, just as well as people here are dressed, and this was the new Mexico. It's the new Australia, it's the new South America—anywhere you want to go—it's a new world that's accepting the gospel and living it and the Lord will be getting a good smile on his face as he sees the progress that we have made. (Missionary Farewell, Scottsdale, Arizona, May 14, 1978.)

Congregations of Saints Are Springing Up. We are grateful, our brethren and sisters, that we have another temple almost ready to be dedicated in São Paulo. We are moving forward and hope to have temples in many lands as we grow. We are gathering in most of the countries of the world. Recently we returned from Poland, where we were well received and had much promise of continuing our proselyting there and bringing those good people into the kingdom of God.

We are now in a new era of Church growth and development. In the early days, if the Saints were to survive as a people, they had to assemble together in closer places. Gathering otherwise, they would have had problems to overcome, more serious problems. But now congregations of Saints are springing up in all parts of the world. They are in almost every country, and they are in high places and in low. We are grateful for them, great leaders and wonderful people in every clime. Many of our members sit in these places of high responsibility and give civic and other leadership to the people of the Church.

It Is a Universal Church

We Are Now a World Church. We are now a world church. We were originally just a United States church, just a New York church and an Illinois church; but today we are scattered far and wide. I remember well when most of the big cities in the United States had no congregations, or if they had one it was a very diminutive, small one. Today there is hardly a city in the whole country of the United States and in Canada and in many other countries where there are not congregations of the people of the Lord.

This is no longer a local church; it is a universal church. It is worldwide, and our missionaries travel to nearly all of the nations of the world with very few exceptions. We are proud of our great missionary system, too. We call these young men when they are approximately nineteen years of age, and we send them to Chile and to Brazil, to Austria and to China, and to Japan and to nearly all of the nations of the world, and we are so proud of the service they perform. It is now your responsibility, my beloved brothers and sisters, to continue on and give the Church great leadership. It takes leaders and it takes followers, but we have plenty of people who can give the proper leadership. (Area Conference Address, Honolulu, Hawaii, June 18, 1978.)

I Have a Great Love for the People of This Church. My beloved brothers and sisters, this is a great experience for me. I have waited for this day and hoped for it and believed for it. I have a great love for the people of this Church, and gratitude for the love expressed by them and by all the people of these valleys. So as I express that love for you and for the memory of the great experiences I've had with you, I bear my testimony: this work is divine, the Lord is at the helm, the Church is true, and all is well. ("The Lord Is at the Helm," General Conference Address, April 3, 1982.)

Peace Be with You. May his joy and peace continue with you. We know it is true. I know the Lord lives and I know that he is revealing his mind and will to us daily, so that we can be inspired as to the direction to go.

We ask this all, with our affection for you, in the name of Jesus Christ, Amen. ("Revelation: The Word of the Lord to His Prophets," General Conference Address, April 3, 1977.)

Index

McIver, Charles D., on education of
  women, 136
McKay, David O., 195, 224–25
  "Every member a missionary," 22,
  60, 241
Magazines, 22
Malachi, 86
Manchester, England, 73, 264
  area conference, 9, 127, 134, 153
Manila, Philippines, area conferences, 36, 81, 204
Marriage, 121, 124, 176, 211
  interfaith, 228–30
  temple, 23, 90, 130, 153, 161,
  174–75, 177, 202, 203, 219,
  225, 226–30, 261
Marsh, Thomas B., 18
Maugham, Somerset, on mediocrity,
  61
Mary (mother of Jesus), 75
Media, 22, 34–36, 174
Melbourne, Australia, area con-
  ference, 11
Melchizedek Priesthood quorums,
  182–83, 261
Member missionary work, 22, 36,
  50, 56–57, 237–56
Mexico, 21, 63, 70, 99, 105, 109, 131,
  242, 265
  dream of progress in, 112–14
  temple in, 114
Mexico City, 264
  area conference, 114, 125
Mexico Hermosillo Mission, 63
Michigan, 31
Migrant workers, 149
Millennium, 115
Minorities, 4, 110
Miracles, 36, 59, 77, 81, 96–97
Mission presidents, 8, 60
  calling of, 54
  instructions to, 48–57
Mission Presidents Seminar, June
  1971, 26
  June 1974, 10, 12, 14, 29, 37, 48,
  50, 52, 101, 111, 141–43, 193
  June 1975, 7, 14, 43, 54, 55, 56,
  62, 66, 67, 105, 162
  June 1976, 10, 27, 49, 50, 53, 54,
  55, 57, 61, 72, 102, 181, 221
  June 1977, 28, 49, 54, 146, 220
  June 1978, 51
  June 1979, 51, 56, 57, 248, 265
  June 1980, 4

Missionaries, all young men to serve
  as, 8, 15, 22, 23–24, 43, 119–33,
  138–48, 226, 232
  conduct of, 197–218
  couples, 119, 123, 136–37, 157,
  180
  decision to serve as, 174–78
  early, 69–73
  financial contributions to, 112,
  131, 225
  financial preparation of, 119, 121,
  123, 131–33, 139, 147, 148, 169,
  174, 179, 226, 239
  forgiveness of, 96
  native, 61, 131–32, 138–51,
  220–21
  lady, 119, 136, 147, 148, 179, 254
  Lamanite, 66, 110
  number of, 4, 5, 16, 24, 36, 43, 61,
  63, 139, 141, 149, 150, 221
  prayers for, 164, 225–26
  preparation of, 23–24, 66, 121–35
  productivity of, 59–64
  returned, 183, 219–30
  stake, 231–33
  training of, 49–50, 52–57
  worthiness of, 119–37
Missionary Committee, 49
Missionary fund, 133
Missionary Training Center, 184–85
Missionary work, commandment to
  do, 3–9, 138
  effectiveness of, 50–51
  every member to do, 237–44
  history of, 69–73
Missions, number of, 4, 24
Missouri, 10
Monterrey, Mexico, area conference,
  173, 214
Montevideo, Uruguay, area conference, 156
Monument Park Stake, 32
Mormon Pioneer Memorial Bridge, 7
Mormon pioneers, 7, 28, 69–70, 167,
  225
Moroni, appearances to Joseph
  Smith, 80
  on power of the Holy Ghost,
  186–87
Mortal death, 76
Mortality, 76–77, 84
Moses, 7, 8, 71, 75, 83, 86, 190
  keys of gathering of Israel restored
  by, 79, 98